PUBLIC JUSTICE AND THE ANTHROPOLOGY OF LAW

In this powerful, timely study Ronald Niezen examines the processes by which cultural concepts are conceived and collective rights are defended in international law. Niezen argues that cultivating support on behalf of those experiencing human rights violations often calls for strategic representations of injustice and suffering to distant audiences. The positive impulse behind public responses to political abuse can be found in the satisfaction of justice done. But the fact that oppressed peoples and their supporters from around the world are competing for public attention is actually a profound source of global difference, stemming from differential capacities to appeal to a remote, unknown public. Niezen's discussion of the impact of public opinion on law provides fresh insights into the importance of legally constructed identity and the changing pathways through which it is being shaped – crucial issues for all those with an interest in anthropology, politics and human rights law.

Ronald Niezen is Professor of Anthropology and Canada Research Chair at McGill University. He has undertaken wide-ranging international research, including work with the UN Permanent Forum on Indigenous Issues and the Arctic Council. His publications include *The Origins of Indigenism: Human Rights and the Politics of Identity* (2003), *A World Beyond Difference: Cultural Identity in the Age of Globalization* (2004), and *The Rediscovered Self: Indigenous Identity and Cultural Justice* (2009).

NEW DEPARTURES IN ANTHROPOLOGY

New Departures in Anthropology is a book series that focuses on emerging themes in social and cultural anthropology. With original perspectives and syntheses, authors introduce new areas of inquiry in anthropology, explore developments that cross disciplinary boundaries, and weigh in on current debates. Every book illustrates theoretical issues with ethnographic material drawn from current research or classic studies, as well as from literature, memoirs, and other genres of reportage. The aim of the series is to produce books that are accessible enough to be used by college students and instructors, but will also stimulate, provoke, and inform anthropologists at all stages of their careers. Written clearly and concisely, books in the series are designed equally for advanced students and a broader range of readers, inside and outside academic anthropology, who want to be brought up to date on the most exciting developments in the discipline.

Public Justice and the Anthropology of Law

RONALD NIEZEN

McGill University

CAMBRIDGE UNIVERSITY PRESS
Cambridge, New York, Melbourne, Madrid, Cape Town, Singapore,
São Paulo, Delhi, Dubai, Tokyo, Mexico City

Cambridge University Press
The Edinburgh Building, Cambridge CB2 8RU, UK

Published in the United States of America by
Cambridge University Press, New York

www.cambridge.org
Information on this title: www.cambridge.org/9780521767040

First published 2010
Printed in the United Kingdom at the University Press, Cambridge

A catalogue record for this publication is available from the British Library

Library of Congress Cataloguing in Publication data
Niezen, Ronald.
    Public justice and the anthropology of law / Ronald Niezen.
        p.   cm. – (New departures in anthropology)
    Includes bibliographical references and index.
    ISBN 978-0-521-76704-0 (hardback) – ISBN 978-0-521-15220-4 (pbk.)
    1. Indigenous peoples–Legal status, laws, etc.–Social aspects.   2. Human rights–
Social aspects.   3. Public opinion.   4. Law and anthropology.   I. Title.   II. Series.
    K3242.N543 2010
    340′.115–dc22
    2010022033

ISBN 978-0-521-76704-0 Hardback
ISBN 978-0-521-15220-4 Paperback

In memory of Ernest Gellner

[T]he best test of truth is the power of thought to get itself accepted in the competition of the market.

Oliver Wendell Holmes Jr,
Abrams v. *United States*, 1919

"The public" is a very strange animal, and although a good knowledge of human nature will generally lead a caterer of amusement to hit the people right, they are fickle and ofttimes perverse.

P.T. Barnum, 1850
In Kunhardt *et al.* (1995: 92)

Contents

Preface

One of the significant recent findings of legal anthropology is that institutions of world governance can only really be understood when considered as producers of their own distinct knowledge and practice. At the same time, it seems clear that ideas about world order produced within these institutions are being taken up in local settings by people and organizations that see in them new possibilities for political leverage and self-determination, correctives to their marginalization by states. Legal anthropology in the era of human rights thus faces the challenge of determining how global concepts of rights and identity are navigated and shaped in practice by those who see themselves as the subjects of rights. Between these foci on the institutions of global governance and the local settings of rights claimants is the problem of *legal norm diffusion*, a key issue that helps to define the sub-discipline of legal anthropology.

My approach to this issue, which has turned out to be *the* central impetus behind this book, involves making a case for including within the central subject matter of anthropology the influence of actors often referred to as "the public" or as I prefer, "publics," groups of actors who are impersonally connected and therefore unknowable through the usual methods of ethnography. Publics are the abstract, invisible intended audiences of outreach engaged in by those with very tangible grievances. And the ideas held by publics do matter, not just because of their possible influence on those who hold power, but because of the possibility that publics themselves might be influenced by claimants of rights. This in itself encourages the repositioning of local knowledge and identities toward their public consumers, bringing about largely unexamined dynamics to the recovery and representation of collective selves.

Without being fully aware of the possibilities of this subject matter, I have touched upon the cultural dynamics of popular persuasion in two previous books, *The Origins of Indigenism* (2003) and *The Rediscovered Self* (2009). In these works the public is there, above all in the dynamics of rights-oriented persuasion, but in a way that for me ultimately raised more questions than answers. If courts and international agencies are called upon to make decisions concerning cultural rights, and occasionally in the process to define culture, what are the sources of knowledge from which they are drawing? If the claimants of cultural rights tend to be on the margins of states, what are the sources of inspiration or compulsion (or both in combination) behind their claims? What are the global dynamics at work in the assertion of identity through the direct and indirect pathways of law, through formal boundary construction and through lobbying with claims and performances to unknown audiences? And what are the implications for identity and for the universal goals of human rights of the need to publicly assert one's collective worth and the reality and significance of one's subjection to injustice?

Describing the place of public persuasion in collective identity formation pushes to the limit the trend in anthropology toward abandonment of the long-held methodological principle of working within a clearly defined community in a single, particular, identifiable setting. Trained in British social anthropology in the 1980s, which was then still very much in the afterglow of the ethnographic models of Malinowski and Evans-Pritchard, I found this a difficult transition to make. Part of what has made my focus on the transnational dynamics of public rights-lobbying possible is the growing awareness in anthropology that the "field" is being redefined, not through the vagaries of intellectual fashion, but through the changing nature of human belonging. I am therefore making use of a kind of ethnography of extrapolation, in which an intangible, anonymous, largely unknowable community can still be seen to act, in some cases profoundly, on the behavior of those whom we know personally.

This book was supported by the Canada Research Chair program and by a grant from the Canada Foundation for Innovation. One of the principal benefits of this support was my ability to make ample use of the research skills of graduate students. I am grateful to those who helped with this project: Julia Bailey, Maria Eugenia Brockman, Paige MacDougall and Sara Thiam. My principal research assistant, Marie-Pierre Gadoua, made an important contribution to this book, going beyond her mandate by (among other things) introducing me to the Oblate priests (discussed in Chapter 6) and in several instances conducting interviews with them. Two anonymous reviewers of my initial proposal gave me confidence in taking my work in a different direction than I first envisioned. Barbro Bankson, Michael Lambek, Sally Engle Merry and Galit Sarfaty each offered very useful, insightful comments on drafts of the manuscript. I am grateful to those (colleagues and students alike) who provided research material or more casually dropped useful hints or suggestions, among them Carol Berger, Jaye Ellis, Dorothy Hodgson, John Galaty, Peter Jackson, Noorjehan Johnson, Ian Kalman, Lior Miller, Scott Matter, Stanley Riamit, Rémy Rouillard, Garett Schromm, Kiven Strohm and Mark Watson. I also benefited significantly from the feedback that resulted from presenting various portions of this book in lectures hosted by (in chronological order): the Max Planck Institute for Social Anthropology (which also housed me over a period of months in 2007 and 2008 and provided me with access to the Institute's rich library); the Centre of Excellence in Global Goverance Research, University of Helsinki; the Institute for Human Rights, Åbo Akademi University, Åbo/Turku, Finland; the National Network for Aboriginal Mental Health Research sponsored by the Culture and Mental Health Research Unit of the Jewish General Hospital, McGill University; the

Preface

Department of Religious Studies at The University of Tromsø; the Ethnologisches Seminar at Zürich University; the Department of History at the University of Iowa; and the Faculty of Law at McGill University. An open forum call-in broadcast of CBC Radio Noon Montreal hosted by Anne Lagacé Dowson provided me with direct exposure to the opinions and insights of the public, an experience I recommend to anyone whose profession involves the communication of ideas.

ONE

The imagined order

The ethnography of the unknowable

Anthropology bases its distinctiveness as a discipline on a method of long-term social interaction, getting to know a community intimately through face-to-face dialogue, together with sustained close attention to the details of everyday life. Knowing this, I am nevertheless setting out here to break with this source of anthropologists' disciplinary identity by discussing social actors who are intangible, abstract, notoriously unpredictable and largely unknowable. In a certain sense, they are figments of the imagination, though they act together in ways that largely determine our cultural, political and legal landscapes. Together, the members of this society are popularly known as *the public* – though there is of course more than one vaguely identifiable public with more than a single repertoire of preferences, and it is usually more appropriate to use the plural term "publics."

It might reasonably be argued that looking at publics is not the business of an anthropologist, that this is the domain of political scientists, sociologists, social psychologists and others who have painstakingly developed methods for probing the dominant trends of opinion, most publicly (and sordidly) in the course of political campaigns. My answer to this is that publics, however intangible, have also become part of the social worlds of those whom it is possible to know intimately. To take this point further, the processes by which people define who they are, above all the ways they articulate and defend their collective rights and shape and represent their distinct cultures, are now often negotiated and mediated in collaboration with distant publics. I am interested in publics because they have become an important part of the social imaginations and dynamics of identity of those with claims of culture.

This is an issue for legal anthropology insofar as the values and tastes of publics have increasingly become points of reference for the rights claims of distinct peoples and communities. Simply because there is primarily a psychical rather than a physical compulsion behind laws that lack judicial enforcement, we should not entirely discount the likelihood that, in Weber's terms, "there is a probability that an order will be upheld by a specific staff of men ... with the intention of obtaining conformity with the order, or of inflicting sanctions for the infringement of it."[1] The question to which we are led by the burgeoning corpus of human rights law concerns the ultimate source of compulsion or power in the realization of collective will. Most analysts of human rights and other bodies of "soft law," lacking enforcement mechanisms through judicial sanctions, would probably agree that popular opinion and activism can and do influence the behavior of the powerful, usually in the direction of conformity with law, and that this can be somehow understood with reference to "popular will," acting in ways that are quite different from judicial decision-making. A basic difference can therefore be drawn between those laws that have built into them a formal mechanism of enforcement, that are supported by the possibility of (ideally) behavior-modifying, judicially applied sanctions, and those that rely more exclusively on popular opinion, compassion, the "politics of shame" or, as I will later discuss, the cultivation of popular "indignation."

[1] M. Weber, *From Max Weber: Essays in Sociology*, ed. H. Gerth and C. Wright Mills (London: Routledge & Kegan Paul, 1948) 180.

Flux and boundary

The central subject matter of this book – that obtuse entity sometimes referred to as "the public" – is situated somewhere in the point of impact of two seemingly incompatible certainties. The dominant paradigm of cultural studies in recent decades has emphasized the invented nature of tradition, the porousness of cultural boundaries, the malleability and often manipulability of the ideological and affective foundations of social membership. Heritage is selected and cultures are constructed. The boundaries of inclusion and exclusion are artificial products of political ambition and/or bureaucratic necessity, often with roots in colonial governance. There is no authentic connection to a primordial past, no inner essence of a people that is not a product of human creativity, no ethnic divisions that are not constructed and, in practice, plastic, overlapping and opaque.

Often ideas of cultural impermanence and invention are connected to hopeful conceptions of cosmopolitan belonging, the idea of people brought together in a mobile, boundaryless condition of peaceable, ecumenical individualism. Since nations are no longer the central reference point for political identity, we are not speaking of the social consequences of trans*national* networks, but of something that might be described as trans-human. In this new world order, social identity is a moral choice. Youth is faced with the burden of this choice, of deciding upon their allegiances and values. The individual is more than ever before freed from the constraints of determined social belonging; and it becomes a task for individuals to navigate the possibilities of self-creation, to choose from their repertoires of identity, to take an active part in determining their personhood. And if culture is ultimately a chosen process, the time has come for divisions between people to be overcome, for people to combine their heritages and social attachments in new ways, on a scale that encompasses all of humanity. This, at any rate, is a central, at times utopian, theme in thought about an emerging global social order.

Another certainty seems on the surface to be starkly contrary to such culture-as-process, cosmopolitan ecumenicalism. During the past several decades we have witnessed the growing importance of reinvigorated identity as a source of group membership. Conceptions (or descriptions) of cultural permeability and change are uncomfortable for or unacceptable to those whose greatest hopes are oriented toward the recognition of their primary source of belonging as an identifiable, secure community. Distinct peoples, through spokespeople and sympathizers, are often publicly represented as bounded entities with discrete histories, encouraging national and international legal systems to accommodate cultural claims in legal proceedings and processes of legal reform.

It is through the inherent mutability of cultural remembrances, identities, and attachments – often mediated and guided by legal formulation of rights-bearing social entities and public affirmation of cultural representation (the subject matter of Chapters 2 and 3) – that distinct societies are bringing their collective self-images into sharper focus. Paradoxically, bonds seen by community members as inherent, timeless and indissoluble have only recently been reformulated, publicly performed and given new political standing.

This means that the unstable conception of culture that pervades the social sciences is in stark contradiction with legal approaches to culture. Transnational organizations and institutions of global governance are primary sources of ideas about cultural coherence and collective virtue, treating heritage as a clearly definable body of beliefs, values and practices rooted in the past, integral to local and distinct ways of life.

At the same time, the institutions of global governance are built upon ideas of effecting change among non-compliant peoples in the interest of furthering cosmopolitan values of peace and development. As I intend to show, there is a tension between promoting the autonomy and identity of distinct peoples and acting on the universalizing ideals of peaceable civilization, human rights and global civic order. Sally Engle Merry is among those who point to a growing tendency in international human rights circles in which activists (and sometimes international institutions and nation states) are prone to engage in sweeping condemnation of "traditional culture" as inconsistent with human rights standards (thus unwittingly invoking nineteenth-century style imperialist arguments that situate cultures on a scale of human progress); while at other times culture is invoked as a source of vital heritage, something to be protected, nurtured and treasured.[2] In both cases, "human rights relies on an essentialized model of culture [that] does not take advantage of the potential of local cultural practices for change."[3] The adaptability of cultural ideals in the context of political contests within communities in transition is all too often overlooked in favor of mistaken attributions of intellectual and political coherence, permanence and undiluted traditional virtues.

Legal anthropology has become a mediator of this tension between flux and boundary. In the study of culture among distinct social strata such as ethnic minorities and indigenous peoples, there is a central intellectual challenge in which social conditions of transnationalism or "delocalization" are causing anthropologists to question the culture concept by emphasizing the shifting, intangible nature of collective identity while, at the same time, distinct peoples, through spokespeople and sympathizers, are publicly represented as bounded entities with distinct histories, encouraging national and international legal systems to accommodate cultural claims in legal proceedings and processes of legal reform. In response to this tension, critical analysis of such concepts as "social justice," "identity," and less familiar terms like "juridification" and "convergence" (discussed in Chapter 7) along with other conceptual tools of legal anthropology, cannot help but lead toward analysis of major social transformations that are currently unfolding and provide an opportunity to appraise efforts to come to grips with them.

[2] S.E. Merry, *Human Rights and Gender Violence: Translating International Law into Local Justice* (University of Chicago Press, 2006) Ch. 1.
[3] Merry, *Human Rights and Gender Violence*, 11.

Law is of course not content to merely describe or comment on the world; it seeks to make itself felt, to act on the world, to be a source of betterment. And this introduces the problem of efficacy: how does the passive orientation of human rights law – its reliance on the "soft power" of public persuasion – translate into immediate, tangible effects in the conditions of peoples' lives? There is another direction from which to approach the same problem: what conditions might have changed the ways that people are influenced by legal thought that allow or encourage a turn toward the reformulation of categories of belonging?

Starting this question is a bit like starting a stone rolling: as it gathers momentum it runs into others and sets them too in motion. It also becomes important to know how ideas about rights that originate in meetings of experts in European and North American centers of power are finding their way to the political, legal and developmental aspirations of peoples (now legally identified as such) and communities on the margins of states. This is a process sometimes referred to as *international norm diffusion*, which in essence challenges us to find the linkages between ideas developed in closed meetings among bureaucrats and experts in capital cities and those among rights-claimants in marginalized communities, and then (and this is the really hard part) to determine, whether, how, and the extent to which the resulting ideas and strategies find legitimacy and support in local constituencies.[4]

Soft power and publics

Human rights ideology, Lori Allen reminds us, "is a cornerstone of global civil society and a key idiom through which stateless groups

---

[4] See, for example, G. Sarfaty, "International Norm Diffusion in the Pimicikamak Cree Nation: A Model of Legal Mediation," *Harvard International Law Journal*, 2007b, 48 (2): 441–82.

and the disadvantaged seek redress across the globe."[5] This is mostly because of the wide recognition in the aftermath of World War II that the alternative to the minimum standards of human rights consensus is moral chaos in an increasingly integrated world. The result of this moral consensus – the current global regime of human rights – is the most widely legitimate source of guidance for the ethical standards of collective behavior. It has more adherents than any one faith, mainly because it does not overtly compete with faith, by virtue of the fact that it does not require of its adherents exclusive membership or loyalty.

Part of the explanation of the near-universal legitimacy of human rights follows from the importance of public appeal as a mechanism of rights compliance. And this, in turn, has created a revolution in the origins and pathways of collective identity construction. A thorough treatment of this topic would have to go well beyond any connection with legal anthropology by outlining the already well-known history of the politics of public persuasion, including the central place of state-sponsored propaganda in the ideological underpinnings of the major wars of the twentieth century. For the purposes of this introduction, it must suffice to briefly outline the origins of the politics of indignation. We can look first to Enlightenment ideas of the capacity of the "public spirit" to unerringly exercise political judgment, elaborated first in England and France and subsequently exported to Germany, and to point to the stark contrast between this "sense of the people" with more contemporary ideas that stress the malleability and manipulability of opinion, emphasizing hegemony as an extension of power.

Jürgen Habermas, in *The Structural Transformation of the Public Sphere*, provides a masterful overview of the intellectual history of public opinion, situated in the tumultuous political transformations of Europe

---

[5] L. Allen, "Martyr Bodies in the Media: Human Rights, Aesthetics, and the Politics of Immediation in the Palestinian Intifada," *American Ethnologist*, 2009, 36 (1): 163.

in the eighteenth and nineteenth centuries. He gives the conservative British parliamentarian Henry Bolingbroke a central place in the early development of the idea of public opinion as a political mechanism, starting with his *Craftsman* articles of 1730 which situated the "Spirit of Liberty" of the people against the corruption of those in power, producing, in Habermas' words, a "direct, undistorted sense for what was right and just and the articulation of 'opinion' into 'judgment' through the public clash of arguments."[6] This was an early expression of the durable idea of public opinion as an essential component of democracy, not only in the electoral process, but also more subtly, with popular will acting as an almost invisible or (depending on one's perspective) insidious source of guidance in judicial decision-making, a kind of hegemony of mass empowerment or, from a minority point of view, of popular tyranny.

As with many turning points in modern history, a formative condition for the politics of indignation can be found in the populism of the French Revolution. The Revolution seems to have put into practice a romantic, demagogic conception of public opinion, reflecting Rousseau's ideal of a public acting according to its natural inclinations, through a consensus of hearts – which ultimately makes superfluous the need for debate. The *volonté générale* was to reveal itself through a plebiscite in permanence, based perhaps on the Greek *polis* or the stirring image of those natural consensual assemblies that must have once taken place beneath the spreading branches of a tree, in which people gathered more for acclamation than the rational-critical processes of public debate.[7]

Keith Baker, in his essay "Public Opinion as Political Invention," demonstrates that in the course of the French Revolution the most widespread conceptualization of opinion changed in a fundamental

---

[6] J. Habermas, *The Structural Transformation of the Public Sphere: An Inquiry into a Category of Bourgeois Society* (Cambridge, MA: The MIT Press, 1991 [1962]) 94.
[7] See Habermas, *The Structural Transformation of the Public Sphere*, 98–100 for a discussion of Rousseau's conception of public opinion.

way, from a philosophical concept describing a dubious, error-laden form of belief that contrasts starkly with the certainty and purity of rational thought, to a political concept referring to an equalizing moral force, the ultimate source of judicial and political guidance, shaping the behavior of citizens and government alike. Public opinion, Baker points out, "suddenly emerged as a central rhetorical figure in a new kind of politics. Suddenly it designated a new source of authority, the supreme tribunal to which the absolute monarchy, no less than its critics, was compelled to appeal."[8] Whether conceived as a source of pre-existing mores, the spirit of a people, that under a just constitution would naturally be expressed in law or imagined as an outcome of a public entrusted with the tools of rational-critical debate that acts as a watchdog and censor of government, a common assumption was that public opinion acted independently, perhaps even infallibly, in a condition of autonomy from the state.

Despite these origins in the Enlightenment ideals that accompanied the emergence of modern states, the influence of popular opinion was slow to emerge as a significant aspect of compliance in international law. The absence of publics was especially significant in the earliest international efforts to regulate the behavior of states toward their own unwanted citizens. The Treaty of Saint-Germain and the Treaty of Versailles (outcomes of the Paris Peace Conference of 1919), intended to establish a new, peaceful order in the aftermath of World War I, were sweeping in their scope, essentially redrawing the map of Europe so that the frontiers of states would, to the fullest extent possible, follow the lines of nationality, and counteracting the behavior of states in their persecution of minorities; but enforcement relied upon agreement and leverage from the Great Powers, the main victor-states of the Great War.

[8] K. Baker, *Inventing the French Revolution* (Cambridge University Press, 1990) 168.

There were no appeals to the will of the people to pressure states in the direction of fulfillment of their obligations, no grassroots lobbying to the fledgling League of Nations, even though the issues involved – especially the resettlement and protection of minorities – were hugely significant, with immigrants numbering in the millions pouring across the redrawn boundaries of Europe and many thousands of new refugees, designated as *apatride* or *heimatlos*, suddenly finding themselves without membership in a state.[9] The League, having put things in motion, had to be content to make itself small, avoid political backlash (especially from the Powers to which it was beholden) and leave it to the states to manage their affairs. To the extent that public involvement was possible in these circumstances, it was indirect and at a remove from the enforcement of law, taking place in a minimal way through the private charitable organizations mobilized to do the things neglected by states in the cataclysms of displacement caused by their actions, things like feeding starving masses and sheltering orphans.

The post-World War II regime of human rights left much more room for public involvement and persuasion – this much almost everyone agrees, despite the influence of new Great Powers in the form of the Security Council and the troika of powerful global financial institutions, the International Monetary Fund (IMF), the World Bank and the World Trade Organization (WTO). And almost everyone agrees that public opinion matters in bringing about human rights compliance (to the lamentably limited extent that states do comply with human rights). But how does this happen? How does popular will modify illegal behavior in the absence of formal mechanisms of enforcement?

First, let us consider the question of public opinion as a source of leverage in rights compliance. Will Kymlicka touches on this when he casually

---

9 M. Marrus, *The Unwanted: European Refugees from the First World War Through the Cold War* (Philadelphia: Temple University Press, 2002) 69–70.

observes that in spite of the non-existence of formal procedures to force governments to comply with new legal standards for minority rights, there are pressures that can be brought to bear to move them in the direction of cooperation and compliance: "States are increasingly monitored and judged for how well they comply with these norms, and failure to comply has resulted not only in criticism, but also, in some cases, in tangible consequences."[10] The "tangible consequences" mentioned by Kymlicka are the easiest part of this process to understand. At the most basic level, for example, many state economies depend on loans and specialized expertise from the IMF or the World Bank, agencies that are part of a powerful complex of intergovernmental organizations, agencies that in varying degrees have been shown to lack transparency and accountability – all while actively promoting human rights and multicultural state governance.[11] Whatever their shortcomings, acting overtly in defiance of those agencies of global governance that in various ways combine rights and economic management is a risk that few states are willing to take, though of course some, such as the Sudan and Zimbabwe, have done just that.

Added to these collective "tangible consequences" are the special international criminal courts established to prosecute war crimes and crimes against humanity committed by individuals in the aftermaths of the most morally corrupt conflicts: Bosnia and Herzegovina, Rwanda, and Sierra Leone. Following on from these temporary tribunals, a permanent criminal court was established in 2002 for the prosecution of genocide, war crimes and crimes against humanity (albeit, with China, Russia, India and the United States declining to join). The International Criminal Court

---

[10] W. Kymlicka, *Multicultural Odysseys* (Oxford University Press, 2007) 4.

[11] Of the global economic institutions, the World Bank has been, to its credit, the most accessible to critical scholarship. See, for example, J. Stiglitz, *Globalization and its Discontents* (New York: Norton, 2003) and G. Sarfaty, "Doing Good Business or Just Doing Good: Competing Human Rights Frameworks at the World Bank," in *The Intersection of Rights and Regulation: New Directions in Sociolegal Scholarship*, ed. Bronwen Morgan (Surrey: Ashgate, 2007a).

based in The Hague, the Netherlands, began its first trial – the prosecution of Congolese militia leader Thomas Lubanga for crimes against humanity – in January 2009, some seven years after its creation, an indication of the political obstacles and glacial movement of international criminal law. Such criminal proceedings, as Arthur Helton points out, have extremely limited capacities: "Enforcement is primarily the responsibility of states, including the formulation of foreign policy, raising potential for profound conflicts of interest."[12] And this takes us back to the influence of opinion as a significant source of rights compliance among states.

It is worth noting that Kymlicka (along with many others) also uses the word "criticism" as a source of the influence of international norms, without exploring this idea further. He seems to be pointing to the fact that the human rights system acts to counteract the harsh reality of state inclinations to violence and injustice through the mechanisms of soft law, that is to say, through the influence – primarily on states – of moral persuasion that makes itself felt largely through the pressures of public opinion.

This means that public opinion is ultimately an important part of the influence and possible effectiveness of international norms that are otherwise not judicially enforceable, including those that have to do with cultural protection. It is the ultimate source of the moral suasion and reputational costs that lie behind the effectiveness of the category of international legal instruments that are not directly enforced by mechanisms of judicial decision-making and power, that, in common parlance, do not have "teeth." The soft power of the UN is such that the moral standards of international law have political and cultural weight disproportionate to its institutional capacity.[13]

---

[12] A. Helton, *The Price of Indifference: Refugees and Humanitarian Action in the New Century* (Oxford University Press, 2002) 125.

[13] The work of Joseph Nye is probably the most influential source of the concept of "soft power" in the UN's (and USA's) civilizational discourse. One of the interesting facts Nye brings to bear on his discussion of soft power in UN diplomacy is that the UN's annual budget for human rights activities is less than the

But criticism – especially popular or public criticism – as a foundation for legal effectiveness is not nearly as straightforward as might initially be supposed. This is the rabbit hole that takes us to some of the odd things that follow from public mediation in rights compliance. Once we find ourselves in the realm of popular criticism as a source of judicially supported moral persuasion, there are several more questions that immediately come to mind. Who is exercising judgment and criticism? Given the specialized nature of expertise in international law, what are the actual, simplified standards on which public judgments are based? How does knowledge about rights and injustice become popularized? And to what extent can it be relied on as a source of support for and compliance of international norms?

Such are the most immediate rights-effectiveness issues that follow from recognition of public involvement in international norm compliance. But there are other questions I want to raise in this book that take us further down the hole in the direction of cultural identity: if criticism is a key aspect of norm compliance, what implicit ideas (or ideals) about culture, and in particular about multiculturalism, are motivating public judgments? More specifically, what are the widely shared expectations of behavior and cultural knowledge that might influence the strategic options and choices of those who are the subjects of collective rights? How do those with collective rights claims try in practice to navigate the new global geography of multiculturalism, and with what degree of success? And finally, what implications does rights-lobbying have for the claimants' repertoires of cultural representation and identity? In other words, what are the consequences of the need to lobby, to

operating budget of the Zurich Opera House. This brings into relief the observation that the moral authority of the human rights movement is greatly disproportionate to its institutional underpinning. See *Understanding International Conflicts: An Introduction to Theory and History*, sixth edn (New York: Pearson/ Longman, 2007) 185.

garner public sympathy, to present a prepared, performed and edited version of social and cultural reality for the consumption of potential sympathizers as preconditions for the successful pursuit of justice or redress of grievances?

The consequences of public mediation in international law have as much to do with failure to garner sympathy and rights activism as with more visible success. Those whose rights and survival are thwarted in the fog of isolation are also part of the new regime of rights and popular activism. Circumstances in which suffering is not visible enough to provoke compassion and culture is not colorful or "authentic" enough to provoke curiosity and admiration create diminished conditions of rights-effectiveness. When a people is unable to give itself constitutional and cultural shape and substance or to effectively communicate its rights claims and its story of rights violations, it faces a likelihood of becoming invisible and therefore of being subject to the will and whims of illegitimate power.

The world's political and cultural geography is being reshaped by stringent conditions for success, conditions that create not only new collective entities, but non-entities (of which refugees are a basic example), forms of human existence that are insecure, incoherent and unimaginable. Membership in a legally defined community with the potential to call upon public sympathies in defense of rights has become the single most important form of belonging, in the absence of which unrecognized masses are commonly consigned to a state of limbo, lacking basic attributes of humanity, somehow indefinably malevolent, casting no shadow. And as spectral beings without credentials of belonging or visible markers of suffering, forced to exist outside their familiar conditions of cultural practice and representation, many also fall outside the narrow pathways of soft law and are subject to violations of rights and dignity: sexual slavery, forced labor, conscription of child soldiers – all the latest possibilities in the seemingly growing repertoire of exploitation and brutality.

Conceptual diplomacy

Anthropologists have long been aware of a basic human capacity to construct categories that bring together patterns of belonging and behavior. In *The Savage Mind* Claude Lévi-Strauss draws upon a wide range of nineteenth-century ethnological material, such as that from the Haddon expedition to the islands of the Torres Straits, to illustrate social-conceptual categories connected to emblematic forms of behavior, manifested in structural analogies between nature and culture: "Thus the Cassowary, Crocodile, Snake, Shark and Hammer-headed Shark clans were said to love fighting and the Shovel-nosed Skate, Ray and Sucker-Fish clans to be peace-loving. The Dog clan was held to be unpredictable, dogs being of a changeable disposition. The members of the Crocodile clan were thought to be strong and ruthless and those of the Cassowary clan to have long legs and to run fast," and so on.[14] Lévi-Strauss admits that such material is in large part fanciful, made up of old wives' tales, but with enough truth and accumulated instances that he feels himself challenged to situate this phenomenon in his overall schema of human thought. He thus goes on to consider such beliefs to be associated with the absence or breakdown of reciprocal relations, particularly marriage exchange, between social groups. In circumstances in which social groups are considered to exist autonomously, as particular manifestations of a wider diversity, "[e]ach social group will tend to form a system no longer with other social groups but with particular differentiating properties regarded as hereditary, and these characteristics exclusive to each group will weaken the framework of their solidarity within the society."[15] A social framework in which natural attributes are built into traditional institutions is, in Lévi-Strauss' view, likely to "split up into a whole lot of independent, hostile bands, each denying that the

---

[14] C. Lévi-Strauss, *The Savage Mind* (London: Weidenfeld and Nicolson; and University of Chicago Press, 1966) 116.

[15] Lévi-Strauss, *The Savage Mind*, 116.

others [are] human."[16] Nature, in other words, can be drawn from only so much as a reference point of social being before the complex, interwoven structures of cosmology and reciprocity begin to unravel.

But what if an analogous capacity to naturalize categories of belonging were part of the legal emergence of social groups or categories with claims to distinct status within a global paradigm of diversity? Are there new possibilities for peace to be established between all people by rethinking the behavioral foundations of categories of belonging? Whatever answers we might find to these questions, one thing is certain: these are not usually the professional concerns of anthropologists but of diplomats, international bureaucrats and (in a broad sense of the term) lawmakers, who recreate or draw upon history-laden ideas of culture and ethnic belonging and give them new, instrumentally oriented life, with the intention of positively constructing the foundations of peace. The institutions of global governance are primary venues for *conceptual diplomacy* – the term I give to endeavors by states and international agencies to establish conditions of peace and prosperity through intervention in the realm of ideas.

One of my more direct predecessors in the study of the issue of juridical influence on ideas is Michel Foucault, especially in a series of lectures he gave at the Pontifical Catholic University in Rio De Janeiro in 1975, collectively titled "Truth and Juridical Forms," and in his next major work that followed, *Discipline and Punish*.[17] At the outset of his Brazil lectures Foucault identifies juridical practices as the most important social activities responsible for the emergence of new forms of subjectivity, which, among other ramifications, find their way into the foundational premises of sociology, psychology, psychopathology and criminology. His emphasis is on the knowledge production inherent in "the manner in which wrongs and responsibilities are settled between men ... by which

16 Lévi-Strauss, *The Savage Mind*, 119.
17 M. Foucault, "Truth and Judicial Forms," in *Power*, ed. James Faubion (New York: The Free Press, 2000); M. Foucault, *Discipline and Punish: The Birth of the Prison*, trans. Alan Sheridan (New York: Vintage 1995).

our society defined types of subjectivity, forms of knowledge, and, consequently, relations between man and truth." In particular, "juridical forms and their evolution in the field of penal law" are seen by Foucault as "the generative locus for a given number of forms of truth."[18] In the Brazil lectures and in *Discipline and Punish* Foucault is centrally concerned with the unrecognized, pervasive and dangerous influence of state-sanctioned juridical power on the organization and control of knowledge, which then constrains and disciplines the behavior of individuals.

There is a key difference between Foucault's connections between juridical power and knowledge and the central premise of this book: I am placing emphasis here, not on the influence of seemingly neutral, politically invisible power on ideas, but on the explicit *exercise* of power *through* ideas. In the institutional analysis I am presenting, the jurists and diplomats of international law are on more equal footing with academicians in the production of knowledge. It is true that in disseminating their ideas they possess the advantage of the influence of their offices; but this is manifested more through legitimacy than coercion. In the legal realm I am describing here, the individual is not disciplined by institutions as much as actively persuaded in contests for the power of mass opinion. And unlike the disciplinary ideas in Foucault's judiciaries, the conceptual constructions of international agencies are not so much concerned with shaping and constraining individuals as they are with defining, formalizing and, in some cases, ennobling and idealizing human categories and communities.

The mobilization of conceptual diplomacy is clearest in the aftermaths of civil war and genocidal violence. Such intra-state violence is almost always preceded by dehumanization of those perceived as enemies. In some cases, the enemy-alien-Other is repeatedly, often strategically, portrayed as a source of pollution, thereby intellectually and emotionally facilitating the work of "ethnic cleansing." For peace to be lasting in such circumstances there has to be more than an imposed

---

[18] M. Foucault, *Power*, ed. James Faubion (New York: The New Press, 2000) 4.

political solution. The ideological foundations of hate also have to be undone, the incommensurable made knowable, the humanity (or at the very least conceptual neutrality) of the enemy Other restored. This is the simple logic of conceptual peacemaking that manifests itself in, for example, jamming hate-mongering radio broadcasts in Rwanda. Such interventions are justified not only by the lived consequences of cultivated hatred, but have a rationale that goes back to the guiding principles of the 1945 constitution of UNESCO: "That since wars begin in the minds of men, it is in the minds of men that the defenses of peace must be constructed."[19] In other words, there has to be an intellectual disarmament before any legal arrangements for peace can be effective.

The nature of cultivated hatred introduces the need for effective public outreach as a necessary condition of stable statehood. This can be seen, for example, in the little known US peace-building efforts in South Africa at the time leading up to the dismantling of apartheid. In this effort, James Michner's novel *The Covenant* provided the US diplomatic staff with a historical background starting in 1652 with the arrival on the Cape of the first Europeans, the Dutch. The staff investigated the origins and avenues to psychological empowerment of all contending groups in South Africa: blacks, Afrikaners, Indians, and two "catch-all" ethnic categories described ambiguously as "Colored" and "English-speaking." The strategy they eventually adopted was largely focused on refashioning ideas of belonging: "South Africa would be well on the way to solving the conflict if the Afrikaners saw their salvation through the Blacks, and if the Blacks saw their greater escalation economically and politically in cooperation with the more economically developed Afrikaners, English-speakers, Coloreds and Asians."[20] These

---

[19] UNESCO, Constitution of the United Nations Educational, Scientific, and Cultural Organization, November 16, 1945.

[20] E.J. Perkins, "The Psychology of Diplomacy: Conflict Resolution in a Time of Minimal or Unusual Small-Scale Conflicts," in *The Psychology of Peacekeeping*, ed. H.J. Langholtz (Westport: Praeger, 1998) 50.

are the "ethnic factors" included by Lawrence Eagleburger (former US Secretary of State under George H.W. Bush) alongside social, political and economic causes of conflict, one aspect of an approach to diplomacy that begins with preventive measures oriented to intervention in conceptual conditions before a conflict erupts into violence.[21] In contrast to the usual processes of forceful intervention and separation of combatants in the aftermath of violence, the central task of US peacemaking in the late apartheid period was ultimately intervention in emblematic, violence-inspiring ideas about group membership and behavior, promoting the capacity of people in conflict to be aware of their enculturation and to cope with primordial sentiments.

Economic development and political reform are therefore seen by some theorists of diplomacy as insufficient ends, but as ideally leading to further-reaching, *intellectual* efforts in the promotion of peace. These are steps toward the transformation of deeply rooted ideas of social belonging and the exclusion, or inhumanity, of others. The ultimate goal made possible by conditions of prosperity – the real prize of lasting, embedded peace – is to be arrived at through *conceptual* change, through change in the collective imagination, to arrive at a politically dominant identity that, while it may not be in perfect accord with the moral paradigm of human rights, has at least done away with the intellectual foundations of dehumanization and hatred of others. Such, at least, is the ideal pursued when forceful intervention is impractical.

The usual way to approach the legal foundations of social attachments and identities is to consider legal categories as reflections of and responses to significant qualities of social reality, as seen in the claims of underrepresented minorities; but it is also possible to find legally elaborated social categories that have first been formulated by

---

[21] L.S. Eagleburger, "Foreword," in *The Psychology of Peacekeeping*, ed. H.J. Langholtz (Westport: Praeger, 1998) vii–ix.

states or international agencies and that are only subsequently translated into social identification, action, claims and popular recognition. Conceptual diplomacy can be a kind of applied legal sociology, but not one intended to serve as a description or interpretation of observable human interaction. Instead, often in sincere efforts to correct error and describe human groups as they really are, it can offer a new reality, above all a reshaping of the perceptions of those in conflict, arrived at by campaigning on behalf of naturalized signposts of identity considered most likely to lead to peace. Institutional initiatives create alternative paradigms to the ideas that accompany violence, paradigms expected to be more conducive to peace than the stereotypes of purposefully inflamed prejudice. This is an approach to peacemaking that identifies and redefines sociological concepts with the goal (explicit or not) of cultivating the positive essential qualities of a category of people through the work of imagination, education, dialogue, mediation, encounter, and occasionally treaty-making.

At least in terms of global paradigms, legal sociology has developed a remarkable capacity to bring its conceptions of reality into being. It is true that international lawmakers who draft peace treaties have often produced short-term, misguided solutions that leave resentments smoldering; but when it comes to conceptual constructions, they do have a distinct advantage over more familiar forms of knowledge production: their ideas benefit from the built-in visibility of their sponsoring institutions. If there is a legal-sociological consensus that Human Category X has a rich history, is a bearer of certain inalienable rights, and is a necessary participant in peacemaking, then reports will be produced detailing the urgent necessity of X-protection, calls will go out to Xs and their supporters, meetings will be arranged, and in short order representatives of Category X will appear as arranged in New York or Geneva, declaim on behalf of the rights of (and rights violations imposed on) Xs and move forward on an agenda of X-building. It matters little whether in creating its programs on behalf of Xs the institutional imagination is scrupulously reflecting reality or whether it is indulging in a flight of fancy with little connection to lived experience; under circumstances in which there is political advantage to be gained by a legal-sociological idea, reality will often adapt to it, vindicate it and give it the imprimatur of truth.

In Chapters 4 and 5, I discuss two globally conceived categories of belonging that illustrate this pathway to identity formation. The international movement of indigenous peoples (the subject matter of Chapter 4) came into being through International Labour Organization initiatives in the 1950s and subsequently became the focal point of the most attended, and quite possibly most vocal, meetings of the Commission on Human Rights (since 2006 the Human Rights Council). The Alliance of Civilizations (discussed in Chapter 5) is conceived at a higher level of abstraction, representing supra-state, "culture-writ-large" entities that do not as easily produce spokespeople and that do not as unambiguously represent the rights of the oppressed. Rather, civilization has become a way of representing history on a grand scale, and hence of reaffirming the dignity of those once subject to the hemispheric oppression of colonial empires.

By concentrating on the "metadialogue" of conceptual diplomacy I do not in any way seek to challenge efforts to focus closely on the syntactic, grammatical and discursive qualities of legal settings that bring together "traditional" and Anglo-American approaches to justice.[22] But I do want to demonstrate that the intellectual schemes elaborated at the highest level of international diplomacy can have a significant impact on globally encompassing conceptions of the cultural and political

---

[22] See, for example, R. Barsh, "Putting the Tribe in Tribal Courts: Possible? Desirable?" *Kansas Journal of Law and Public Policy*, 1999, 8: 74–97; J. Clifford "Identity in Mashpee," in *The Predicament of Culture: Twentieth-Century Ethnography, Literature, and Art*, ed. James Clifford (Cambridge, MA: Harvard University Press, 1988) 277–346; J. Richland, "'What Are You Going to Do with the Village's Knowledge?' Talking Tradition, Talking Law in Hopi Tribal Court," *Law and Society Review*, 2005, 39 (2): 235–71.

makeup of the world, which, in turn, encourage the public emergence of more particular, rights-oriented conceptualizations of culture and belonging.

From the perspective of a legal anthropology that is willing to take publicly shaped concepts like "indigenous peoples" or "civilization" seriously, it has become indispensable to consider the intellectual sway of institutions that are more political and legal than scholarly or scientific. For a variety of reasons (including postmodern and postcolonial advocacy of disengagement from public policy, expressed in closed, impenetrable forms of discourse), bureaucracies of global governance are today the most publicly influential sources of opinion-shaping ideas about cultural history and human belonging. Even more surprising when we closely examine these legal-conceptual origins is the fact that the impetus behind knowledge production in this international context is often anything but institutional, routinized and pedantic (though it may ultimately have these qualities in abundance), but has every bit as much to do with spiritual longing, cultural romance, the inner wellspring of human creativity, and, in common with "salvage" anthropology, the feeling of loss of these things, nostalgia for knowledge and ways of life disappearing from the repertoire of human possibilities – all this on the part of lawmakers, diplomats and bureaucrats who seem to draw upon ideas of human betterment, the essence of human groups and categories, and the rhetoric and performance of the claims of culture.

The personification of the state

At the same time that distinct peoples, minorities, communities and other collective claimants of rights and identity are gaining self-awareness and influence, the state, often seen as oppositional to distinct legal (above all constitutional) status of marginalized groups, has become a more significant moral actor than ever before. This follows simply and directly from the legitimacy and influence of human rights in international law, which bring to bear on states all of the ideals and responsibilities of correct behavior normally attributed to individual persons, not just legal compliance, but beyond that – in defiance of the actual strategically self-interested or outwardly rapacious behavior of states – new expectations of benevolence and altruism oriented toward the well-being of others. These "others," these beneficiaries of state virtue, can be understood through a broad interpretation of the concept of the "international community," which extends to all those peoples whose conditions of life can be improved through the promotion of peace and human development.

Aspirations for the improvement of the moral behavior of states are the essence of human rights standard setting; and states, as self-interested actors largely in control of the venues of international law, are closely involved in the process of what we might call moral self-definition and identity construction. Like individuals, states rarely measure up to the highest shared ideals of behavior and personal accomplishment. Given a global reality in which states are the principal moral entities answerable to human rights standards, when communities marginal to states reach out to alien publics for recognition and sympathy, they are usually doing so with reference to a state (or a corporate state proxy) as an immoral actor, as a source of suffering and injustice. And in doing so, they are called upon to self-reference and represent themselves to others as a collective entity subject (historically and/or currently) to the abuses of a state, in other words to articulate claims to collective rights, virtue and victimhood – all with implicit or explicit reference to a state.

The soft law of public persuasion and indignation is not entirely an informal process. It also has recourse to remedies that formalize and at times ritualize the guilt and atonement of states. This takes the form of the public apology or the truth and reconciliation commission. In Chapter 6, I discuss an example of these processes drawn from Canada's response to far-reaching injury caused by the state's policy of aboriginal assimilation through Indian residential schools and the mechanisms of atonement that have followed from recognition of this harm as a major human rights violation. The ceremonialized public state apology and the truth and reconciliation commission have become the preferred mechanisms for the recognition and correction of mass collective injury wrought by state policy. These mechanisms call upon states not only to acknowledge this harm but to modify their public representation of state history. They call into being expressions of humility that are uncharacteristic of states, that are, in fact, often performed reluctantly, through clenched teeth, even though the most significant criterion of success in this venture is the communication of sincerity to a skeptical, keenly observant audience. And, oddly enough, they are also sometimes performed with markers of sincerity, with voices quavering with emotion and gestures of remorse and supplication. In any case, formal mechanisms of atonement, mediated by public opinion, call upon states to be moral actors, to be self-critical and self-developing entities.

At the same time they call upon the victims of state action to cohere around remembrances of suffering, to aid in the process of reshaping the past by becoming historically coherent, to produce an assembled narrative out of those experiences of harm that can be sympathetically understood, while leaving hope for a future of mutual recognition and collaboration.

But every exercise in coherence produces exclusions. In this case the public imagination has difficulty grasping the vexed nature of intergenerational suffering and the widely ramifying effects of assimilationist or genocidal policy. Publics are in some circumstances inappropriately narrow and judgmental and in others excessively optimistic and indulgent; and these are qualities that are consequential for those whose cultural/legal identities are shaped, even in part, through public mediation.

There is an emphasis on the great importance of human diversity in many initiatives on behalf of minorities; but at the same time, all pathways for the claims of truth and justice considered in this book lead in the direction of culturally corrosive forms of juridification, the formalization of concepts, categories and defense strategies of social membership and survival. To put this last point more broadly, world governance initiatives toward collective justice are producing ideas about identity, culture and tradition that have important effects on the ways that social belonging is expressed. Law revolutionizes whenever it is used as an instrument of preservation. This results in a paradox in which strategies for cultural protection are increasingly reliant upon culturally corrosive, globally uniform expressions of cultural integrity and strategies of defense. But, as I argue in Chapter 7, the outcome of this paradox is inconsistent with a simple model of cultural convergence, in which there is a progressive, civilizing shift from "status to contract" or a cumulative, extending influence of legal/bureaucratic norms and legitimacy. Instead, the influence of laws, especially human rights standards and institutional reforms, now have the effects of reinforcing tradition, securing ethnic boundaries and emphasizing the broadly appealing poetic and spiritual qualities of those who are the subjects of wrongs.

This is the basic starting point of what I am setting out to discuss in this book: legal institutions and processes are not simply instrumental agents of social order, but are also products and producers of imagination. And legal thinking, as product and producer of imagination, is not based, as is commonly assumed, exclusively on reason, order, factuality or the systematic application of rules through propositional language structure. Law can also be a vehicle for expressions of nostalgia, longing for intimacy, and a need for variety of experience through encounter with difference. And such longings can be seen with particular clarity in the intersection of international law and the public pathways of cultural rediscovery and collective identity. The dynamics of new international norms of human rights and multiculturalism lead us toward a consideration of the reconfiguration of collective life, the adaptive rediscovery of self, largely in response to the preferences and inclinations of public consumers of justice and culture.

TWO

The power of persons unknown

The golden record

Largely because of their intangibility, publics exist largely in the imaginations of those who are reaching out to them, as the unknown recipients and arbiters of appeals to justice. They are in good measure whatever a spokesperson imagines their audience to be when they stand in front of a microphone and/or a camera. Because of this, outreach to publics is almost always in some way like sending a message in a bottle, oriented toward a future audience of unknown provenance and uncertain sympathies.

The "message in a bottle" quality of social justice lobbying can be heuristically demonstrated with the example of the "time capsule" phonograph record on the Voyager 1 space probe launched in 1977 and now hurtling somewhere in the interstellar void, containing, among many other items, messages of peace from humanity on the part of then US president Jimmy Carter and UN secretary general Kurt Waldheim. The golden record is eventually to be discovered, its designers hoped, by an extraterrestrial public elsewhere in the universe, or perhaps by an equally alien species of future humans traveling far from earth, their planet of origin. Carter addressed this possible audience with the following statement:

We cast this message into the cosmos ... Of the 200 billion stars in the Milky Way galaxy, some – perhaps many – may have inhabited planets and space-faring civilizations. If one such civilization intercepts Voyager and can understand these recorded contents, here is our message: We are trying to survive our time so we may live into yours. We hope some day, having solved the problems we face, to join a community of Galactic Civilizations. This record represents our hope and our determination and our goodwill in a vast and awesome universe.[1]

The space probe message is an exaggerated instance of the anonymous nature of publics, which nevertheless reveals a more common quality to be found in outreach to those who are distant in time and space: representations to publics of all kinds consist not only of hoped for, relatively immediate responses to a crisis of injustice, but also of messages to a more distant futurity, with often implicit aspirations for human betterment.

There is a simple logic to the Voyager 1 human outreach project that follows from the challenge of self-presentation to an alien public: a simple description of humanity and its environment has to be selected out of a vast array of possible information. Limited by the capacity of information storage available in the 1970s, a committee of experts had to decide what was to be included, out of the incredible variety of human experience and planetary phenomena, as representative of the earth and the human self. It is easy to understand their predicament as they met to address this problem. They eventually decided on photographs of planet earth and representative samples of other planets in the solar system; architectural monuments such as the Sydney Opera House, the UN headquarters in New York (privileged with two images: one in daylight and another at night), the Golden Gate Bridge and (unaccountably) the Toronto airport; and in terms of images of humans there is a representative sample of appearance and activities, such as bushmen stalking a gazelle, the face of a Guatemalan peasant, a portrait of

---

[1] http://en.wikipedia.org/wiki/Voyager_Golden_Record#Contents. Accessed December 16, 2008.

an extended family from rural America, and an Olympic gymnast. In the audio portion of the record, it seems only natural that whale songs be included in the repertoire of earth sounds and given a prominent place as "whale greetings" alongside "UN greetings." The didgeridoo of indigenous Australians is of course not to be left out. Then there are the obligatory classics by J.S. Bach and Louis Armstrong. And this leads to a further variety of human musical accomplishment, selected, it appears, according to geographical distribution, the society's degree of technological development, and, reasonably enough, the Cold War divide.[2]

In terms of understanding the process of public representation, as much can be learned from the excluded information as from the chosen. Notably absent are sounds and images that many would consider unpleasant: bats, for example (everyone hates bats); or anything remotely associated with experiences of grief and suffering. As a species, humans have demonstrated a penchant for violence that seems almost natural, and whatever one might argue about human nature, warfare has certainly been an essential part of human history; but the golden record gives no indication to its potential alien audience that the species has been anything but peace-loving and uninterruptedly prosperous. Religion too has been bracketed out, perhaps because any one image calls for all faiths to be represented equally (and hence compromising the limited information storage capacity) or perhaps because of the humanist inclinations of those on the committee, or both.

Representation to an alien audience raises a very basic question that applies to all public outreach: what gets included in the archive of self-presentation and what does not? Social justice activism, involving outreach to unknown consumers of information who are then possible sources of sympathy and action, involves much the same problem

---

[2] The complete inventory of golden record data can be consulted at: http://goldenrecord.org. Accessed December 16, 2008. I am grateful to Peter Jackson for drawing my attention to the Voyager 1 time capsule project.

of culling images and ideas from a range of possibilities. It calls for a strategic, selective representation of justice claimants. What that is distinctive about our customs is most likely to appeal to those who are possibly willing to act on our behalf? And what do we do as a people that can and should be given recognition and connected to rights claims?

Rights claims intended to address injustice and suffering call for a form of representation that answer questions about the consequences of harm. What are the most essential events in our history that communicate to others our sense of injustice? In answer to this (in contrast to the sanitized representation of humanity on the golden record) the depiction of violence and suffering is sometimes essential; it is the ultimate source and expression of the abuse of power, ideally communicated through emotionally stirring, even disturbing, depictions of the afflictions of the innocent.

But in terrestrial social justice activism, as opposed to the time capsule, publics are not merely the ghostly subjects of abstract hope. They can become momentarily tangible, able to respond in the here-and-now to outreach in direct ways, through correspondence, unannounced visits, rallies, protests or newspaper editorials. Public outreach is not always mysterious and impersonal, but can manifest itself in direct ways, providing another sense of the term "public appearances," perhaps better described as the seemingly spontaneous appearance of publics. Such appearances, including smaller but often cumulatively influential sound bites in the media, are significant for social justice campaigns in that they can reinforce a sense of grievance and provide confidence among activists in a cause that might otherwise seem unattractive and futile.

More common are those publics that remain anonymous, yet identifiable because they selectively respond to the information sent in their direction. They will probably always remain in some measure obscure, diverse, porous, lacking homogeneity, inclined to change, acting like processes rather than noun-like things. Their vagueness and instability are some of the qualities of publics that make them important for understanding the hidden dynamics of social justice activism. But at the same time, they can be provoked or stimulated into action: their members can write to newspapers and blogs or construct Web pages that express the reasoning and at times the emotion behind their indignation; their spokespeople can appear, sometimes with no previous introduction to their collaborators, at arranged venues to voice shared opinion directly to decision-makers and other members of other publics; they can ultimately merge others into a temporary collective entity that itself becomes newsworthy, with public visibility in their mobilization around a cause; and ultimately they can, just possibly, through the build-up of a critical mass of public expression, bring about positive change to a dispute or crisis marked by the systemic abuse of power.

Tarde's sociology of imitation

Like many important concepts, the idea of publics (in the plural) has its very own public figure with a rightful claim to a significant place in intellectual history. Gabriel Tarde, writing in France at the turn of the nineteenth to twentieth centuries, developed the idea of publics as a central part of the emerging discipline of sociology. This is useful for our purposes because a century-old conception of publics highlights those traits of Euro-American publics that have only recently come to prominence. Tarde's sociology of public makes it easier to identify those aspects of the representation of rights and culture that are truly new, or that have only recently grown in significance; and at the same time it makes it easier to see those processes of public influence and interaction that have emerged more slowly and been with us longer than is commonly assumed.

There is a sense in which Tarde is the Jules Verne of sociology, constructing much of his analysis around an imagined social order based upon the anticipated effects of yet-to-emerge inventions. He saw the indefinite public as "the social group of the future," brought into being by three mutually auxiliary inventions: the printing press, the railroad and the telegraph, which together comprised the "perfected means of locomotion and instantaneous transmission of thought from any distance."[3] These inventions had already in his time enhanced the power of the press to the point at which it had become politically formidable, bringing into being a new foundation for common ideas and new social bonds originating in peoples' "awareness of sharing at the same time an idea or a wish with a great number of other men."[4] Ideas communicated rapidly through new technologies readily become the shared foundations of religious, economic, political and national groups. "Our age," he proclaimed, "is the era of the public," and then added the important but rhetorically deflating rider, "or of publics."[5]

Tarde anticipated the close connection between the themes of identity and communication, now very much in the forefront of culture and media studies. He observed in an 1893 essay, "The public and the crowd," that "not all communications from mind to mind, from soul to soul, are necessarily based on physical proximity. This condition is fulfilled less and less often in our civilized societies when *currents of opinion* take shape."[6] Opinion, as Tarde defines it, is "a momentary, more or less logical cluster of judgments which, responding to current problems is reproduced many times over in people of the same country, at the same time, in the same society."[7] He felt that newspapers in particular had a profound impact on opinion and hence on the dynamics of society. Almost a century before the pioneering work of Benedict Anderson, which connects nationalism to the rise of commercial print media, Tarde pointed out that newspapers "transformed, both enriched and

[3] G. Tarde, *On Communication and Social Influence*, ed. Terry Clark (University of Chicago Press, 1969 [1901]) 280.
[4] Tarde, *On Communication and Social Influence*, 278.
[5] Tarde, *On Communication and Social Influence*, 281.
[6] Tarde, *On Communication and Social Influence*, 278.
[7] Tarde, *On Communication and Social Influence*, 300.

levelled, unified in space and diversified in time, the conversations of individuals," with important implications for their forms of belonging.[8] At its worst, however, the popular press represented to Tarde "the double progress of pornography and slander, which have become the two breasts nourishing the newspaper."[9] The *Chronique judiciaire* is a particular target of his outrage, for instigating crimes through the "contagion of murder." To him, this point seemed obvious, "For not a murder is committed but the press becomes aroused – except when it is a question of murdering two or three hundred thousand Armenians, which it fails to tell us about."[10] His outrage is connected to a heightened sense of the responsibility of those who manage a product – publicly shared information – that is formative not only of opinion but of society itself.

Thus, Tarde's sociology is premised on a highly plastic dimension to social institutions and laws that emphasizes the coalescing of social life around the ideas and acts of individuals. Under circumstances in which inter-mentality is not an outcome of direct, personal communication, public opinion, and the political mobilizations influenced by it, grow in significance. A consequence of the plasticity and growing reach of opinion was a paradox in which social sameness and difference simultaneously become more salient: "As nations intermingle and imitate one another, assimilate, and morally unite, the demarcation of nationalities becomes deeper, and their oppositions appear more irreconcilable."[11] "Therefore," Tarde concludes with a very contemporary-sounding paradox, "even though the absolute difference between nations diminished, their relative and conscious differences grew."[12]

Tarde's innovative understanding of the workings of publics is easily glossed over because much of what he says seems self-evident from the

---

[8] Tarde, *On Communication and Social Influence*, 304.
[9] Tarde, *On Communication and Social Influence*, 266.
[10] Tarde, *On Communication and Social Influence*, 266.
[11] Tarde, *On Communication and Social Influence*, 306.
[12] Tarde, *On Communication and Social Influence*, 306.

perspective of the mobile, globally networked world of the twenty-first century. But Tarde's publics are actually a small part of a much more ambitious project. His wider goal was to set out the foundational premises of the emerging discipline of sociology. He supported his version of the nascent discipline of sociology with an extended discussion of the analogies between social analysis and sciences which (as he took pains to demonstrate) had all begun to converge on monads and microcosms as the most important sources for unlocking the secrets of the universe. In Tarde's *monadologie* the individual takes on the explanatory role of the atom or cell, with a result that was completely at variance with the emphasis by his influential colleague at the Sorbonne, Emile Durkheim, on the moral power of society. For Tarde, individuals are the elementary agents of society: "there can only be individual actions and interactions. The rest is only a metaphysical entity, mysticism."[13] A social group is therefore simply "a collection of beings, brought together by the fact that they are in the process of imitating one another or, without imitating one another presently, resemble one another in that their common features are previous copies of a same model."[14] Following from this premise, Tarde elaborates what is sometimes called a constructivist approach to social belonging in which nations, for example, "are merely entities long considered to be real beings in the ambitious and sterile theories of so-called philosophical historians."[15] His starting point in understanding nationalism is a critique of the essentialist idea or assumption "that it springs spontaneously from the genius of a race,

---

[13] Tarde, *On Communication and Social Influence*, 140.

[14] "une collection d'êtres en tant qu'ils sont en train de s'imiter entre eux ou en tant que, sans s'imiter actuellement, il se ressemblent et que leurs traits communs sont des copies anciennes d'un même modèle." G. Tarde, *Les Lois de l'Imitation* (Paris: Les empêcheurs de penser en ronde/Éditions du Seuil, 2001) 128. My translation.

[15] "Les nations ne sont que des entités longtemps prises pour des êtres véritables dans les théories ambitieuses et stériles des historiens dits philosophes." Tarde, *Monadologie et Sociologie* (Le Plessis-Robinson: Institut Synthélabo pour le progrès de la connaissance, 1999) 36. My translation.

the entrails of the people, that anonymous and superhuman actor." [16]
Once these sorts of explanations are exhausted we are left with the real,
formative sources of history and social life. We are led toward "the kind
of clearer and more rational explanations, which interpret any historical event only through individual actions, notably through the actions
of inventive men that have served as a model to others and been reproduced in thousands of copies, like mother-cells of the social body." [17]
The combined influences of extraordinary individuals can fuse to form
a collective product, which only has an appearance of exteriority, but
which is in reality merely the result of psychological synthesis. This phenomenon, which defines the essence of social interaction in families,
classes and nations, he termed "inter-mental psychology." A central task
of sociology thus turned toward understanding the complex dynamics
of interaction between individuals, their means of communication and
forms of imitation. Given that individuals in complex industrial society are often separated from one another by the very nature of urban
life and institutional specialization, how do they cohere? How do common sentiments of belonging bring people together? How do observable trends in belief and opinion take shape among individuals who
do not know or interact personally with one another? How, through
indirect exchanges between individuals, are social institutions created
or reformed? How are ideas with implications for collective action conceived and propagated? Approached from this direction, social solidarity in complex societies cannot be dismissed as inconsequential, fleeting
or as a given that arises simply from the nature of society, but becomes
the central question in the agenda of sociology. It is seen by Tarde as an

---

[16] "qu'elle a jailli spontanément du génie de la race, des entrailles du peuple, acteur
anonyme et surhumain?" Tarde, *Monadologie et Sociologie*, 36. My translation.

[17] "un genre d'explications plus claires et plus positives, qui rend compte d'un
événement historique quelconque par des actions individuelles seulement, et
notamment par des actions d'hommes inventifs qui ont servi de modèle aux
autres et se sont reproduites à milliers d'exemplaires, sortes de cellules-mères du
corps social." Tarde, *Monadologie et Sociologie*, 36. My translation.

outcome of changeable ideas rather than more immutable institutions or basic forms of social existence. The driving forces of society are to be found in processes of innovation and imitation among creatively active and receptive individuals rather than acting independently from human agents.

This is a sociology that in some respects seems current, in which publics are formed by new media of travel and communication, and in particular are influenced in their behavior by the editorial decisions and opinions of the press. But there is another sense in which his ideas, applied to contemporary dynamics between media and publics, falls short: there is relatively little conception of publics *being* influenced for strategic purposes. Collective ideas in Tarde's sociology are expressed, perhaps selected out with a view to profit, but not cultivated. Publics mobilize and produce opinions and ultimately laws, but they are not strategically acted upon. In his world, the press may be misguided, and thereby morally misdirect its readership, but the press does not actively attempt to move its public toward a specific political or moral stance. Its choice of subject matter is guided more by assumptions about what the public wants to hear, what it is inclined to consume, than by goals of mass mobilization and political awakening. Despite Tarde's keen awareness of the press's shortcomings, there is in his sociology an innocence concerning the relationship between the media and their publics. Perhaps his trust in publics can even be said to cross the line from innocence into politically naïve, blind optimism. He was not concerned about the possibility of the powerful influencing or monopolizing of the media that shape opinion, but on the contrary found that the press suppresses the conditions favoring the absolute power of governing groups. "A newspaper reader," he pointed out hopefully, "is much more in control of his intellectual freedom than a lost individual swept up in a crowd." [18]

---

[18] Tarde, *On Communication and Social Influence*, 282–3.

Despite this shortcoming, Tarde's conception of the formative power of publics merits greater attention. Under the rapidly changing circumstances of late modernity in which no society is fully isolated from others, and in which inter-cultural dynamics are becoming an increasingly important part of cultural identity, Tarde's sociology, or at the very least his emphasis on the concept of publics, has become increasingly relevant. It is not entirely clear to me how this happened. Perhaps the world itself has changed in ways that have vindicated his intuitions and corrected his myopia. My sense is that Tarde has become more significant than he was in his own time above all because of the increasingly obvious place of public opinion in processes of collective rights and recognition, new pathways toward the expression of cultural difference. His work suggests that we may have underestimated the influence and reach through time and space of shared ideas, assumptions and sentiments in the constitution – and constitutionalization – of social and cultural life.

The human rights movement represents the most recent history of the emergence of influential publics, in this case publics that are attuned to ideals of a common humanity, universal standards of human dignity and a just world society. A common denominator among the publics drawn to and forming around human rights is that they see the state and the societies it contains, not as sources of consistent security or objects of patriotism, but as potential perpetrators of serious harm to the human ideals of dignity, prosperity and justice. The rights revolution, and the humanitarian ideas that go with it, are central to the effectiveness of the politics of indignation. Justice lobbying is most effective among those publics in which humanism and ideals of global justice have been given room to develop, in which they are part of the day-to-day processes of information consumption and interpretation. The concepts and sentiments of ideal conditions of human belonging have an increasing, and under-recognized, influence on the priorities and implementation policies of global power.

The persona of mass publics

Delving into some of the basic features of mass Euro-American publics reveals the limitations and dilemmas of strategic appeals to popular will. In view of this challenge, I am purposefully limiting myself to those basic qualities that I see as bringing out some of the little-recognized predicaments of social justice activism. To accomplish this portrait, I am relying on my participation as an ethnographer in several social justice campaigns on behalf of indigenous peoples, supplemented here and there by abundant literatures that concentrate on one or another aspect of the public persona. So here, as I see it, are a few of the common features of those publics that have become reference points for activist efforts toward persuasion, popular influence and, to the extent that it exists, the practical leverage of soft power:

1. *Publics are persuadable.* This is the quality that propels efforts to sway popular ideas. Even though some publics are adamantine in their beliefs, all are to varying extents subject to influence, if not persuasion. At their worst, publics are not criminal masterminds, but are better characterized as sidekicks or collaborators in the schemes of those with influence over them, those more knowledgeable, ambitious and unscrupulous – and with a certain amount of access to media. The positive side to this is that, like many a passive participant in malfeasance, they are capable of correction, with only minor inclinations toward recidivism.

A corollary of persuadability, however, is the idea that public opinion acts at the bidding of, and is ultimately inseparable from, power interests. This can be seen in the now conventional approach to hegemony, usually traced to Marx via Gramsci via Foucault, which holds that power in conditions of late modernity relies more on combinations of institutions and ideas that intrude further than ever before into the private lives of individuals, creating forms of compliance and obedience that are unperceived and hence beyond the reach of political action. There is an element of fatalism to those conceptions of hegemony which hold that diffuse, ideologically manifested power interests are virtually undiscoverable, intuited only by an enlightened few whose central insight is to tell us with certainty that hegemony exists. To reveal hegemonic workings with any amount of precision would of necessity compromise the idea of an unfathomable, unreachable, and hence unreformable, realm of power.

But the basic premise of hegemonic disempowerment also finds expression in more activist ideas that try to cultivate an enlightened public by exposing the conspiracies of media control to the light of day. A variant paradigm of the usurpation of public opinion relies less on the idea of nebulous, unknowable hegemony, but holds that the culprits behind the capturing of opinion are identifiable, that a central feature of late modernity – *the* defining source of political abuse – is the arrogation of any possible popular sense of justice or injustice by the combined, at times collusive, powers of states and an increasingly concentrated commercial media. Cynicism toward public opinion in the context of mass democracy can already be seen in Max Weber's definition of it, written with a backdrop of the systemic hyper-nationalism of World War I: "communal conduct born of irrational 'sentiments' … [n]ormally … staged or directed by party leaders and the press."[19] Recent iterations of this idea tend to be expressed with somewhat less measured rhetoric, as through expressing frustration that awareness of the manipulations of centralized media have inexplicably not reached mainstream consumers of information. Pierre Bourdieu, for example, rails against the "symbolic drip-feed" of compliant and complicit journalism, which he considers the main source of the legitimacy of unchecked liberal free-market capitalism.[20] A similar position is taken by Edward Herman and

---

[19] M. Weber, *From Max Weber: Essays in Sociology*, ed. H. Gerth and C. Wright Mills (London: Routledge & Kegan Paul, 1948) 221.

[20] P. Bourdieu, *Acts of Resistance: Against the Tyranny of the Market* (New York: The New Press, 1998) 35.

Noam Chomsky in *Manufacturing Consent*.[21] Their propaganda model of the mass media and public opinion describes the media as centrally owned and controlled, serving and propagandizing on behalf of powerful political interests that are well positioned to select the priorities and definitions of newsworthiness, and more generally to constrain media policy, ultimately shaping the information and opinions offered to consumers. The central outcome of this collusion is a public that is simultaneously credulous and confused, unable to make sense of the world because of its regular consumption of misdirected information, a public that is therefore politically de-fanged, neutralized and compliant.

There is undoubtedly a kernel of truth to this scenario, which is only partly brought into question by the obvious point that the supposedly conspiratorially power-enmeshed media are, aside from their many failings, also responsible for producing and marketing the best-selling book that offers Herman and Chomsky's uncompromising critique of the media (Pantheon Books, a division of Random House, Inc., owned by the private media corporation Bertelsmann AG, which operates in 63 countries and employs over 100,000 workers).

This self-evident point takes us in the direction of a more substantive argument: the conspiratorial aspects of the relationships between states, centrally owned media and publics are also greatly attenuated if we consider what might be called the popularization of the tools of propaganda. This follows from the simple fact that the technologies of communication with publics are no longer (if they ever were) monopolized by states and have become more widely available than ever before. Herman and Chomsky acknowledge this, and point to a variety of instances in which the scope of resistance by dissident groups and protest movements has been enlarged by Internet activism, including the famous 1998 protest against the World Trade Organization's secretive formulation of global

[21] E. Herman and N. Chomsky, *Manufacturing Consent* (New York: Pantheon, 2002).

trade policy and the peasant uprising in Bolivia in 2000 in response to a scheme sponsored by the World Bank for the privatization of water. Herman and Chomsky nevertheless minimize the Internet's utility as a critical tool, pointing to the uneven global distribution of access to information technology and anticipating "the private and concentrated control of the new broadband technology" which threatens to "limit any future prospects of the Internet as a democratic media vehicle."[22] In making this argument, however, they resort to an illegitimate discursive technique in which established facts are denied with reference to yet-to-be-manifested conspiracies.

For the moment, global trends are clearly in the direction of increased access to information and communications technology, which has every appearance of keeping one step ahead of universal control by power interests.[23] This means that we are witnessing a revolution in the dynamics and range of influence of public opinion, in which widely shared ideas are more commonly cultivated on a small scale with a view to justice and social good. Because of wider access to the tools of information production and distribution it is more possible than ever before to make limited-range, at times cumulatively massed, efforts to persuade unseen audiences, to influence or "raise" public awareness, with the potential to become a catalyst of judicial and political criticism and reform.

It is now commonly recognized that the increased availability of tools of communication and information goes together with the fact that nongovernmental organizations (NGOs) have in recent decades become the building blocks of civil society, growing exponentially both in number and in the reach of their political influence. They have thus become intermediary producers and consumers of information and

---

[22] Herman and Chomsky, *Manufacturing Consent*, xvi.
[23] Both the uneven global distribution of information technologies and their exponential growth are illustrated in the United Nations Development Programme, *Human Development Report 2001: Making New Technologies Work for Human Development* (Oxford University Press, 2001).

instigators and organizers of activism, situated between claimants of collective rights and anonymous publics (very much in the plural), with the leverage needed (the organizers hope) to influence the holders of power in corporations, states and the institutions of global governance. NGOs have become primary resources for expressing grievances, rights claims, local culture and micro-nationalism. But they cannot exert influence without capturing a part, sometimes a very small part, of this strategic reservoir of public attention and support. Donations, petitions and membership lists are measures of an organization's influence, its ability to persuade and call people to action. The involvement of NGOs in public persuasion, in the solicitation of compassion, indignation and activism, is the source of most significant changes that have taken place in recent decades in the dynamics of social justice and the politics of culture.

2. *Publics are self-interested.* This point seems to run up against the most visible outpourings of sympathy through action, guided by altruism and occasionally the heroic self-sacrifice of remarkable individuals. Certainly the donations and interventions following the cataclysmic 2006 tsunami and the 2010 earthquake in Haiti, for example, were not, taken together, selfishly motivated. But publics qua anonymous opinion-sharing collective entities are inclined toward the protection or furtherance of their own interests before they open up to the plights of unfortunate others. The most influential publics are therefore those large-scale interest groups, the silent self-interested majorities, which serve as the reference points to or common denominators of political action. Efforts to cultivate sympathy for a cause that runs up against the perceived interests of such a broad public are unlikely to succeed, despite what one might wish to think about human proclivities to altruism.

3. *Publics tend to be hypocritical.* That is to say, relative to the causes in which they are active, they do not readily become indignant toward injustices in which they are implicated, even if only through political affiliation. The idea of media control by dominant powers takes us

only so far in attempting to understand the social justice preferences of publics. There is another dynamic at work here that has less to do with control of information and more to do with the discomforts of self-examination following from information successfully communicated.

Indignation and activist involvement tends to be easier to mobilize in circumstances that lie outside the immediate scope of political responsibility of those concerned. Pride and self-interest (following point 2 above) add an element of hypocrisy to the choices behind righteous anger and empathy. For example, it is easier for the public in Turkey to become incensed about Israel's handling of the political aspirations of Palestinians than about their own government's stonewalling on the issue of Kurdish autonomy. Much the same transnational tendencies in the sense of injustice can be seen within both the Arab states and Israel itself. And (here I am selecting an example so that I am not implicated in the phenomenon I am describing) popular opinion in Canada, where much of the political identity is based on the promotion of human rights and development overseas, tends to be less receptive to information about abrogation of treaties and so-called Third World conditions in Canada's own aboriginal reserves. This does not mean that such self-examination cannot be encouraged; only that cultivating indignation in an inward direction, toward a public's own political community, tends to be difficult. Expressing indignation about injustices occurring elsewhere is easier than acting on wrongs for which one might, however indirectly, share responsibility. There seems to be more to this tendency than the straightforward exercise of preferences. There can also be a kind of displacement at work in which publics rally around transnational causes as a way to avoid the discomforts, responsibilities and sacrifices involved in self-examination and self-correction. Acting on indignation about injustices occurring elsewhere can be a salve applied to the sense of responsibility for wrongs occurring within one's own realm of political identity, wrongs that reflect back toward the sense of self.

4. *Publics are curious*. Perhaps a better way of putting this is that they are attentive to the anomalous. This means that a strategy for gaining recognition and political traction in public representation of a social justice claim is communication from sites that in and of themselves garner recognition, often heightened by disjuncture through the mere presence of cultural performers. Times and locations that have pre-formed symbolic content, and above all that predispose audiences to attention and sympathy, are often used by activists as a way to communicate directly with a public, or in Tarde's terms, with a public via a crowd. More than this, a carefully selected point of entry for conveying a message gives the news media something to work with, a "hook" or a "handle" on which to focus a story.

An example that comes to mind is a campaign within a campaign that I witnessed when the aboriginal reserve community of Cross Lake, Manitoba, faced what appeared to be a sudden ecological crisis, with large numbers of dead fish suddenly appearing in a shallow inlet of the Nelson River adjacent to a residential area.[24] A lawyer for the community based in Toronto, communicating by email and telephone, saw this as an opportunity for public exposure and immediately began a response, first encouraging me and employees of the Band Office to get images of the fish floating belly-up in the reeds and sending them to the law office and to the community's lobbyist based in Minnesota. The next step in the plan, accepted by the Chief and Council, was to gather some of the fish in garbage bags, eventually to further decompose en route to Winnipeg, and then to dump them on the main stairway of the provincial parliament, with speeches to be given before the public and the press. Here we have an example of public space used as a focal point for media attention. The intended site of this planned protest was

---

[24] I elaborate on the circumstances and results of this research project in greater detail in Chapters 5 and 6 of *The Rediscovered Self: Indigenous Identity and Cultural Justice* (Montreal and Kingston: McGill-Queen's University Press, 2009b).

significant as a primary source of the recognition of government; and of course the attention-getting disjuncture was to be the act of pollution, fouling the stairway with rotten fish, an act that would have been justified (so the Band's lawyer argued) by the attribution of responsibility to the government in office, with an implicit reason: these dead fish were caused by your neglect; now you can have them. This strategy had progressed to the point of gathering some of the fish in garbage bags, ready to be driven south, when a report was issued by the environment ministry explaining that the dead fish were caused by a combination of a blocked culvert under a roadway, which disconnected the inlet from the main body of the Nelson River, and an algae bloom that took oxygen out of the water and suffocated the fish, which in turn was occasioned by seepage from a nearby waste processing system, both of which were the responsibility (though the situation could not reasonably have been recognized, nor its consequences anticipated) of several successive Band administrations. The bags of dead fish found their way to a landfill and the issue was forgotten.

The key to acting on such opportunities in a way that resonates with mass audiences, whether strategically intentional or not, is the manipulation of symbolism in a way that creates a separation from ordinary, taken-for-granted perceptions of inhabited space. One of the advantages enjoyed by delegations of the indigenous peoples' movement (discussed further in Chapter 4) is the facility with which participants are able to create these kinds of anomalies and provoke curiosity, often with their mere presence, dressed colorfully in a setting that represents modernity: the Ainu singing and drumming outside a metro station in Tokyo, minimally clad tribesmen with spears and feathers confronting Brazil's FUNAI officials seated behind desks and microphones, and even the multitudes of indigenous delegates in meetings taking place amidst the concrete and glass of the UN headquarters – such images, while eventually becoming familiar and weakening with use, are devices that at one point attracted the attention of publics, that invited them to find out why the anomaly had occurred, and ultimately to symbolically restore order to the universe.[25]

5. *Publics have short attention spans.* An idea or a piece of information presented once is soon forgotten, disappearing into the seemingly infinite mass of information to which a literate person (especially one with an Internet connection) has access. The goal of activist campaigns, as a self-styled human rights lawyer once explained it to me, is to create a background hum of publicly-accessible information, that is to say, to generate enough individual bits of noise in the media so as to produce a sound that cannot be ignored. This calls, first, for personal representation to the public, appearing before and appealing to audiences anywhere and everywhere, from church basements to Earth Day summits. This then provides material – or, from the press's point of view, a public interest incentive – for the production of news stories, feeding into a regular, multi-venue output of material sympathetic (one hopes) to one's cause, again without discrimination as to the size of the venues' subscription base, listenership or viewership, anything from local newsletters to national or, at best, international television coverage. The greatest challenge of social justice activism consists in creating this background hum in competition with other rights-claimants for the attention of publics.

This is made complicated by desensitization to suffering, "compassion fatigue," the cumulative consequence of the barrage of information and appeals to fractured consumers of information. The fickle nature of mass publics poses a tremendous challenge to social justice activists in terms of garnering recognition and commitment in competition with other worthy causes. How does one effectively testify to remote others? How does one get the attention and sympathy, and possibly arouse the

[25] I am grateful to Mark Watson for drawing my attention to the symbolic strategies of the Ainu in Tokyo. Images and discussion of indigenous protest in formal settings are amply provided by A. Ramos, *Indigenism: Ethnic Politics in Brazil* (Madison: University of Wisconsin Press, 1998).

indignation, of those whose starting point is (one must assume) disengagement and skepticism?

To succeed in being provocative, a public appeal must ultimately succeed in being seen in preference to others. This means not only having a strong claim to sympathy through a compelling cause; it also means presenting that cause in such a way that it will be seen. A cluttered, overcrowded exhibit makes each work of art intrude on the others. Perception calls for empty space, removed from rival claims to attention.

If this book were a how-to guide for social justice activism directed toward organized communities or NGOs with a compelling grievance and little public lobbying experience, my advice would be to leave to one side the unlikely goal of direct mass mobilization and instead to identify and concentrate efforts of persuasion on specific publics, which willingly provide room for appeals to attention and sympathy: church groups, aid organizations, university campuses, and the like. These are the sites of publics most likely to be receptive to the information one wants to convey, that is to say, most likely to perceive and act upon a compelling message by disseminating it further, to ever-widening audiences.

The ultimate sign of a campaign's success is when the public response to a media campaign itself becomes a story, which then feeds back to a more general public and provides assurance to barely convinced individuals that their opinions are shared by many others, and can justifiably be converted into action. Only by repeatedly conveying a message to targeted audiences does one create that most desired goal of media campaigns: to ignite an autonomous, media-worthy reproduction of opinion that by its very nature is inclined to spread and gather its own attention.

6. *Publics are emotionally responsive.* That is to say, they respond more favorably to information that triggers emotion than to appeals to reason. This means that they do not readily pick up on mixed messages or

even stark contradictions in the information they consume. They have a tendency to compartmentalize, receiving and responding to information in tidy, separate packages. If the information they receive appears authentic and triggers emotion in one context, then that is all that matters, even if a contradictory view later makes an equally effective appeal to their emotions.

The tendency of publics to respond to an affect-laden human experience has an effect on (and is affected by) appeals to social justice and the ideological foundations of human rights. In responding to these appeals, the feelings that seem to be commonly expressed by publics (and then to generate further affect in them) can be described as a love that moves in one direction, unreciprocated, toward an object of pity, and sometimes beyond into the oceanic feeling of shared humanity, of brotherhood or sisterhood. Under these circumstances there are direct connections between suffering, sympathy, action and remedy.

But stirring emotion in response to, say, an unfulfilled promise in a formal agreement, is far more difficult because in this circumstance injustice occurs in the context of legal language that is purposefully devoid of emotion, and the wrong is an act of omission that cannot be unambiguously identified and connected to a condition of suffering. Provoking emotion in sympathetic others calls for tangibility and intimacy and the innocence of sufferers, all of which are absent when a crisis exists only as an injustice, as words on paper. Public demands for authentic experience, perhaps as an antidote to the saturation of media with political discourse, lead them to turn to affect, to the most visceral experience of sympathy, as a source of moral guidance.

7. *Publics have an abiding sense of fairness, with inclinations to indignation when rules of fairness are violated.* The phenomenon of indignation – defined in the *Oxford English Dictionary* as "wrath excited by a sense of wrong to oneself or, especially, to others" – has in my view become the central source of energy in movements of political and legal reform. Expressed as a shared complex of ideas and sentiment,

indignation is the most immediate public response to injustice, and ultimately to the effectiveness of soft law. Like other forms of public emotion, it relies on simple ideas – in this case taking the form of stark hypocrisy, blatant contrasts between laws and behavior, all with readily perceptible consequences for fairness and good governance. Given the untidy nature of almost all instances of political and/or judicial abuse, it calls for a process of simplification, conceptual distillation and direct communication. It is usually cultivated by intermediaries between untidy facts and public consumers of information.

Of course such faith in the infallibility of the public sense of justice is in stark contradiction with my discussion (above) concerning the publics' persuadability – some might go so far as to say their gullibility. This makes it all the more important to investigate the actual ideas and behaviors of publics, at least insofar as they are qualitatively identifiable. It is in the strategic cultivation of popular compassion and indignation that we are likely to find the most interesting and odd connections between injustice, public persuasion and cultural representation. Even if the publics involved in these relationships remain largely anonymous, we can still illustrate their importance by looking carefully at how rights and identities are perceived and presented by identifiable, strategically-minded actors.

Compassion involves a sense of understanding, of sympathy with the suffering of others, whereas indignation leads to activism through a sympathetic but ultimately self-interested sense of political harm or injustice. Indignation may be more difficult to cultivate, but is ultimately a much greater prize for those with political goals because it has a more direct connection to collaborative activism. Injustice is not just a formal contravention of law; it can be the source of a powerful sympathetic emotion, sometimes expressed through a sense of personal moral outrage, even toward distant injustices involving unknown actors. And, like compassion, it can be stimulated into growth by strategic representation. Now, more than ever before, small-scale organizations are able to communicate their members' basic moral commitments to strategically identified publics, to harness their idealism, compassion and sense of justice with testimony and images of distant suffering.

8. *Publics tend to be ismatic*; they form around specific collective causes or "isms" that become items in repertoires of identity, like femin*ism*, liberal*ism* and so on. This suffix can be applied whenever members of a movement oriented toward rights and social justice acquire a relatively clearly defined sense of history, exclusivity, inherent virtue, political ambition and the ongoing nature of their struggle.

New forms of communication and opportunities for transnational networking encourage and facilitate the engagement of isms with legal processes of human rights standard setting, negotiation with states and use of courts in asserting rights and pursuing autonomy; but, at the same time, they enable movements of unilateral autonomy and hard-line religious extremism that directly refuse engagement with states and legal regimes of autonomy and that separate themselves as fully as possible from the cultural influence of the global consumer society. Paradoxically, transnational networks of solidarity can in some circumstances support the erection of isms with little public appeal, marked by rigid social boundaries based on redefined and reinforced collective values.

Again, public involvement in isms would not be possible, or at least not occur to the same extent, without the empowerment of soft power through the rise in legitimacy of human rights and the near-simultaneous rise in numbers and influence of nongovernmental organizations. There has been a shift in recent decades from an emphasis on state-centered nationalism in public persuasion to a more diffuse, strategic consciousness-raising and public involvement in humanitarian causes inspired by the ideals of global development and human rights. This brings us to the final, related quality of the character of publics.

9. *Publics are drawn to universal ideals, with a capacity to act on them with evangelical fervor.* This of course is a trait with a long history,

inherited from the cosmopolitanism of the Stoics, the millenarian expectations of Reformation Christianity, through the most fervently held ideals of the Enlightenment and the enduring legacy of the civilizational philanthropy of the nineteenth century. All of this is background to the public's penchant for persuasion by ideas that correspond with deeply held convictions in the form of universal paradigms of liberation or utopian aspirations. Occidental publics in particular are inclined to act on the belief that their vision of human good will not come about unless and until it is communicated, propagated, acted on and universalized in concert with sympathetic others. Given that there are rival visions of human good (including the absence or negation of such a vision), this kind of universalist conviction ultimately seems to result from (and in) a basic core of moral hubris and self-defensive enclosure.

All of this means that the most globally influential publics, taken together and characterized as an individual personality, have the qualities of a typical, perfectly normal, conflicted, hypocritical and half-formed teenager: somewhat (but not entirely) credulous, curious, easily distracted and self-interested, with a keen, sometimes extravagant sense of justice, tending to succumb to emotion and to push his or her view of universal values on others. As I will discuss in more detail below, each of these traits has an effect on the processes and possibilities of social justice activism; and taken together they produce stark dilemmas in the publicly mediated law and politics of difference.

Witnessing and new media

To maintain an effective degree of information sharing and action, activist movements established in response to political crises and with ambitions toward autonomy are required to be highly social, to network actively, to recruit and organize members, to fundraise and, even in clandestine organizations, to "publicize" their work. The task of communicating the rightful, recognized place of a community of sufferers of political abuse and/or injustice is therefore a tremendous challenge. Provoking indignation and political action within a strategically identified public calls first for communication oriented toward persuasion. This challenge calls for the same kind of selectivity in public representation as in the eye-witnessing of film or photography. It calls for images or artifacts of testimony to be selected with a view to their communicability, appeal and potential to evoke strong emotions in others. It is a challenge that at times elevates testimony to an art form, a kind of narrative poetry comparable to great literature. Those whose identities are built on intergenerational suffering and marginalization have a story to tell. Their starting point is a situation of isolation, not only from the recognition and services of the state, but from the public that is the most immediate source of the states' power. How, under these circumstances, is the story to be told, and the marginalized people represented?

One of the clearest examples of NGOs using new technologies to harness the power of indignation can be seen in the use of video (especially video made available on the Internet) to document human rights abuses. There is of course almost universal recognition of the inevitability of contestation of views, critical scrutiny and skepticism toward specific items of visually recorded testimony; but because of its immediacy, its ability to convey and provoke emotion, and its perceived capacity to transcend journalistic filters, visually recorded testimony engages publics with a legitimacy that surpasses that of all other forms of evidence.

Public receptiveness to visual media might go some way toward explaining the success of the "shooting back" initiative by the human rights organization B'Tselem, the Israeli Information Center for Human Rights. (The main title, which comes from the first line of the Book of Genesis, is Hebrew for "in His image," interpreted to mean that everyone is in God's image, that everyone is equal.) This organization began documenting rights violations in 1989 through the work of researchers who were sent to every large city in the West Bank.

The first information they gathered took the form of transcribed narratives offered by Palestinians who claimed to have been subject to rights abuses. They also produced several films, again based mainly on testimony from Palestinians who had been victims of abuse. But these carefully produced films were limited in their effect; and the activists felt a sense of frustration that human rights abuses were occurring which, according to every shred of evidence and intuition, were part of daily life in the West Bank but were not being perceived or understood by the Israeli public. A turning point came when the organization hit on the idea of supplying video cameras to Palestinian families throughout the West Bank to document their treatment by Israeli soldiers and settlers. Oren Yakobovich, coordinator of B'Tselem's video department, in an interview posted on the Internet by the human rights NGO Democracy Now!, describes the content and effect of the first video clip shot by a Palestinian to be posted on the Internet by B'Tselem:

What you're going to see is a clip from a settlement called Tel Rumeida in Hebron. What we will see is a settler from this settlement ... pushing Palestinians that basically are living across the street, on the other side of the road, pushing her back to her home, calling her "whore," cursing her very viciously. And all this time you see the soldier standing next to the woman doing nothing, not interfering ... The sister of the Palestinian who's being cursed is the one that's filming. Basically, there is a kid there, sixteen years old, holding a camera while her sister is being attacked by the settler. You see that the settler is coming to the camera, trying to push her into the house. And her sister is just next to her filming.

When [the Palestinians] gave me the camera, they gave me the tape, they didn't talk about this video, because for them it's casual. They didn't think there was anything special in this video. While we watched it in the office in B'Tselem, we said like there's something very strong here that we need everybody to see ... And then we put it out on one of the Israeli Internet-used channels, and very fast there was a lot of – about hundreds of talk-backs and hundreds of clicks on this video. Of course, [an] hour after, I got a great response from the rest of the networks in Israel, news networks. The day after, it was everywhere in Israel.[26]

The video reached a wide enough (and indignant enough) audience in Israel to be addressed by Israeli Prime Minister Ehud Olmert. Soon thereafter, it was picked up by major networks in the United States and Europe, and eventually globally. In practical terms, this publicity did little to end the situation of conflict between Palestinians and settlers in Hebron, but it did appear to reduce the level of violence in the occupied territories simply through awareness by settlers and soldiers of the potential presence of cameras recording their behavior.

It is interesting to note that different audiences picked up on different aspects of the video clip as their central source of moral outrage. The most immediate and obvious source of abuse documented in the clip, which I assume contributed to making it a global news item, is the individual *being* abusive – the settler haranguing, insulting and pushing the Palestinian teenager. But the Israeli audience concentrated its attention on something quite different. The settler they took for granted. Even though her aggression was in this instance extreme, such was the kind of behavior that Israelis had come to expect from the settlers in Hebron. To them it was unfortunate, but, like inclement weather, not something one could reasonably expect to be expeditiously remedied. But what the Israeli audience picked up on, according to a spokesman for B'Tselem, was the soldier witnessing the abuse and not intervening: "Our problem is the policy, the lack of law enforcement, that the soldier is standing there and doing nothing, and the police are there close by and doing nothing ... And this is what the debate is about."[27]

---

[26] Democracy Now! "Shooting Back: The Israeli Human Rights Group," December 26, 2007, www.democracynow.org/2007/12/26/shooting_back_the_israeli_human_rights. Accessed September 18, 2007.

[27] www.democracynow.org/2007/12/26/shooting_back_the_israeli_human_rights. Accessed September 18, 2007.

So what we have here is a public community of Israeli citizens reacting sharply to a manifest instance of the unequal distribution of the benefits of the state, in this case the protection of the law. The video clip prompted a strong reaction among them mainly because it was seen as authoritative, truthful, bypassing the distortions of politically interested testimony and journalistic opinion to give insight into a situation of rights abuse through an immediate example, as it occurred. The contents of the clip transcended the posturing of religious and political communities in conflict and presented Israeli citizens with a starkly clear issue: are Palestinians the legitimate subjects of rights under the state of Israel? And if so, are we willing to tolerate the unequal application of those rights in response to religious and political differences? There may be those Israelis who consider Palestinians to be endemically disloyal and undeserving of the protections of the state (hence the debate), but the majority seem to have been moved by a sense that basic principles of rights, equality and compassion had been violated in the course of this incident by the non-intervention of soldiers and police.

It is significant that there is no portrayal of the distinct culture of Palestinians in the B'Tselem-sponsored video clips. Certainly there is no romantic search for cultural virtue and authenticity visible in them. The source of the injustice that Palestinians face, and of indignation in their viewership, is the violation of their rights qua individuals – individuals of a particular kind – youth who are innocent of the violence happening around them or simple farmers caught off guard in the act of working in their fields or orchards – those who are apparently being targeted for abuse for no other reason than the accident of their birth.

The more direct engagement of Palestinians in a global effort to represent themselves as human rights-bearing subjects of victimization and suffering tends to turn toward more graphic depictions of violence in the occupied territories. Given new opportunities to represent themselves and their plight, the Palestinians are engaged in a global contest for sympathetic attention which, as Lori Allen describes it, "uses visual proof of damaged bodies and images of human suffering as primary tools. Through a focus on bodies and the blood, guts, and flesh to which so many are reduced by Israeli violence, the physical common denominators all human beings share are thrust before the world's eyes" in an effort to make "connections between suffering and political entitlement." [28]

As I write these lines another example of the activist use of video has almost literally fallen into my lap. A quick scroll-through of my email inbox reveals an item from *Sermitsiaq*, billing itself as "Greenland's best-selling newspaper," that has somehow gotten through my server's formidable junk mail filters and caught my attention among a miscellany of work-related messages. The newspaper has set up a fixed camera to take images of one of Greenland's largest glaciers, the Ilulissat Ice fjord, a UNESCO world heritage site, making available to the public evidence of the effects of global climate change. What I find interesting about this example is that the images it presents are compelling in a very particular way. There is of course little action in the video evidence. What it shows, after all, is a glacier, the epitome of slowness, even as it shifts and sends off icebergs and, ultimately, melts into oblivion at an alarming rate as measured against other geological speeds. More than this, though, is a sense I feel in viewing this site's images that the wind-swept glacier represents the utter absence of humanity, nature in one of its purest forms. It combines two essential elements that are most often sources of the appeal of video evidence. The first, and most apparent, is a sense of wrong. The time-interval images implicitly represent harm wrought by human agents. Ultimately it might be possible to identify the actions causing this harm and the human agents with the greatest degree of responsibility for them. In this instance, the practices

---

[28] L. Allen, "Martyr Bodies in the Media: Human Rights, Aesthetics, and the Politics of Immediation in the Palestinian Intifada," *American Ethnologist*, 2009, 36 (1): 162.

and policies responsible for bringing an unacceptable reality into being are attributable to a large population, making it unlikely that there can be any connection between the images and a judicial remedy, but very often, as we will see below, images can include an (often) implicit appeal to justice.

The second source of appeal here is the more positive side of indignation. It is derived from a sense of wonder and awe toward the difficult-to-grasp forces of the world, combined with a kind of anticipatory nostalgia toward its future loss. It connects injustice to a depiction of fragile phenomena – simultaneously unfamiliar and wonderful – that are threatened by misguided human actions. The central subtext of this kind of message is that the shrinking of the range of possible knowledge and experience, which diminishes what it means to be human, is being wrought by wrongs and injustices committed by identifiable agents. Who wants to live in a world that has converged into one landscape, one grey culture, in which everything is immediately familiar or readily knowable? There is a human capacity for curiosity, for self-development or (captured by the under-recognized German term *Bildung*), which is violated by the wilful diminishment of possible experience.

There is not only an ideal of a just world society at work in the most responsive publics, but also a more positively-oriented ideal of inter-cultural communication and collaboration. If we go back to the Enlightenment sources of humanism, this represents an ideal of self-improvement or self-cultivation with a common human dimension. One cannot learn a great deal from those whose ideas and values are incommunicable and incommensurable, or, moving in the other direction, from those who most resemble us, who have little to teach us that is not already familiar. Nor do we like to learn from those who are hostile toward us (even if this is a missed opportunity – the cliché is probably true that we can learn more from our enemies than from our friends). Some publics more than others are moved in ways that go beyond their self-interest by acting on a desire to learn from encounters with difference. This source of popular mobilization hinges on the idea that we have the most to learn from cultural variety, that different (but not entirely incommensurable) others might possibly hold the secrets of human betterment or survival. The significance of this ideal for campaigns of social justice should not be overlooked. As I will discuss further below, the ideal of self-improvement through communication and influence from the inherited knowledge of exotic others is a central source of the connection between local collective grievance and public indignation.

Lobbying efforts oriented toward provoking a public sense of outrage in furtherance of a moral cause use technologies of communication to emphasize, in varying combinations, such negative and positive sources of popular response. In some cases (as in the Rodney King video that first fully revealed the far-reaching potential of film as a tool of justice) moral outrage follows from a sense of institutionally entrenched violations of rights and basic principles of equality, without any kind of appeal to cultural nostalgia.

The opinions and activist engagements of publics have become resources necessary for the success of NGO activities. And because of this, the distinctiveness or individuality of a mobilizing group or community is frequently arrived at through wide, often transnational, communication of ideas about justice, dignity, political rectitude and human good, acted on in response to the emotional triggers of the consequences of the violation of these ideals, captured and embodied in images of suffering resulting from wrongful action.

Invisibility

The public is not the only intangible community that has become significant for the dynamics of cultural representation. Another abstract category of the invisible consists of those who are overlooked or excluded from media attention and activist intervention because, through the very nature of their cause and identity, they do not have access to the thematic fulcrums that tend to mobilize publics. The downside of cultural rights lobbying is especially to be found in dark corners and narrow alleys, among the dispossessed, where the public gaze is sightless or apathetic, that is to say, where there is neither the visible horror of violence nor the color and joy of cultural play.

From the standpoint of human rights universalism it is enormously consequential that human categories such as refugees, asylum seekers and immigrants have difficulty representing suffering and a distinct way of life that resonates with justice activists or cultural preservationists, a situation that engenders vacuums or failures of remedy. This is particularly true of long-term refugees, for a variety of reasons. For one thing, refugee societies tend to be chronically uprooted and broken, unable to command sympathy beyond their immediate crisis of dislocation. They are those who find themselves, as one historian puts it, "entirely outside the web of national community" and, we might add, outside the usual pathways of collective recognition and identity.[29] It is true that in the initial throes of homelessness, hunger and insecurity, refugees do garner sympathetic attention. Roads filled with people on the move, carrying infants and the little that they own, or crowded around food distribution points, arms outstretched in supplication, have become staples of war photojournalism. They represent the consequences of political immorality and the seemingly expanding limits of the human capacity for cruelty. They are, especially in the early stages of their displacement, the epitome of the illegitimate suffering of the innocent. In their condition of humiliation and loss they provoke a strong impulse to help, brought into being through the channels of distant suffering, sympathy and charitable intervention.

But refugee status has often become a chronic condition that, in the absence of the political will of warring states or factions, lasts long past

---

[29] M. Marrus, *The Unwanted: European Refugees from the First World War Through the Cold War* (Philadelphia: Temple University Press, 2002) 4.

the moment of displacement. And the enduring inheritance of violence and displacement diminishes people's capacity for expressing either compelling suffering or collective virtue through cultural difference. Having been displaced, they have no access to their territory, little usable knowledge of their environment, and produce almost nothing. They are dependent and generic. They have little to show that might place them in the category of possessors of traditional knowledge, little that others might admire. The crises that they represent are "humanitarian," suggesting that they cannot be classified in any way other than through their species membership, that they possess no common attributes of distinctiveness. They are simply marginalized human beings who are biologically alive.

It was the experience of the Holocaust and the mass displacements of warfare in Europe that seems to have informed the UN's definition of refugees, formulated in the 1951 Convention Relating to the Status of Refugees. According to this Convention, a refugee is one who:

owing to well-founded fear of being persecuted for reasons of race, religion, nationality, membership of a particular social group or political opinion, is outside the country of his nationality and is unable, or owing to such fear, is unwilling to avail himself of the protection of that country; or who, not having a nationality and being outside the country of his former habitual residence as a result of such events, is unable or, owing to such fear, is unwilling to return to it.[30]

Probably no other instance of legal classification has proven to be so catastrophically inadequate for the purposes for which it was intended. The central weakness of the definition built into the Refugee Convention is its emphasis on the "outside" position of refugees. Their situation is defined as one in which they are driven from their country of residence and nationality and forced into untenable conditions of life on

---

[30] United Nations, Convention Relating to the Status of Refugees, July 28, 1951, 189 U.N.T.S. 150.

foreign soil. The thinking of state governments is evident in a definition that tacitly overlooks the possible existence of "internal" refugees and appears to assume that states play no part in the displacement of their own citizens. The reality of armed conflict, particularly in the latter half of the twentieth century, however, has been one in which states engaged in civil conflict have acted at best with disregard, and at worst with strategic rapacity, toward the displacement of their own citizens, resulting in some 20 or 25 million internally displaced persons in the first years of the new millennium.[31] The Convention's emphasis on "persecution" as a factor in the creation of refugees is a further limitation, excluding many forms of brutality used to drive people from their homes.[32]

Refugees seem to comprise a new form of human existence that defies clear categorization. These are the masses that represent a model of awkwardness, confusion, powerlessness and demoralization, presenting the international community with "the stock figure of the unwanted suppliant."[33] Those who are displaced by violence not only lack the visible, tangible artifacts of suffering; they fall outside the recognized limits of belonging. They are forgotten, deterritorialized, in a semi-permanent condition of liminality between culture and death. They are, in Mary Douglas' terms, "matter out of place," a kind of political pollution.[34]

Being a refugee is not a chosen marker of identity any more than it is a chosen condition. No one declaims as a refugee on behalf of other

---

[31] These rough estimates are cited by A. Helton in *The Price of Indifference: Refugees and Humanitarian Action in the New Century* (Oxford University Press, 2002) 126 and 128.

[32] In response to this reality, Gibney proposes an alternative working definition of refugees, as being, "Those people in need of a new state of residence, either temporarily or permanently, because if forced to return home or remain where they are they would – as a result of either the brutality or inadequacy of their state – be persecuted or seriously jeopardize their physical security or vital subsistence needs." M. Gibney, *The Ethics and Politics of Asylum: Liberal Democracy and the Response to Refugees* (Cambridge University Press, 2004) 7.

[33] Marrus, *The Unwanted*, 10.

[34] M. Douglas, *Purity and Danger: An Analysis of the Concepts of Pollution and Taboo* (London: Routledge, 2002).

refugees. It is an imposed category of belonging elaborated in response to changing global patterns of forced displacement.

Even if they find a way to represent themselves to the world outside the camps, the obstacles that semi-permanent refugees must overcome in order to provoke sympathy are formidable. Unremitting dislocation does not readily take the form of exportable, emulable virtue. In being removed from their homes and/or territory, the dispossessed are hindered in the performance of their way of life. They are unable to rediscover and reveal themselves to others, to make an argument through the expression of culture for their worth and dignity as humans. To those who are normally ready to act against suffering and injustice in defense of others, the causes of their misfortune and essence of their being are largely imperceptible and unimaginable.

As a collective entirety, their innocence may be called into question – sometimes because any innocence they might have had was well and truly destroyed by the circumstances of their lives. Failures of government are concealed by the fact that, in the long term, refugees come to incarnate the vices of oppression, the human condition in the absence of anchorage to place, transmission of values, or the sanctioned rhythms of maturation. Boredom and dependency are conditions in which violence and criminal networks flourish. The high walls and electrified barbed wire fences of UN compounds are testimony to the seething resentments and insecurity of some refugee facilities. In conditions of forced settlement, at a remove from the cause of their displacement, the UN protectors readily become perceived as captors.

Arthur Helton, a Senior Fellow for Refugee Studies and Preventive Action at the Council of Foreign Relations in New York, describes the Dadaab refugee camps in northeast Kenya, housing some 128,000 refugees of mainly Somali origin, as a "care and maintenance" arrangement for a "huge but largely invisible refugee population," in a global system of refugee arrangements that are fast becoming a "norm by default."[35] "Human insecurity," Helton reports, "is the defining characteristic in the camps around Dadaab. Banditry and violence remain pervasive between the complex network of Somali clans which are represented among both the refugee and the local community." Perhaps his most poignant observation is that, "The rape of women has become synonymous with the Dadaab camps. When I first visited the camps in April and May 1993, the issue was just emerging as a critical dimension of the insecurity in the camps. A UNHCR [United Nations High Commissioner for Refugees] rape counsellor then reported 107 cases of rape in the two months before my visit."[36] In response to the finding that most of the rapes occurred when women left the camps to forage for firewood in the surrounding territory, the US government funded an initiative in 1995 to provide firewood to the Dadaab refugees, an initiative that was then taken up in a regular program by the UNHCR (which, due to the usual budget constraints, was able to provide only 30 per cent of the needed supply), and which became the focal point of a micro-credit lending program financed by Ted Turner's United Nations Foundation, intended in the context of the Dadaab camps to support small-scale women's enterprises with the ultimate goal of giving them the earnings needed to buy wood without having to leave the camps, protecting women from the high risk of rape when venturing in the bush outside the camps.[37]

Taken together, the defining circumstances of refugees mean that the United Nations High Commissioner for Refugees, probably more than any other UN agency, faces the challenge of influencing popular opinion as a condition for the successful accomplishment of its mission. State governments are disinclined to invest in the repatriation or asylum of populations that become an unassimilated "foreign body." Prejudices and strategic misinformation directed toward refugees are

---

[35] Helton, *The Price of Indifference*, 156–7.
[36] Helton, *The Price of Indifference*, 157.
[37] Helton, *The Price of Indifference*, 157–8.

a hindrance to fundraising efforts and the pursuit of almost any initiative other than the maintenance of camps. In Colombia, for example, a four-decade-long internal armed conflict, mainly between left-wing guerrillas, right-wing paramilitaries and government forces, has produced the largest population of displaced persons in the western hemisphere (two to three million) and, after the Sudan, the second largest displaced population in the world, a population that lives not only with the circumstances of protracted violence but also the stigma and insecurity of their refugee status. In addressing public mistrust of both displaced persons and international agencies, UNHCR initiatives in Colombia emphasized "capacity building," a shorthand term for indirect involvement, in part by reinforcing the civil society institutions such as church groups that have a legitimate role in philanthropic intervention, and by "strengthening the protection regime" through "documentation campaigns, human rights training, [and] pedagogy projects."[38] UNHCR efforts in Colombia, in combating the negative stereotypes directed toward refugees, have attempted to "boost public awareness of the refugees' plight through radio advertisements, photo exhibits and educational programmes."[39] The first and most important step toward addressing the plight of the displaced is to reconfigure popular misconceptions about them.

Because of their public invisibility (or the hostility they sometimes engender when visible) and states' indifference toward them, refugees supported by UNHCR programs sometimes rely on the intermediation of celebrities to garner attention, donations and commitments to intervention programs. Tenor Luciano Pavarotti (d. 2007), fashion designer Giorgio Armani and screen actor Angelina Jolie are among the celebrities who have served in various capacities as UNHCR "ambassadors." From

---

[38] UNHCR, *The State of the World's Refugees: Human Displacement in the New Millennium* (Oxford University Press, 2006) 171.
[39] UNHCR, *The State of the World's Refugees*, 81.

May 28 to June 15, 2003, "Pavarotti and Friends" held their tenth fund-raising extravaganza in Modena, Italy, an event titled "SOS Iraq," with proceeds going toward Iraqi refugees. Maestro Pavarotti, in his capacity not only as a musical superstar but as the UN Secretary-General's Messenger of Peace, performed alongside artists such as Bono, Queen, Eric Clapton, Deep Purple, Ricky Martin, Andrea Bocelli, Lionel Richie, Laura Pausini, Zucchero and Mana to an enthusiastic crowd and millions of television viewers on the RAI Uno channel, raising more than two million euros through ticket sales and private donations.[40]

Armani, named UNHCR Goodwill Ambassador in 2002, focused his efforts on behalf of refugees through holiday campaigns at Emporio Armani stores, most notably in 2006 when he designed a mug, referred to as a "Christmas gift of hope," in support of the UNHCR.[41]

And, since taking on the role of Goodwill Ambassador in 2001, Jolie has made noteworthy efforts to apply her Hollywood star power toward shaping world opinion toward refugees, above all by visiting camps and pointing to her impressions of the nature of suffering among them. After a visit to refugee camps in Ecuador in 2002, she wrote: "What was really shocking was that every individual person you meet will tell you that their immediate family was [affected]. Somebody's child was killed, somebody's husband. Someone was beaten."[42] She was also cited in a *National Geographic* interview, which appeared just before she was to launch the 2009 World Refugee Day (June 20) celebrations in Washington, DC: "The trauma children face as a result of being

---

[40] UNHCR, "'Pavarotti and Friends' Celebrate 10th Anniversary, Raising Over 2 Million euros for Iraqi Refugees," May 28, 2003, www.unhcr.org/cgibin/texis/vtx/news/opendoc.htm?tbl=NEWS&id=3ed4c33a4. Accessed June 9, 2009.

[41] UNHCR, "Giorgio Armani Creates a Christmas Gift of 'Hope' in Aid of UNHCR," December 20, 2006, www.unhcr.org/45896c514.html. Accessed July 25, 2009.

[42] UNHCR, "Good Will Ambassador Angelina Jolie Ends Ecuador Mission," June 10, 2002, www.unhcr.org/cgi-bin/texis/vtx/news/opendoc.htm?tbl=NEWS&id=3d04d46e4. Accessed August 29, 2009.

uprooted from their homes, often very suddenly, is devastating, and affects the rest of their lives. The very young children still have dreams. But the young teens have very little hope. They are more realistic. There is nothing for them to do in the camps, and they seem defeated. It is very sad." [43]

Sad too are the ironies inherent in these efforts. The world's most visible individuals are needed to draw support for the most invisible; the most creative are needed to support the masses whose very form of existence suppresses creativity; and those who symbolize the pleasures of high art are the intermediaries of those whose existence is reduced to the dull routines of survival. These are structural ironies, in which the heightened visibility of a compassionate few has (in the absence of sufficient commitments from states) become necessary to stir the attention and compassion of the many, in efforts to provide for the continued existence of the unseen.

The conditions behind the invisibility of refugees illustrate some of the key features of publicly mediated justice. Although ideas of popular will as the foundation of enlightened democracy and justice rely on a knowledgeable, well-intentioned public, such qualities simply cannot be counted on. Using media to appeal to an unseen audience is like making a supplication to a flawed, quasi-scient deity, not knowing if or through what devices it might respond. With anonymity as an essential part of their nature, publics express their ideas only voluntarily, often impulsively, and are rarely meaningfully accountable for the real-world consequences of their opinions. They consist mainly of persons unknown, who are rarely identified or sought out to clarify or defend their ideas. Yet for good or ill they are an avenue to the exercise of justice, arbiters of legitimate causes and consumers of a limited range of expressions of collective identity.

---

[43] National Geographic, "Angelina Jolie on her UN Refugee Role," http://news. nationalgeographic.com/news/2003/06/0618_030618_angelinajolie_2.html. Accessed June 9, 2009.

This is why (as I will discuss further in Chapter 3) those organizations that want to promote the legitimacy of distinct collective rights will often turn to the romance of difference, emphasizing the unique and uniquely worthy essence of a people or category of people, the subjects of actual or hoped-for distinct rights, as a source of popular persuasion.

THREE

Cultural lobbying

Cultural justice

The complexity of the politics of indignation arises mainly from the fact that those who are oppressed often have to do more than make a claim as the collective subjects of illegitimate violence, forced displacement, or other forms of injustice. They can (and sometimes must) also lobby for attention and action by emphasizing their cultural virtue, as a sub-unit of wider conceptions of distinctiveness and its fragility in the face of injustice. Indignation among many consumers of information follows from a sense that the range of possibilities for cultural exploration and personal growth has been compromised – often by judicial bias or indifference toward the abrogation of rights that protect distinct, attractive, spiritually elevating ways of life.

This combination of ideas and sentiments toward culture is connected to, and possibly originates from, the "salvage anthropology" prevalent in the nineteenth and twentieth centuries, based on the idea of the urgent need for the preservation of knowledge about savage lore and life before their inevitable disappearance. Preservation had, at first, a primarily scientific motive. Primitive customs were to be recorded so that knowledge about them would be available to future scholars. There is just such a impulse toward cultural preservation in the origins of many ethnological museum collections started in the mid-nineteenth century in Europe and North America, continuing through the races that dominated twentieth-century anthropology to collect the fragile and disappearing intangibles of language, symbolism, myth, ritual and even (in the case of Franz Boas) cultural patterns of body movement.

In the new clothing of rights and identity, however, the urge to collect and preserve is more than ever before driven by the needs of *self*-knowledge. It is a way of re-establishing connections to the past, to forbears, to an essence once broken by colonial displacements. It is a source of collective recovery from the emotional injury and abuse of marginalization and state-sponsored efforts toward cultural erasure and assimilation. And it is part of the armature of rights of self-determination, anchored as they are to claims and arguments of authenticity and distinctiveness.

Cultural preservation has gone public – in a very different way than the edification through glimpses into primitive life intended through early museum collections, with their imposed categories and cluttered sterility. If law in its myriad forms is exercised through systematic argument and judgment, then cultural rights entail the presentation of arguments concerning the right to preserve a culture. More significantly, it entails judgments in response to those arguments, involving popular will. Cultural rights make the identification and preservation of vital heritage a collaborative process, involving experts, activists and publics as arbiters of performative cultural persuasion. Collective rights are commonly asserted through strategically oriented and organized representation of culture, with emphasis on the distinctiveness of rights claimants, juxtaposed with the injustice that threatens this difference. Cultural lobbying has thus overtaken ethnography (and in the process often infiltrated it) as the essential vehicle for the transmission of ideas about human difference.

At the same time, effectively reaching a limited reserve of public sympathy has become more competitive. This is partly a result of the recently dramatically widened access to communication and information technology, at work, for example, in the cell phone video images of the Burmese government's repression of protests led by Buddhist monks in 2007, which otherwise, given the government's efforts to strictly control the media, would have been largely invisible to anyone outside the country. But publics cannot be receptive to every item among an increased volume of rights-violation images, nor can they respond favorably to every representation of jeopardized distinctiveness. The availability – some might say the "democracy" – of technology goes along with an over-saturation of visually represented rights-appeals; and out of the mass of campaigns and the images that go with them, caring consumers of suffering and injustice must choose the objects of their attention and intervention. In these circumstances, the unimaginable must somehow be made real, simple legislative acts of dispossession made concrete, mental anguish expressed, and immaterial losses manifested.

The nature of impersonal audiences is also changing: although we are accustomed to hearing about the persuadability and manipulability of publics, there are many who approach information critically, in the direction of greater awareness of the arguments and artifices used to influence their opinions. This skeptical reserve (in the sense of withholding judgment) is directed toward both information that reflects state-centered views and interests and the more dissident representations by claimants of rights and cultural authenticity. One of the most appealing kinds of information involves drawing aside the curtain and exposing the wizard, revealing the secrets of illusion, falsehood and hypocrisy and raising the standards of belief. In the realm of social justice lobbying, this is occurring in much the same way that movie audiences are increasingly attuned to the production of special effects, demanding ever more convincing illusions of reality. Consumers of suffering and injustice are calling for higher standards of truth and greater evocation of feeling, searching out failures of authenticity, while still requiring emotional impact in the information they consume.

Under these circumstances the central place of public opinion in the dynamics of human rights is fraught with difficulty. The global scale of displacement and the exacting requirements of persuasion present a similar problem to that of "compassion fatigue" – to which we can add "culture fatigue" and "indignation fatigue" – in humanitarian intervention. If a people or community is only one among many worldwide being oppressed – raided by state "security" forces, removed without consultation or compensation to make room for an extractive project, or subject to any other kind of one-sided violence – how does it attract the attention of a public? How does it stand out in competition with others with similar or greater claims to justice? If the members of a community of the oppressed do not collectively stand out as victims deserving of sympathy in competition or comparison with others, if, in other words, there is not enough blood and hunger in their immediate experience to provoke strangers to action on their behalf, how do they make an effective claim? How do they capture the attention of the consumers of suffering, of those who are willing to be moved to compassion and indignation? The very nature of the politics of indignation brings into being a global victimology, in which collective sufferers compete for the attentions of increasingly jaded publics, often inured to depictions of misery and bored by performances of virtue.

How might this jadedness be overcome? First, as a condition of their active support, publics inspired by the values of human rights call for the innocence of the victims of political abuse to be established. With the possible exception of child soldiers, there is little sympathy in the global human rights public for combatants. One can, as an aspirant toward a peoples' autonomy, point to specific instances of a state's abuse of power, but there are usually counter-examples that political rivals can invoke, usually through accusation of impetuosity, intolerance and unprovoked violence from their enemies. Even depictions of charred remains in the twisted wreckage of an exploded car raise questions of context: how are we to know for certain that this unrecognizable victim of violence was innocent during the time that led to their death?[1] Might not they too have been a player in a corrupt, power-motivated vendetta, fueled by hatred? For an effective, non-violent engagement with the politics of indignation, a case must be made to public consumers of information that violence and injustice and their consequent suffering are one-sided, that a conflict or crisis can be understood as divided along the lines of the powerful and those who have been systematically oppressed. Counter-violence obscures this paradigm, while the portrayal of victimization and cultural virtue brings it into sharper focus.

Once the innocence of the claimants is broadly accepted, the claim to justice can move on to questions of responsibility. Among the innocent victims of a political crisis, suffering did not just happen but was *done* to them. Indignation follows from an understanding that the claimant-narrator's loss (which more widely represents those of his or her people) has a perpetrator, someone responsible, someone toward whom a call to justice can be directed. This means that intervention involves not only alleviating the immediate suffering of those caught in the middle of a struggle for power – the homeless, the hungry and the wounded – but most importantly it also involves seeking over the long term the sources of responsibility for the most historically decisive abuses of power. Indignation is every bit as powerful as sympathy in motivating publics to collaborative action. Provoking this sentiment means unmasking the states' defences, countering propaganda, revealing to the light of day the motives and responsibilities of power applied wrongly, against the innocent. Under these circumstances, the public is called upon to do more than send a check or online donation. It is asked to think, to evaluate, and to judge, and then perhaps to act against the expressed interests of a state that has committed injustice, quite possibly to become a dissident political actor.

---

[1] I am referring here to a photograph discussed at length by L. Allen, "Martyr Bodies in the Media: Human Rights, Aesthetics, and the Politics of Immediation in the Palestinian Intifada," *American Ethnologist*, 2009, 36 (1): 161–80.

Collective claims to justice also call for something more than depictions of violence, more than the all too familiar visual artifacts of oppression in public outreach; they call for public demonstrations of the dignity, distinctiveness and worth of a people. This in turn requires public representations of those particular qualities to which a public – or better: numerous widely distributed publics – might respond favorably. Media representation of a culture, often an adjunct to legal lobbying, calls for the most essential qualities of that culture to be defined and displayed. It initiates a process of selection and translation of the key features of a peoples' innermost being for public consumption. The central question of identity – "who are we?" – becomes reframed for export: "what do we practice, produce, know and believe that others might understand and appreciate?" It invokes, in other words, the art and artifices of simultaneous claims to victimhood and authenticity.

Let us consider two examples, from very different socio-political contexts. In much of the remainder of this chapter I will discuss the aboriginal/indigenous rights claims pursued by the Crees of northern Quebec and the women's rights claims of the Samburu of north central Kenya. These two cases lend themselves to comparison of the distinct forms of collaboration and the distinct challenges faced by victims of rights violations and activists involved in rights lobbying in Euro-America and Africa. And each of these examples in its own way illustrates the consequences for cultural identity of the strategic use of culture in campaigns of social justice.

Northern exposure

The James Bay Crees, perhaps in common with other hunting societies, tend to take a relaxed attitude toward disciplining their children. There seems to be something about living with several families crowded together in a split-log, moss-insulated hunting lodge that leads to a suppression of feelings of frustration or animosity and a greater willingness to openly contribute to collective welfare. This may seem counter-intuitive – human experience tells us that crowding and lack of privacy lead to short tempers – until one realizes the importance that collaboration had (particularly before village sedentarization and the introduction of new transportation technologies) under circumstances in which quickly constructing a lodge, gathering firewood, not to mention finding and killing game, were group efforts necessary for everyone's survival. "The bush is a natural disciplinarian," I was once told by a Cree social service administrator, followed by the explanation that when a family is camped in the forest, there are few distractions (other than those brought from the village), and no outlets for teenage rebellion. And the improper use of an axe has its own sanction, with built-in possibilities for a positive lesson in closing a wound with tamarack resin and a needle and thread.

In the village setting – even with its particular vices, conveniences and more impersonalized relationships – hunting ethics still manage to find expression. I was once with an experienced hunter in his home in Chisasibi, Quebec, as he was taking care of his grandchildren, spending part of his time making a sling shot from a rubber gasket (salvaged, he said, from heavy-machinery scrapped by Hydro Québec). Meanwhile, his three- or four-year-old grandson, playing outside in the sand and dirt adjacent to the house, kept taking off his shoes, and occasionally came into the house barefoot. The older children he was playing with protested that they could do nothing to convince the boy to keep his shoes on. His grandfather twice stopped what he was doing, took him outside to find his shoes, and tied them back on with a gentle admonition to keep them on because there was broken glass in the sand (the detritus of more than one drinking party). The third time the boy appeared in the house barefoot, the grandfather again went out to find the shoes. As he returned he was thoroughly dusting them off by hitting them together and blowing on them. Then he rummaged in a cupboard until he found a roll of duct tape. He sat the boy down and tied the shoes on as usual, then wrapped a generous amount of tape around the shoes to cover the laces and attach them to his grandson's ankles. Problem solved – all without a hint of annoyance and not a word spoken.

But the wordless discipline inherent in the hunting ethic of child-raising did not fully protect the Crees from an intergenerational disconnection that seemed to follow from imposed mega-project development and village relocation. The youth crisis in Chisasibi came to my attention with my first assignment in 1988 as a new Cambridge University PhD graduate in social anthropology for the then-fledgling Cree Board of Health and Social Services of James Bay. I had answered an ad for a social service consulting job in the *Montreal Gazette* and was hired right away, even though I was an Africanist with a specialty on Islamic reform and Qur'anic education in Mali. (This happened, I was later told, not just because of my Cambridge credentials, but because I could be paid less than a more qualified candidate with an MD.) My assignment was to fly to the (then) eight James Bay Cree communities to do a survey of the social service files and to talk to (I cannot remember anyone using the word "interview") social service workers about the challenges they faced. I flew in an assortment of small planes, in seemingly every conceivable weather condition (including a snow storm in which the pilot and co-pilot – I could overhear their conversation – were temporarily lost), and a even greater variety of co-passengers: Cree families flying to Montreal for medical services, doctors and nurses on temporary assignment, and once a styrofoam cooler labeled "live organs."

I began working for the Cree social services in a period of social transition: the James Bay and Northern Québec Agreement, negotiated in the aftermath of the La Grande River hydroelectric project (dubbed by its advocates in the Quebec government the "project of the century") was only then coming into full swing; and as part of this and several supplementary agreements two of the communities (Chisasibi and Nemaska) had been recently relocated; the Cree administrations such as the Cree School Board and the Cree Board of Health and Social Services were relatively new; and the James Bay Cree government's political NGO, the Grand Council of the Crees (Eeyou Istchee), was still in the early stages of its activist engagements.

My sweeping and sudden introduction to James Bay Cree society entailed in this first research assignment was for me a lasting source of insight into the disarray and dangers of imposing drastic change on a people in ways that add to earlier dislocations. Of course, entering a new social setting from the perspective of its social service files will inevitably result in a distorted perspective; one will tend to focus on the pathologies, on the things that go (sometimes terribly) wrong. I had to remind myself as I sat hunched over open file drawers and borrowed desks for days on end that I should not let myself be unduly influenced by the contents of the entries in the state-sanctioned forms, of family violence, binge drinking and drug addictions, suicide attempts, struggles to arrange child custody, chronic depression, and (though not an official entry, it was often implied by the facts) lost childhood. This, I kept telling myself, was not who the Crees were. The social service files were mostly telling the stories of the marginalized and forgotten, the families on welfare, with no useful task other than waiting in line for a check once every two weeks. These were exceptions in a recently formed coalition of aboriginal communities that were otherwise, in relative terms, models of success.

Even so there was something different about Chisasibi. Just days before I arrived, a young man had miraculously survived shooting himself in the head with a high-powered rifle, missing his brain by millimetres, and the noise of it still resonated in half-furtive conversations in the social service office. Of course, each of the communities had its own sad stories. Every one of them seemed to have particular families that were broken and kept on breaking. But there was a distinct impression expressed by many of its residents that Chisasibi had more than its share of troubles, and in particular that something had gone wrong with the young.

Chisasibi had been relocated to the mainland on the northern coast of the James Bay from Fort George Island after construction of a hydro-electric installation several miles upstream on the La Grande River. The high volume of water, caused by periodically opening the spillways on the LG-1 installation, was expected to rapidly erode the island, situated squarely in the river's current. A referendum was held on the relocation, and the community was predictably divided in a contest of rival hopes and fears. The "yes" votes won and Chisasibi (Cree for "big river") was constructed and occupied.

But even with Chisasibi's new amenities: an arena, school (with a corrugated cinder block exterior, evidently designed to prevent graffiti), a hospital, a community center with shops, stores and a hotel, and eventually a tepee-shaped recreation building with a bowling alley and restaurant; even with rows of new suburban-style houses and the relocation from Fort George Island of older houses with sound structures and unforsakable memories – even with these things the youth seemed unsettled and adrift. The crisis was manifested in such things as the binge drinking and vandalism associated with "walking the road" – the term for night-time gatherings of up to fifty teenagers on the three or four miles of Chisasibi's paved perimeter road – with evidence left behind in daylight hours in the form of broken glass and the defensive strategy of installing heavy gauge wire mesh on first floor windows. The main store, the "Northern," kept its cans of aerosol hairspray and anything else that could be used for a "high" under lock and key. Even bottles of ink – sometimes used for home-made tattoos – had to be specially asked for.

In my conversations with social service workers and other residents of the village a consistent refrain was that in the years following the relocation young people's connection to the older generations in their families seemed broken. It was common for people to say that the youth had lost their identity; but in retrospect this does not seem to hold true. Youth identity seemed to be commonly equated with ideas about what a Cree *should* be, and in this form it was surely interrupted. But the problem (to my later thinking) went further than this. It was not that they had no constructed self-image – an impossibility – but that their identity was formed independently from transmitted values; it was constructed – or so it seemed – around the absence of a future, formed and manifested in a drive toward intense social interaction and risk-taking that sometimes crossed the line into the negation of life.[2]

Whatever its causes and manifestations, the social service files reflected a youth crisis, with greater intensity in Chisasibi in the aftermath of relocation. This, at any rate, was the conclusion of a paper I later drafted on the social consequences of displacement among the Crees following large-scale hydroelectric development.[3] A comparison of social service interventions for hunters and their families with those full-time residents who were unemployed and a separate comparison of social service intervention rates for Chisasibi (a relocated community) with Mistassini (of roughly equal size and largely unaffected by the project) put this observation into the language of numbers. Even though the small sample size made the conclusions only suggestive, these few basic statistical comparisons underscored the things that people were saying: that families were broken by the loss of connection to the land, that in particular the loss of meaningful activity through imposed change had compromised the relationships between generations. This was – I was inclined to agree – the most likely explanation for Chisasibi's high frequency of family violence, mental illness and self-destruction.

[2] I elaborate on this approach to aboriginal youth identity in "Self-Destruction as a Way of Belonging: Understanding Cluster Suicides among Aboriginal Youth in Canada," in *Healing Traditions: The Mental Health of Aboriginal Peoples*, ed. Lawrence Kirmayer and Gail Valaskakis (Vancouver: University of British Columbia Press, 2009d).

[3] This paper was subsequently published as, R. Niezen, "Power and Dignity: The Social Consequences of Hydro-Electric Development for the James Bay Cree," *Canadian Review of Sociology and Anthropology*, 1993, 30 (4): 510–29.

And it was this conclusion that for me opened the passageway to the world of cultural rights and public persuasion. Though they seem only remotely connected, the experience I had as a social service researcher fed seamlessly into a connection with the Grand Council of the Crees and its now-famous campaign in the early 1990s to stop the second phase of hydroelectric development in northern Quebec: Hydro Québec's planned mega-project on the Great Whale River.[4]

The idea of Hydro Québec as an exporter of power and industrial leader may have appealed to Quebec nationalists, but the Crees, in their opposition to the planned project, could count on support from native organizations throughout Canada and the United States, extending into the international movement of indigenous peoples. Their resistance to the Great Whale River project appealed to a broad array of local and international environmental groups; and they had support from anthropologists and other social researchers, mostly in Canadian universities, some of whom left academe and entered the employ of the Grand Council of the Crees. Despite this base of domestic activism, which at least gave them a foothold in mounting a campaign to stop the Great Whale River project, the particular challenge they faced was the fact that much of the energy produced by the planned Hydro Québec facilities was to be exported to the United States, in particular to consumers in New England, who tended to be blithely unaware of the Canadian politics of hydro power. Without reaching this audience

---

[4] I have discussed various aspects of Chisasibi's crisis and the Cree lobby campaigns in several publications, but it is worth briefly reiterating this material here in the context of the early phase of the Crees' struggle for public recognition and prevention of the environmental and social impacts of hydroelectric development. See especially: Niezen, "Power and Dignity"; R. Niezen, *Spirit Wars: Native North American Religions in the Age of Nation Building* (Berkeley and Los Angeles: University of California Press, 2000); R. Niezen, *The Origins of Indigenism: Human Rights and the Politics of Identity* (Berkeley and Los Angeles: University of California Press, 2003); and R. Niezen *Defending the Land: Sovereignty and Forest Life in James Bay Cree Society*, second edn (Upper Saddle River: Pearson Prentice Hall, 2009a).

of power consumers, the Crees would have little leverage in efforts to stop the project. This fact encouraged the Crees to internationalize their campaign.

There was one key aspect of the Cree campaign that has tended to be overlooked. It involved collaborative relationships with an array of paid professionals: lawyers, researchers and lobbyists. The assignments that these intermediaries take on often call for them to remain in the background; and even when they do appear before a microphone, their contributions are secondary. This is of course true of any campaign, whether political or commercial. A cardinal rule of influencing peoples' opinion is never to reveal the effort one is making to do so; but the invisibility of the artificers and artifices of persuasion is particularly noteworthy in campaigns of cultural justice, as though (and it is probably true) the personnel and means used in representing a claim of authentic difference are inherently corrosive of that claim.

The Crees did not just come out of nowhere to suddenly mount an effective resistance to the designs of government and industry. In particular, they had an advantage through the way that their funding regime from the federal and provincial governments was structured, first for the purposes of negotiating the James Bay and Northern Québec Agreement in the 1970s (at which time the Grand Council came into existence as a negotiating entity) and later in the Agreement itself. The Grand Council of the Crees is an independent NGO with funding guaranteed in a treaty relationship. Much of this NGO's effectiveness lies in the fact that it is able (within limits) to hire professional facilitators, on a scale much greater than the Band governments administered under the Indian Act. The Crees thus began their campaign with an effective base of professional expertise in law and methods of persuasion, ultimately funded by the very governments that they were calling to account.

There can be no doubt that the relationships between the Crees on the one hand and the government of Quebec and Hydro Québec on the other were at this time explicitly adversarial. This is shown quite simply in the fact that they contested one another in court, where the Crees had only limited success. As Abel Bosum, former chief of Oujé-Bougoumou and spokesperson for the Grand Council, explained, "when an indigenous treaty is violated, when an indigenous territory is flooded to provide hydroelectricity, when an indigenous forest is clear cut ... our people are forced to turn to authorities who have a vested interest in the outcome. We must pretend that they are the purveyors of neutral and unbiased justice."[5] Outside the courtroom, this contest often took the form of media representations in which each side – through spokespeople uttering mostly carefully and collaboratively prepared dialogue – would make a point and perhaps respond to the other's claims. Newspaper stories would carry statements from each side in a measured balance of opinion and television interviews would include a Cree "talking head" and one from Hydro Québec, ideally with equal time in front of the camera. Such, at any rate, was the ideal form of unbiased news journalism.

One of the principal reasons for the Crees' success in their rights campaigns can be found in their ability to disrupt this media pattern of balanced coverage, to provoke, sometimes by their mere presence in unexpected places, a kind of symbolic dissonance, to do things publicly that generated curious, sympathetic, concerned attention to which there could be no equal response. This first came to my attention in hearings that took place in 1992 in the Massachusetts State Legislature concerning a bill that would remove state pension funds from investment in Hydro Québec. Supporters of the bill invoked the utility's poor relationship with the Crees and the expected environmental and social impacts of the proposed mega-project on the Great Whale River. I was included on the speakers' list to present my (then) draft article on the

---

[5] A. Bosum, "The Human Rights of Indigenous Peoples at the United Nations," Workshop on Indigenous Peoples' Rights, The John F. Kennedy Library, Dorchester, MA, December 10, 1994.

social impacts of the first mega-project in the James Bay region, the La Grande River project which had resulted in the village relocation from Fort George to Chisasibi. I had been previously contacted by the Crees' lobbyist, who had somehow gotten wind of my research, and who explained to me that the overwhelming preponderance of material on the effects of large dams was focused on the environment, but that very little had been done to specifically link displacement to social crisis, and that my paper should therefore be presented to the hearings on the divestment bill.

The main representative of the Crees to the State of Massachusetts legislative hearings on the divestment bill was Matthew Coon-Come, dressed in an embroidered and fringed moose-hide jacket. He stood when he was introduced and began his discourse, without preamble, in Cree, a language that only he and a few others in the room understood. For around a minute the members of the legislative committee, assembled facing the room along a raised, richly paneled dais, exchanged glances and shifted in their seats. The tension in the room seemed to build the longer Coon-Come spoke, but was instantly released when he switched to English and explained the nature of his greeting in his own language as an expression of respect. He then went on to use a form of discourse more in keeping with expectations: an argument or plea about the importance of the land for his people and the threat to it posed by Hydro Québec's plans to build a series of large dams on the Great Whale River, one of the last truly wild rivers in North America, with much of the energy produced to be exported via transmission lines to New England.

The use of indigenous languages in the context of non-indigenous forums is now commonplace, but the non-verbal response Coon-Come provoked by speaking Cree in the early 1990s points to its strategic origin. It was a way of establishing the point that he represented a distinct culture that had maintained its vitality. It made a tacit argument for authenticity and the potential of large-scale "development" to cause cultural loss and suffering. It did so in the context of a legal venue of a dominant society conducted in a dominant language, and it therefore disrupted the taken-for-granted flow of authority. It was ultimately an argument for self-determination: the Cree language represented a people with a living heritage and a political organization that had selected and sent a representative to participate in a legal process in another country in defence of territory and livelihood – the attributes by definition of a self-determining people.

All of this is manifestly clear. But what about the big picture? How might this event contribute to the Crees' specific political goal: to stop the hydroelectric project on the Great Whale River? To answer this, we should consider not only the words and ideas but the emotions generated by discourse. The symbolic dissonance provoked by the fluent use of Cree in an English venue seemed striking to the audience present; it focused their attention and created a momentary sense of expectation. By heightening emotion it stimulated curiosity and contributed to the newsworthiness of the event.

And newsworthiness was the ultimate goal: to produce and provoke sound bites that might put the words "Cree," "Hydro Québec," "environment" and "controversy" together in the same sentence, to influence public perception of the moral dimension to their consumption of energy; and to do this not just once, but again and again, in venues ranging from the *New York Times* to community newsletters, from speeches to the crowds of Earth Day summits to campus gatherings of rights activists, to create a "background noise" of information, opinion and awareness. Major initiatives like the divestment bill are a strategic focus, but in the age of publics, rights are ultimately defended by the unfolding of chairs in seminar rooms and church basements.

In the course of their campaign to stop the Great Whale River hydroelectric project, the Crees frequently employed the technique of situating themselves and their claims into sites with heightened political and cultural significance. The State of Massachusetts divestment bill is an example. Other divestment efforts, this time targeting academic faculty and staff pensions, took place at major universities in New England. (One such meeting at Harvard that I attended in the early 1990s filled a room with several hundred students.) Representatives who embodied Cree language and culture made their presence felt in a variety of major public institutions.

Cree delegations made regular appearances at annual meetings of the United Nations Working Group on Indigenous Populations in Geneva and at meetings arranged for the drafting of a Declaration on the Rights of Indigenous Peoples. Here the Crees made their presence felt through a high degree of professionalism. In the midst of an at times almost carnivalesque celebration of indigenous difference, the Crees wore dark suits and ties. (At meetings sponsored by the Assembly of First Nations in Canada, the Crees were referred to as the "Quebec mafia," because of their preference for dark pinstriped suits.) Their discourse in these meetings tended toward a use of legal logic in making arguments in favor of the self-determination of indigenous peoples. In the context of the Great Whale campaign, assertions of self-determination applied especially to the right to make decisions on the use of their territory and resources in the face of Quebec's plans for hydroelectric development.

One of the Crees' most striking exercises of cultural rights lobbying involved the construction, using materials, knowledge and labor of Crees and Inuits of northern Quebec, of a hybrid eight-person canoe/kayak, called an *odayek* (combining the Cree words "*uut*" and the Inuit "*qayaq*") which was flown to Amsterdam in the week preceding the 1992 hearings of the International Water Tribunal (IWT). The IWT is an independent human rights venue, sometimes referred to as the "Amnesty International" for water, which produces opinions on environmental disputes involving water resources; and though its judgments carry no legal sanction, it has a reputation for thoroughness and impartiality that lends itself to moral persuasion. A Cree/Inuit delegation, representing those whose territory would be most directly affected by the Great Whale mega-project, paddled the *odayek* along the picturesque canals of Amsterdam's center, under low bridges and around tour boats, stopping occasionally to talk to curious onlookers and give interviews to reporters. The IWT ruling, which expressed the view that Quebec should not move ahead on its massive hydroelectric project on the Great Whale River without first undertaking a thorough environmental assessment, was based on the facts presented before it, but was also fully consistent with the opinion generated by Cree lobbying.

There were two major outcomes to the Cree campaign, one immediate and one delayed. The immediate outcome was New York governor Mario Cumo's 1992 decision to pull out of New York Power Authority contracts for the purchase of energy from Quebec, which has every appearance of being connected to Quebec premier Jacques Parizeau's decision in 1994 to permanently shelve the hydroelectric mega-project on the Great Whale River.

A later outcome was the shifting of plans for hydroelectric development to the Rupert and Eastmain Rivers, further to the south of the James Bay region, this time in consultation with the Crees, and this time with advance commitments to environmental mitigation and compensation. The New Relationship Agreement, known in the Quebec media as the Paix des Braves, includes royalty payments over a period of fifty years amounting to some 3.6 billion Canadian dollars – this for a population of approximately 13,000 Crees. Without question, the staggering sum involved in this agreement would not have been even remotely conceivable without the Cree leadership's proven success in rights campaigning.

The Paix des Braves sheds new light on the campaign to stop the Great Whale project in the early 1990s. The messages the Crees brought south were constructed around the need to appeal to their listeners. The historical and cultural repertoire from which they drew included themes of millennial occupation of territory, intimate environmental knowledge, and the personal qualities of patience and spiritual connectedness that go with it. Their self-characterization centered on the depth of their history on the land, their superior ability to act as its stewards, and its importance for their continued well-being.

Less was said about injustice and suffering, about the dependencies and disconnections of the relocated village setting. And to my knowledge nothing was said in the Cree campaign of the urgent need for employment, especially for youth, of a burgeoning population that could no longer be supported from the land. This later became the focus of a debate internal to Cree society, especially in the period leading up to the 2002 referendum on the Paix des Braves, and ongoing with less intensity since, but was not raised as an issue in the campaign of the early 1990s even though the unemployment challenge loomed even then.

In making this choice of representation the Crees and their advisors are to be given credit. The information they conveyed to audiences in the south was clear, uncomplicated, direct and strategically effective. It also illustrates for us some of the basic features of cultural lobbying. Their campaign represents one of the informal mechanisms of collective human rights, which attach positive value and hope to particular communities or categories of people who somehow conform to a popular ideal. The diffusion of international norms to the Cree communities and their public audiences took place through a relatively new opportunity by those who are marginalized by the state to transcend the political obstacles of state agencies and the legal obstacles of state judiciaries. The Crees and their advisors were able to do this by situating Cree cultural difference in the forums and ideas of rights, especially human rights, as part of an organized campaign to enlighten, persuade and provoke the sympathy and indignation of an international public.

Southern exposure

The new pathways of collective rights and representation are further illustrated by the grievances, claims and lobbying activities of the

Umoja Uaso Women's Group near Archer's Post, Kenya, a village-based women's shelter that offers protection to women and children not only from domestic abuse, but also from traditionally inscribed Samburu roles and rituals that define womanhood, such as excision and arranged marriage. In a visit to McGill University in 2005, Rebecca Lolosoli, founder and chairperson of the Umoja Uaso Women's Group, talked to me about her wide-ranging activities as head of the organization, which included gathering information on potentially useful rights instruments and processes and presenting her own experience and her organization's history to a wide range of audiences, an effort intended in part to raise the international profile of the Women's Group. She participated, for example, in the 2001 World Conference against Racism, Racial Discrimination, Xenophobia, and Related Intolerance in Durban, South Africa; and when I met her she had just been a panellist at the 2005 session of the Commission on the Status of Women in New York. (As with many participants who come from village settings to UN meetings, she reported to me the usual experience of loneliness, claustrophobia in hotel rooms, and an inability to find a familiar diet, in her case sufficient quantities of warm whole milk and fresh cow blood.) In October 2006, she went on a speaking tour across the United States, accompanied by Vivian Stromberg, executive director of MADRE, a human rights NGO established in response to the victimization of women during the civil war in Guatemala and now more globally dedicated to the promotion of rural women's rights. Together Stromberg and Lolosoli shared "ideas and strategies, successes and challenges, and the inspiring story of the women of Umoja" and offered participants the opportunity to purchase Samburu beadwork.[6]

Although Samburu representatives have participated in indigenous rights forums, the most obvious source of rights claims and public

---

[6] MADRE, www.madre.org/programs/pe/speakers_fall06.html. Accessed March 31, 2009.

appeal invoked in support of the Umoja Uaso Women's Group follows from the values and opportunities made available by the global women's movement, particularly the human rights instruments, organizations and forums developed in the late twentieth century's human rights revolution, which identify women around the world as commonly subjected to identifiable patterns of abuse and which have called for the promotion of security and equality through the elaboration of rights as part of a global movement of cultural and political reform.[7]

The increased participation of Kenyan women in transnational activism and public life has been a trend of the new millennium, with a focal point in a constitutional review process that accompanied and followed the 2002 election. Women's NGOs and human rights organizations were energized by the opportunity to influence constitutional reform; and even with a draft constitution in place, a coalition of women's groups mounted a campaign in 2003 titled Safeguard the Gains for Women in the Draft Constitution. The political process in Kenya was infused with issues of gender justice in a process understood by one activist as "engendering" the state, with women facing "a unique political chance to alter their unequal social and political positions by narrating and initiating particular actions to make the Kenyan state more accountable in gender-based matters."[8]

Even in this climate of change, the foundation of the Umoja women's village would not have been possible, or at least not as successful in its

---

[7] The focal point of human rights claims and activism on behalf of women is the United Nations, *Convention on the Elimination of all Forms of Discrimination against Women (CEDAW)*, GA Res. 34/180, 34 UN GAOR, 1981, Supp. (No. 46) at 193, UN doc. A/34/46; 1249 UNTS 13; 19 ILM 33 (1980). UN activities on behalf of women are coordinated by the Division for the Advancement of Women in the Department of Economic and Social Affairs; see www.un.org/womenwatch/daw. Accessed September 9, 2009.

[8] J. Muteshi, "Women's Advocacy: Engendering and Reconstituting the Kenyan State," in *Human Rights NGOs in East Africa: Political and Normative Tensions*, ed. M. Mutua (Philadelphia: University of Pennsylvania Press, 2009) 137.

outreach, were it not for the emergence of female circumcision (often referred to as female genital mutilation, or FGM) as a focal point of human rights claims, with connections to the rights of the child and the global women's movement. The *New York Times*, for example, published an article in 1996 describing the rite of passage among the Samburu, revealing to its readership both the act of the rite of passage and the attitudes behind it: "The girl bled a stream of blood onto the hide and dirt, but she did not cry or move. Some of the younger women in the crowd turned away in revulsion. The older women scolded the exciser, who was not experienced and took more than five minutes to do her job. Someone suggested that another exciser should be called, but the girl muttered: 'Just finish it. Just finish it.'" The article concludes with an interview with the girl's mother that reveals some of the common ideas behind the ceremony: "We don't care about pleasure ... All we care about is that our daughter is clean, as the community wants her to be. Our happiness will be to see our daughter going through circumcision when she is not pregnant and to see her get a husband of her own."[9] Prior to the establishment of the Umoja Uaso Women's group the tension between the values of tradition and the violation of the universal rights of female children by the practices of excision and infibulation became a global issue; and through their resistance to practices of female circumcision or FGM, the dissident Samburu women had a significant audience of potential sympathizers, even before their village became a reality.

To this rights-versus-tradition background must be added allegations of the rape of Samburu and Maasai women by British soldiers from 1972 to 2003, the period during which they were stationed near Archer's Post

---

[9] J.C. McKinley, "At a Ceremony in Kenya, A Harsh Rite of Passage for a Brother and Sister," *New York Times*, October 5, 1996, http://query.nytimes.com/gst/fullpage.html?res=9E00EEDB103FF936A35753C1A960958260&sec=health&spon=&pagewanted=all. Accessed August 22, 2008.

for military training. The rape allegations surfaced when Martyn Day, a British lawyer specializing in high-profile claims against corporations and governments, was investigating the circumstances in which unexploded British ordnance had killed and maimed hundreds of Samburu and Maasai herdsmen, having accumulated over the course of three decades of training exercises in the same Kenyan territories subsequently used for pasturage. In 2003, on the heels of a joint inquiry into the rape allegations by British military police and Kenyan authorities, Leigh, Day and Company began preparing a class action suit against the British Defence Ministry on behalf of 650 women from Archer's post and nearby Dol Dol who claimed to have been raped by British soldiers. But in 2006 a three-year investigation by the Royal Military Police cleared British soldiers of the alleged rapes, concluding that dozens of complaints of rape in Kenyan police files were forgeries, while conceding that not all the claims were faked. The circumstances of systemic abuse by the British military, followed by international litigation and ultimately significant setbacks for the Samburu women in their pursuit of justice, make up another part of the rights claims and public appeal of the Umoja Uaso Women's Group.

As I will soon illustrate, the claims of rape by British soldiers are not the only grievance emphasized in the village's scripted public discourse. It is striking that public mention of the rapes is usually accompanied by accounts of their secondary victimization by husbands, by the men who abused and rejected them because of the shame caused by what they saw as their wives' condition of impurity. The women who set out to establish their own protective village setting therefore often speak of themselves as oppressed by their own people's conservative attitudes and traditions. This unusual situation is clarified when we see that European conceptions of rights and social reform are creating space for Africans to engage in experimental forms of activism, based in large measure on the ready communication and widespread legitimacy of universal standards of human rights. The changed circumstances of their lives, along with new, transnationally communicated ideas of collective justice, have made it possible for Samburu women to radically reassess their social roles not only in terms of a status as victims but more broadly in terms of new opportunities afforded by what they have learned about rights and the powers of law.

In a few short years the Samburu women of the Umoja village have developed a sophisticated awareness of the advantages inherent in various levels of legal change, not only in international human rights norms, but more immediately and practically in the context of a Kenyan state extending its reach into the Samburu and Maasai pasturages. The women of Umoja support themselves in large measure by running a cultural center and camping site for tourists visiting the adjacent Samburu National Reserve. The women's village therefore combines the functions of women's shelter and tourist camp, with many of the women "residents" spending the day there and returning to their homes in nearby villages at the end of the day. With the money they earn they have been proactive in purchasing private land being put up for sale in a sweeping land reform sponsored by the Kenyan government. Their success therefore follows from skilful exploitation of every new opportunity that becomes available to them, from the local navigation of land reform to the more complex collaborative exchanges involved in the transnational communication of grievance and, inseparable from this, the promotion of positive cultural experiences for foreign tourists, interns and journalists.[10]

---

[10] The appeal of the Umoja women, as representatives of the global women's movement, is evident, for example, in an article published in 2005 by the *Washington Post*: "What started as a group of homeless women looking for a place of their own became a successful and happy village. About three dozen women live here and run a cultural center and camping site for tourists visiting the adjacent Samburu National Reserve. Umoja has flourished, eventually attracting so many women seeking help that they even hired men to haul firewood, traditionally women's work." E. Wax, "A Place Where Women Rule; All-Female Village in Kenya Is a Sign Of Burgeoning Feminism Across Africa," *Washington Post*, July 9, 2005, A.01.

This positive side of rights claims is a relatively unrecognized aspect of the international legal order, which tends to emphasize the injuries and suffering of the innocent in humanitarian crises. But cultural lobbying – the display of collective virtue in campaigns of public outreach associated with rights claims – is every bit as important. In navigating the new national and international regimes of rights, the Umoja Uaso Women's Group has been able to cultivate and draw upon ideas of inherently sacred ways of life and primordial wisdom that have become part of a recently globalized conception of cultural difference.

An indication of the reach of positive cultural values as a source of leverage came to me from a report written by a student intern sponsored by McGill University who, along with three others, spent part of the summer of 2006 volunteering and conducting research in the Umoja Uaso women's village. Among their many experiences, the interns witnessed the ebb and flow of visitors to the village, mostly tourists on their way to the nearby Samburu National Reserve. This traffic of cultural consumers once included an Al-Jazeera film crew preparing a story for the Arab language news network, which requested that the four college interns stay out of the camera's view while they shot footage of "daily life" in the village. And, what is more, the journalists seemed oblivious to the irony of being entertained with a song normally performed during circumcision ceremonies. The sights and sounds of primordial difference were all that mattered.

The juxtaposition of messages of cultural virtue and of suffering comes across clearly in a video clip sponsored by Manta Productions, a French public relations firm that specializes in video productions for small businesses and nongovernmental organizations. A seven-minute video clip posted by Manta Productions on YouTube, titled "Umoja, le village interdit aux hommes" ("Umoja, the village where men are forbidden"), offers images of peace, tranquility, joy, movement, song and color: a woman quietly singing to herself as she makes a beaded bracelet, a young boy demurely wrapped in a towel washing himself from a basin, a group of women dressed in bright, beaded finery singing and dancing and playfully interacting with the camera. Between such moments the screen fades to black and displays in white lettering and plain prose the back-story, the horrors that have been only partially overcome to produce this idyllic setting:

> From 1970 to 2003, 1600 women were raped by British soldiers stationed in northern Kenya.
> Feeling dishonoured, husbands beat and rejected their wives.
> To survive, some of the women organized themselves and created ...
> Umoja, the village where men are forbidden.[11]

There follows an interview with Rebecca Lolosoli in which she focuses on an unfair sexual distribution of labor as a central source of grievance with Samburu men – "You do everything, but nothing belongs to you. You are just their slave. You do all the work" – followed by an indication of the hope to be found in resistance oriented toward the autonomy of women: "The men are now very angry with Umoja. Because we own our land. We work for ourselves and we have our money. We sell our things and the woman has her own money."[12] To conclude, the screen

[11] "De 1970 à 2003, 1600 femmes ont été violées par des soldats britanniques en stationnement dans le nord du Kenya; Se sentant déshonorés, les maris ont battu et répudié leurs femmes; Pour survivre, certaines femmes se sont regroupées et ont créé ... Umoja, le village interdit aux hommes." My translation. Mantaprod, "Umoja, the Village where Men are Forbidden," www.youtube.com/watch?v=V7RIaroskuU. Accessed October 21, 2008.

[12] Mantaprod, "Umoja, the Village where Men are Forbidden." In taking this approach to gender differences, the Umoja women's group is at variance with Africa-wide trends observed by Filomina Steady. African women's organizations, Steady observes, "tend to give priority to social and human-centered goals rather than to narrow feminist preoccupations about gender equality alone. A large part of their effort is not spent on agitating for women's rights or in challenging men." F. Steady, *Women and Collective Action in Africa* (New York: Palgrave Macmillan, 2006) 1. This distinct quality of Umoja can be readily understood by its day-to-day function as a women's shelter, but it could well be that resistance to traditional male roles and behavior resonates strongly with the community's feminist sympathizers.

again fades to black and reveals a word-collage of the Samburu women's sources of suffering and grievance: "Excision; organized rape; traffic of women and children; forced marriage; sexual slavery; slavery of girls."[13]

Evidence that the film communicated effectively with its public can be seen in the consistently positive commentary posted by Internet viewers, of which the following written prayer in the thread that follows the YouTube Umoja video is an example:

Thank you God for women like this in the world. Empower them, and abolish all slavery. Please punish these evil, lazy, oppressive, asinine men. Make them realize that for half the population to be forced to do it all yet get the least, while the other half (men) does little as possible is a recipe for the failure of a whole people to thrive. Slavery and oppression of the female half of population is the source of evil. Dear God bless these noble, intelligent, beautiful, brave women, Amen.[14]

The ability of the Umoja women to move their audiences is abundantly clear from this kind of response. But what do they gain from this kind of sympathy aside from the (at times prayerful) appreciation of strangers? An answer does come to mind: their exposure is ultimately a source of protection from those who wield the power to define and enforce traditional roles. It gives them the ability to cause offence against the male-dominated order (with a diminished but not completely absent risk of retribution) by redefining the place of women in the sexual division of labor, status hierarchy and avenues to prosperity. It connects their survival, including protection from violent retaliation by men, to political answerability. And that answerability, in turn, is a by-product of the global legitimacy of human rights, of public scrutiny through the lens of a moral code that makes it

---

[13] "Excision, Viol organisé, Trafic de femmes et d'enfants, Mariage forcés, Esclavage sexuel, Esclavage des fillettes." My translation. Mantaprod, "Umoja, the Village where Men are Forbidden."

[14] www.youtube.com/watch?v=V7RIaroskuU. Accessed October 7, 2008.

in the Kenyan state's interest to tolerate, if not facilitate, the survival and success of the Samburu women dissidents.

The Umoja women's participation in cultural lobbying raises another question: when rights-claimants wear finery and sing and dance for a camera in the furtherance of their claims, is there no longer any sacred element to the event itself? Does it happen that words and movements that were once identifiable markers of ritual become, in the context of cultural rights lobbying, mere performance? Is the camera under these conditions an instrument of disenchantment?

The distinction between sacred ritual and secular performance should not be made too starkly. In the circumstances of the women's village, performance is not simply undertaken for those present, but is also, perhaps primarily, for the benefit of a distant, abstract audience with the power to shape the community's fortunes. Ceremony in this context is a kind of prayer to remote agents with control over destiny. The camera becomes invested with power as the vehicle for the transmission of messages of supplication to another, unseen realm. In their performances for distant publics the women of Umoja are doing exactly what ritual has always done: rejecting the dogma of chance and protecting themselves from danger by appeal to a powerful impersonal force.

African appeal

The analogy with ritual does have its limits because ultimately there are human agents on the other side of the camera; and it is to some extent possible to identify them and to tease out the dynamics of publicly mediated rights claims. The question we are led to is this: to whom are the Samburu women appealing? More specifically, what audience makes up the potentially sympathetic public in Kenya that might directly apply pressure on the government to initiate or support reform? Tracing the connection between Rebecca Lolosoli, through the sounds and images of her utterances on camera as captured by sympathetic, media-savvy activists, to their destination among the consumers of expressions and images of cultural virtue, rights-claims and suffering, reveals that there is a different dynamic occurring in the Samburu women's activism – and by extension within the public outreach of many other rights claimants in Africa, Asia and elsewhere in the "South" – from those in the Euro-American "North" who are better able to reach "domestic" publics. The images and opinions recorded and transmitted by the Women's Group and their allies appear to be consumed and acted on by distant publics, mostly in Europe and North America, which then support the activities of mostly European and North American nongovernmental organizations committed to change within Africa.

What might be the distinct conditions in Africa that influence the social justice claims of those pointing to conditions of oppression and marginalization?[15] The most obvious approach to this question might turn to the level of literacy and the technological impediments to the consumption of information. There is globally a wide disparity in the use of information and communication technology. Above all, there continues to be a striking North–South (or if one prefers, temperate–tropical) difference in terms of access to information technology. Clearly, the Internet is

---

[15] The discussion in this chapter of the different pathways and possibilities of public persuasion in Africa and Euro-America offers an alternative explanation for Oona Hathaway's finding that disingenuousness toward human rights treaties is less likely in democratic states, "not only because democracies are arguably more likely to have a true normative commitment to the principles embedded in the treaties but also because democratic governments will likely find it difficult to engage in expressions that are inconsistent with their actions." Hathaway supports this interpretation by invoking the liberalist claim that "liberal democracies contain powerful domestic interest groups that mobilize to pressure their governments to comply with their international legal obligations." O. Hathaway, "Do Human Rights Treaties Make a Difference?" *Yale Law Journal*, 2002, 111 (8): 1935–2042, at 2019. Without taking a further step and enquiring into the nature of these interest groups, or into what amounts to different conditions for the effectiveness of publics, the comparative issue of human rights compliance will remain obscure.

an increasingly important part the communicative effectiveness of dissi-dent peoples and communities.[16] If media-based lobbying is a key strategy for defense against unwanted mega-projects, forced resettlement, envir-onmental degradation, or policies of linguistic and cultural assimilation, then those who exist on the margins of technology and literacy will also have fewer of their own resources for promoting cultural integrity.[17]

But in Africa the dynamics of cultural lobbying have as much to do with the nature of civil society – with the institutions and associations that articulate between the state and society – as with the technological means of reaching sympathetic audiences. And there is no simple way to capture the essence of African civil society, influenced as it is by distinct colonial histories, structures of state power, forms of Euro-American NGO activism and uneven policies and priorities of agencies of global governance. There are, however, some unique qualities of sub-Saharan African civil society (if we choose to call it that) that can be seen in the dynamics of social justice lobbying.

One of the most profound discontinuities brought about by colo-nial administration was the categorization and classification of human differences, the naming of "bands," "tribes" and "cultures," or perhaps more significantly, the endowment of these categories with strictly defined political significance, making them self-referential and self-reproducing, as sources of security and pride in the con-text of limited autonomy. Terrence Ranger, in his classic essay, "The Invention of Tradition in Africa" argues that in East Africa in the pre-colonial period, "competition, movement, fluidity were as much fea-tures of small-scale communities as they were of larger groupings."[18]

---

[16] Though such information rapidly becomes obsolete, the uneven distribution of information technologies is strikingly documented in: United Nations Development Programme, *Human Development Report 2001: Making New Technologies Work for Human Development* (Oxford University Press, 2001).

[17] See R. Niezen, *The Rediscovered Self: Indigenous Identity and Cultural Justice* (Montreal and Kingston: McGill-Queen's University Press, 2009b) Ch. 3.

[18] T. Ranger, "The Invention of Tradition in Africa," in *The Invention of Tradition*, ed. Eric Hobsbawm and Terrence Ranger (Cambridge University Press, 1983) 249.

Boundaries between groups were shifting and socially contextual. Only later do we find that "The dogmas of customary security and immutably fixed relationships grew up in these same societies."[19] Jean-Loup Amselle, concentrating his research in West Africa, applies the term "ethnological reason" to the thinking behind such administratively reinforced ethnic categories, a form of reason that is not limited to the work of professional anthropologists, but that can be seen more broadly as part of the intellectual background to colonial occupation.[20] It is also (this point is essential) reflected back, used by African intellectual themselves as guideposts to power and liberation. The formations of power around rival tribal groups, in large part an outcome of colonial histories that encouraged ethnic essentialism and boundaries, make it a challenge to assert claims for distinct rights that successfully cross tribal boundaries, especially in circumstances of reconfiguration and redistribution of land and resources. Often the grievances and uncertainties of postcolonial statehood have given rise to the potent temptation to draw upon cultivated hatreds as a basis for unity, expressed through pre-emptive exclusion of those who do not or will not belong, who might have their own claims to statehood, or more commonly have a foundation for collective life distinct from loyalty to the state. And under circumstances of politically circumscribed ethnic identification, the justice claims of one group are not readily exported to others.

This further suggests that the nature of civil society, and even state politics, tends to follow pathways of kinship and patronage that are commonly overlooked by Euro-American NGOs in their efforts in Africa to build local networks and formulate strategies of public outreach. This possibility has been explored by Mikael Karlström in a

[19] Ranger, "The Invention of Tradition in Africa," 249.
[20] J.-L. Amselle *Mestizo Logics: Anthropology of Identity in Africa and Elsewhere* (Stanford University Press, 1998).

close observation of social reform under Uganda's National Resistance Movement after it came to power in 1986. Karlström argues that in the Ugandan context of political reform, and in sub-Saharan Africa more generally, kinship (especially clanship in Uganda) "as an axis of solidarity and association" has been unjustifiably "excluded from the objective-categorical conception of civil society."[21] He reports that the Baganda are comfortable with their hierarchy of ranked lineages and clan leaders, which supports the institution of a king as "head of all the clan heads" and "produces the most stable, cohesive and responsive political order possible," with structural checks and balances that have worked more effectively in engagement with the state than the imported system of competing political parties.[22] Basing his conclusions on the perspectives and institutional effectiveness of the Baganda themselves, Karlström argues for African idioms of kinship and local governance, in their immense variety, to be included in the study of, and engagement with, relations between local populations and the state.

But the failure of some of their own Samburu institutions and hierarchies to meet their basic needs is precisely the reason that the founders of the Umoja Uaso Women's Group felt it necessary to appeal to European and American audiences through the values, organizational models and mediations of human rights. Under circumstances in which locally influential networks of kinship and local politics fail to provide security or accommodate new aspirations for equality and prosperity, help may be sought from outside organizations (themselves sources of new aspirations), organizations that are often run by rights brokers who offer strategic possibilities that transcend those of all available local structures. The example of the Umoja Uaso women's village adds an

---

[21] M. Karlström, "Civil Society and its Presuppositions: Lessons from Uganda," in *Civil Society and the Political Imagination in Africa: Critical Perspectives*, ed. J.L. Comaroff and J. Comaroff (University of Chicago Press, 1999) 107.

[22] Karlström, "Civil Society and its Presuppositions," 107.

important qualification to Karlström's kinship-centered approach to African civil society: local aspirations need not be pursued exclusively within local avenues of power; and kinship roles can be circumvented, called into question, even permanently altered, by the extended reach of human rights values and their boundaryless agents.

The outcome of these transnational collaborations is not always positive. Some ethnographers have shown how rights-based outreach strategies can become vexed and their goals compromised, due in part to the demands and distortions of cultural representation to remote audiences.[23] Jaqueline Solway is among those who have recently published trouble-in-paradise counterpoints to the overly optimistic and selective views of justice campaigns in Africa.[24] In the case she describes, the manifest outcome of a dispute between the Bushmen and the state of Botswana is a victory for human rights: the Bushmen won a judgment from the High Court that received worldwide attention and demonstrated the Botswana judiciary's remarkable independence. The court awarded the Bushmen many of the concessions they were seeking, including a right to return to the Central Kalahari Game Reserve from which they were being removed by the state.

The manner with which the Bushmen achieved this court victory, however, is instructive: a strategic affiliation between the Bushmen and the British-based NGO Survival International (SI) selectively overlooked the Botswana government's motives behind the relocations: to

[23] See, for example: D. Hodgson, "Precarious Alliances: the Cultural Politics and Structural Predicaments of the Indigenous Rights Movements in Tanzania," *American Anthropologist*, 2002, 104 (4): 1086–97; G. Robert and S. Sholto-Douglas, *The Bushman Myth: The Making of a Namibian Underclass*, second edn (Boulder: Westview, 2000); and R. Sylvain, "Disorderly Development: Globalization and the Idea of 'Culture' in the Kalahari," *American Ethnologist*, 2005, 32 (3): 354–70. Cultural dilemmas from the point of view of development advocacy are emphasized in S. Saugestad, *The Inconvenient Indigenous: Remote Area Development in Botswana, Donor Assistance and the First People of the Kalahari* (Uppsala: Nordic Africa Institute, 2001).

[24] J. Solway, "Human Rights and NGO 'Wrongs': Conflict Diamonds, Culture Wars and the 'Bushman Question,'" *Africa*, 2009, 79 (3): 321–46.

counteract the effects of livestock and human settlement in the Game Reserve, to promote tourism and in the process (as Solway describes it, paternalistically) to cultivate the virtues of progress, as manifested in new villages and opportunities outside the reserve. Instead, SI emphasized the place of diamond mining as the government's central motive behind the relocations, making rhetorical links between Botswana's "diamonds" and "genocide," with explicit comparison to the already well publicized role of the illicit diamond trade in Sierra Leone's civil war, highlighted by the 2006 Hollywood film *Blood Diamond*. Diamond mining was at no point central to the relocations in Botswana because it does not require extensive use of land, yet it was made *the* issue by Survival International and their allies in their publicity campaign. Nor did the SI campaign accurately represent the lifestyle and aspirations of the Bushmen themselves, which include raising livestock, practicing agriculture, hunting with horses and guns, and ideally establishing conditions for reliable formal sector employment (including diamond mining). Instead the campaign emphasized the more widely recognized cultural virtues of the Bushmen, their innocence toward modernity and their intimate connection to the natural world. This was expressed a variety of media, including a Web-posted open letter to *Blood Diamond* star Leonardo DiCaprio that emphasized their desire to just "go home, and hunt and gather and live in peace like we have always done." [25] Moreover, as Solway reports, "SI and its collaborators have also done their best to compromise Botswana's hitherto impeccable human rights record and to threaten Botswana's economy, which is heavily dependent upon diamond exports ... SI also portrays Botswana as a pariah state and aims to spoil Botswana's desirability as a tourist destination." [26] In other words, the campaign in support

[25] This is from an open letter to Leonardo DiCaprio by Roy Sesana, spokesperson for the First Peoples of the Kalahari, cited in Solway, "Human Rights and NGO 'Wrongs'," 323.

[26] Solway, "Human Rights and NGO 'Wrongs'," 324.

of the Bushmen took on a high-stakes, pressure-tactic orientation, in response to which "Botswana ramped up its efforts to present its own side. They hired an expensive PR firm and senior officials, including the President, have travelled to plead the government's case to as many high-profile international audiences as possible." [27] To some extent Botswana's counter-PR worked: Leonardo DiCaprio did not endorse the SI campaign and the High Court judgment excluded the diamond issue as a reason for its findings. The ultimate outcome of the court victory, however, was a disaffected, increasingly authoritarian government that defined its obligations toward the Bushmen narrowly and punitively, requiring permits of many Bushmen who wished to return to the Game Reserve, requiring proof of identity at the gates, restricting the amounts of water and construction materials brought into the Reserve, forbidding domestic animals, and calling for special hunting permits that limited hunters to "traditional" methods. The Bushmen who were permitted to live in the Reserve, in other words, could live there in the manner of the stereotypes they and their allies publicly promoted, or not at all.

This example illustrates the fact that the African human rights movement depends heavily upon conditions that support transnational relationships of collaboration based upon the cultural and social justice ideals of Euro-American publics. Not surprisingly, the cultural geography of collective rights in Africa reflects the preferences of these publics. The most prominent claimants of cultural distinctiveness are those who possess qualities that appeal to the Western imagination, whose pedigrees of representation go far back in the history of the European popular imagination, to the human encounters of the earliest explorers, the likes of Ibn Battuta, René Caillé and Mungo Park. Encounters with those same exotic people were later regularly featured in adventure stories, news reels and documentaries. Whether or not they have succeeded

[27] J. Solway, "Human Rights and NGO 'Wrongs'," 324.

in having their grievances addressed, pastoralists like the Maasai and Samburu in East Africa, the Tuareg of the West African Sahara and Sahel (the "blue men of the desert" of whom the French tend to be especially enamored), and hunter-gatherers like the Mbuti ("Pygmies") of the Congo region and the San or !Kung Bushmen of southern Africa have each represented themselves as "indigenous" and found places in the limited repertoire of international cultural preservation initiatives. There is, in contrast, little inspiration to be found in slums and refugee camps. While many Africans are more often subject to the imperatives of development, a limited number of widely recognized peoples are able to draw on the ideas and emotions of those looking for picturesque qualities in those they support, some kind of vicarious cultural entertainment value, ultimately connected to global visions of diversity as a source of the enrichment of life.

Largely through the activities of NGOs and their engagements with publics, the creation of politically viable cultural communities has become an inter-cultural process. Cultural survival is promoted within parameters of potentially shared knowledge. The processes and assumptions behind collective justice lobbying are themselves cultural phenomena (but with the largely abstract publics involved, these cultures remain tantalizingly obscure for those who study culture). We can therefore expect the receptiveness and actions of publics to vary and to be subject to all the complexities of historical change, influence of other traditions, and of course the uncertain and shifting boundaries of cultural belonging. An important part of effective self-representation in campaigns of justice involves an acquired ability to learn and interpret the complex cultures of alien publics, something the James Bay Crees and the Samburu women have accomplished with an unusual degree of success.

The publicly idealized victims of rights abuse are those who have retained their dignity and unity. But the oppressed are usually divided in various ways; and the local leadership challenge becomes one of establishing enough connections among individuals to create an impression (or illusion) of unity. For them, the task of public persuasion moves in two directions: toward potentially compassionate outside others and toward the demands of local constituents. The most significant division to be overcome in any distinct people is between those who are in the forefront of the political representation of difference and those who are a-political, who don't understand the advantages to be gained by the restless strivings for rights and recognition. The new, formally educated leadership is often faced with the challenge of communicating their values and goals to a widely dispersed and diverse constituency. Often while they are representing their community to distant publics, their community as a collective rights claimant is coming into being.

The fact that their publics are primarily transnational rather than domestic means that African rights-claimants are competing through global networks to provoke the sympathy and indignation of publics in those few states with significant international interest and influence. This fundamentally changes the dynamics of rights lobbying. It greatly increases the importance of intermediaries, those organizations that speak for innocent others and specialize in interpreting the tastes and inclinations of overseas publics, while limiting local control over the strategies pursued and messages conveyed by these intermediaries. This, in turn, increases the extent to which collective rights lobbying becomes inter-culturally negotiated, attuned to the expected preferences of remote, unknowable audiences.

We should therefore be cautious in applying the concepts "legalism from below" or "juridification from below" to campaigns of cultural rights, even though we may be in admiration of the dexterity with which new pathways to justice are being navigated. The necessarily collaborative dimension to rights lobbying means that there is a transnational dynamic built into efforts to cultivate a rights-compliant caretaker state. Normative ideas of global order are communicated via intermediaries, based on broadly legitimate visions of the rights and entitlements of citizens. And these ideas, in turn, involve collaboration with those more distant still, the consumers of rights and culture, the most politically active publics of Europe and North America.

The usual way of assessing the consequences of collective human rights is to consider the manifest content of law, with examples drawn from situations of disjuncture between human rights norms and cultural attachments. But I am emphasizing another, more generalized aspect of this process: the moral leverage of collective human rights is refracted through the preferences and judgments of remote consumers of information. The publics involved in this process are knowable mostly through extrapolation. For the most part, they are distinctly non-manifest, something like invisible black holes in distant galaxies, the presence of which astronomers can only infer through wobbles in the orbits of visible stars. This intangible form of human belonging is a primary target and source of energy that moves cultural lobbying and social justice activism, that makes its presence felt in the struggles, strategies and self-perceptions taking shape before our eyes.

FOUR

The invention of indigenous peoples

Introduction

In this chapter I present evidence that conceptual diplomacy, the (re)configuration and naturalization of categories of belonging in international law, operates at such high levels of abstraction that it has, like many other things, gone global. In particular I want to discuss a long-term diplomatic initiative by the United Nations – the elaboration of the rights of indigenous peoples – to illustrate a pathway toward identity formation and public persuasion that does not straightforwardly give names to established social entities, but begins with the creation or re-conceptualization of a category of belonging, which only through public exposure and approval can then acquire leaderships, memberships, traditions, loyalties and rights claims. Conceptual diplomacy is applied not only in specific situations of conflict but in more nebulous categories of belonging that transcend state boundaries. It is occasionally invoked in response to abstract circumstances of conflict, disconnected from any particular situation of crisis. It can be based on intangibles, while remaining in essence ameliorative and preventive, aimed toward improving conditions of peoples' lives and preventing violence by cultivating cultural understanding and appreciation of human difference to a global audience.

The agendas of international institutions do not reveal or reflect cognizance of the history of the terms they use or the cultural innovations introduced by conceptual-diplomatic efforts. An overview of past use of the key concept "indigenous peoples," followed by an outline of current popular usage, should make it clear that this term has been reformulated to become an institutionally managed, publicly promoted, state-transcending category of identity, taking initial form through legal/institutional imperatives and processes and then indirectly influencing the conditions of peoples' lives through the cultivation of ideas.

Self-determination and self-definition

The most basic concept at the origin of the emergence of indigenous peoples as a legal category is the self-determination of peoples. Without this, the promotion of collective rights that stand apart from, and require reconciliation with, the rights of states would be inconceivable, or at least impracticable in the face of state monopolies of power. The international movement of indigenous peoples thus has its ultimate origin in the Byzantine conceptual apparatus of international law, beginning with the elaboration of the right of distinct peoples to self-determination.

The self-determination of non-state peoples is an insecure foundation for rights and recognition because the international human rights regime was conceived with a strong focus on the rights of individuals and the responsibilities of states. While it is oriented toward universal application, the human rights system builds into law a moral system that has its central point of origin in the Enlightenment project (pursued most influentially by Hume and Kant) of attaining knowledge that transcends the prejudices of custom and the interests of those in power. This is, almost by definition, a project that privileges the solitary thinker, removed from all conditions that we would recognize as socialization. As Ernest Gellner points out, in the epistemological tradition of Enlightenment philosophy, the problem of knowledge was formulated "in terms of a discriminating cognitive élitism," which held that all individual minds, but not all cultures and systems of meaning, were equal. In other words, "all minds were endowed with the potential of attaining a unique objective truth, but only on condition of employing the correct method and forswearing the seduction of cultural indoctrination."[1] This epistemological starting point is in basic agreement with the principal multicultural goal of some states, which inclines toward equalizing the conditions of life and opportunities of all individual citizens. Those who are especially burdened by poverty and disease are often those who are also the targets of racism, sexism, and other forms of discrimination. Liberal states and organizations take pride in combating these scourges of equal opportunity. Those who have been relegated to second- or third-class status can be defended, and their lives improved, by greater inclusion and equality, reinforced by identical rights and immunities.

But against the illustrious history of human rights individualism, collective rights have been formulated and asserted with increasing influence in the postcolonial era. This can be seen as based on another Enlightenment tradition, or at least an intellectual tradition that emerged distinctly at the time of the Enlightenment, one that rejected cognitive elitism, that morally privileged human life in the absence of civilization by placing value on the intimacy and color of rugged simplicity, on the romance of difference and the purity of human origins. Herder's understanding of human history in particular is tinged with nostalgia for a lost condition of solidarity, in which prejudice was not so much an act of hostility as a positive expression of belonging, a sense of comfort among those who lived together in close agreement and harmony, with shared principles of belief and behavior. This intellectual tradition has been equally durable and influential to that of individualism – and

---

[1] E. Gellner, *Postmodernism, Reason and Religion* (London and New York: Routledge, 1992) 37.

not only in the discipline of anthropology.[2] The longing for spiritual meaning in collective life has also entered the realm of global governance and can be seen with particular clarity in the guiding values behind the management of diversity. It constitutes another direction from which the legal foundations of belonging are being reshaped on a global scale: through public manifestations of difference conjoined with claims by distinct peoples to self-determination, arguably the least understood, most vociferously debated, and increasingly influential principle in international law.

The "We the Peoples" of the UN Charter was formulated in the years after World War II when it was still possible to argue, however misguidedly, that only natural boundaries separated distinct cultures.[3] Geographical distinctiveness, manifest in the landscapes of islands, deserts, forests and mountains was seen as the central source of unique lifestyles and identities, much like the ecological niches of flora and fauna. Today it is much easier to see that other forces are at work in the reformulation of identities, that some of the strongest claims of difference are made by the marginalized and deracinated, by those who would otherwise be absorbed, eliminated and forgotten by dominant societies. Cultural identities are stimulated by their denial; and the landscape of social justice has overtaken ecology as the most important source of human differences.[4]

---

[2] I discuss Herder's approach to comparative anthropology more fully in "The Aufklärung's Human Discipline: Comparative Anthropology according to Kant, Herder and Wilhelm von Humboldt," *Intellectual History Review*, 2009c, 19 (2): 177–95.

[3] Fredrik Barth in his famous introduction to *Ethnic Groups and Boundaries: The Social Organization of Culture Difference* (Bergen/Oslo: Universitetsforlaget; London: George Allen & Uwin, 1969) contrasts his approach with such a simplistic view of geographical and social isolation.

[4] Jean-Loup Amselle, for example, discusses the revival of African tribal identities as a product of colonial imaginings and the resurgence of postcolonial "regionalism" which "completely overturn the picture one might have of precolonial African societies." ["bouleverse totalement la vision que l'on peut avoir des sociétés africaines précoloniales." My translation.] J.-L. Amselle, "Ethnie et

Self-determination is, according to a number of legal scholars, indisputably entitled to treatment as *jus cogens*, a peremptory norm from which no derogation is to be tolerated, beyond the reach of negotiation or modification through treaties. It is in this sense in company with genocide, wars of aggression, slavery and piracy.⁵ But relative to these other familiar exclusive-club-members of international law, self-determination would be a recent inductee with no Hollywood credentials, a kind of highly attractive and mysterious dark stranger, commanding respect through charisma and promise, but not particularly forthcoming. What is its past and of what does it consist?

Erica-Irene Daes makes a revealing reference to what she calls the "new" United Nations law of self-determination, pointing out that the right to self-determination in the formulation of the UN Charter was a desiderata rather than a legal right, but that the Charter then initiated a "revolutionary process" realized through processes of decolonization in the latter half of the twentieth century that spilled over from postcolonial nation building and gave a strong impetus to minority peoples' claims of self-determination.⁶ The specific reference point for this revolution is Article 3 of the Declaration on the Granting of Independence to Colonial Countries and Peoples, adopted by the UN General Assembly on 14 December 1960: "All peoples have the right to self-determination; by virtue of that right

espaces: pour une anthropologie topologique," in *Au coeur de l'ethnie. Ethnie, tribalisme et État en Afrique*, ed. J.-L. Amselle and Elikia M'Bokolo (Paris: La Découverte: 1999) 43.

5 See, for example, K. Parker, "Understanding Self-determination: The Basics," in *In Pursuit of the Right to Self-Determination: Collected Papers and Proceedings of the First International Conference on the Right to Self-Determination and the United Nations, Geneva 2000*, ed. Y.N. Kly and D. Kly (Atlanta: Clarity, 2001) 63–73; H. G. Espiell, *The Right to Self-Determination*, UN doc. E/CN.4Sub.2/405/Rev.1.U.N. Sales No. E.79.XIV.5 (1980).

6 E.-I. Daes, "Striving for Self-determination for Indigenous Peoples" in *In Pursuit of the Right to Self-Determination: Collected Papers and Proceedings of the First International Conference on the Right to Self-Determination and the United Nations, Geneva 2000*, ed. Y.N. Kly and D. Kly (Atlanta: Clarity, 2001) 50–1.

they freely determine their political status and freely pursue their economic, social and cultural development."[7] With its legal origin so recent, it could be reasonably argued that, even taking into account the revolutionary process of decolonization of the latter half of the twentieth century, the practical consequences of the law of self-determination have continued to ramify broadly and are in political terms still making themselves felt.

There appear to have been two interrelated sources of the elaboration and extension of the ideals of self-determination to a wide range of minority communities in the post-World War II era. The first (already discussed in Chapter 3) consisted of the ideas of belonging that were an essential aspect of colonial projects, the naming of "bands," "tribes" and "cultures," accompanied by their endowment with formal legal and political significance, in the context of limited opportunity and autonomy.

Then there were the postcolonial aspirations of political inclusion that followed the dismantling of overseas empires, built on the unstable inheritance of colonially elaborated tribalism. In the postcolonial era, we are witnessing the rise of political and territorial claims that follow from the formalization of these cultural categories (in much the same way that European nation-states became formalized in the course of World War I). During the last two decades of the twentieth century, self-determination became the legal focal point and source of all other claims to distinct rights among minority peoples. The transnational indigenous peoples' movement in particular can be seen as a clear manifestation of the localization of nationalist sentiments, a process that Anthony Giddens once anticipated as a consequence of globalizing modernity.[8]

---

[7] United Nations, *Declaration on the Granting of Independence to Colonial Countries and Peoples*, GA Res. 1514 (XV), UN GAOR, 1960, UN doc. A/4684/1961.

[8] A. Giddens, *The Consequences of Modernity* (Stanford University Press, 1990) 65.

But the intellectual legitimacy of self-determination can be found further afield than its obvious connections to the project of decolonization. It can also be seen in cosmopolitan designs for bringing together the entire range of human difference in a single regime of peaceable world governance, one that is more than respectful of distinctiveness, but that takes on the task of furthering the human project by identifying, promoting and protecting unique ways of life and bodies of knowledge. If the essence of humanity cannot be found by sweepingly imposing a uniform socio-political design, it must be found in the common denominator of human diversity. If the model of state-mediated peace and prosperity was so adamantly rejected by those on the margins of states, this must be so because the model itself did not correspond with the fundamental nature of what it means to be human. Human nature is pliant clay that takes on a miraculous variety of social forms, and there is no possibility for absolute, immutable, perfect human happiness above the cultural reach of individual peoples and communities. If a universal foundation for law is not to be found by rational means, by beginning with abstractions and generalities on the nature of humankind, then distinct cultures must have a more significant place in the project of creating a harmonious, culturally ecumenical world.

Whatever its intellectual origins, the recent emphasis in international law on shoring up distinct ways of life through distinct rights introduces a number of clearly recognizable tensions in the human rights regime elaborated in the post-World War II era. For one thing, the basic goal of the human rights movement – to define and implement a foundation of moral standards applicable to humankind across the boundaries of religion, race, class, ethnicity and national affiliation – leads to difficulty accommodating those who value human differences that are contrary to the standards of human rights, who emphasize the merging of individuals in systems of ascribed status. The human rights system is often criticized or even repudiated by cultural relativists, who find fault with the emphasis it places on individual rights, even (or especially) within its programs of diversity.[9] And for this reason, they have insisted upon a broadening of universal values to include greater, more tolerant, more sweeping protections of distinctive cultural traditions.

Another paradox inherent in the expanded scope of self-determination in human rights is a more central theme of this book: if, in accordance with the postcolonial turn toward the rights of peoples in international law, a distinct people possesses cultural rights as a central component of their self-determination, then it is incumbent on international agencies to become involved in the understanding of culture and the affirmation of cultural rights. After all, without situating rights within clearly understood, institutionally-interpreted categories of people, self-determination can have little effect. But self-determination is inseparable from the idea of self-definition, above all from representing one's collective difference for all to see, from the publicly-visible elaboration of one's own collective political and cultural identity. Acting on claims of self-determination by the once-unrecognized involves representation of collective difference to public others, making manifest to as large an audience as possible the markers of "peoplehood," such things as distinct language, territory, subsistence base, knowledge, ritual and governance.

Given this basic premise of self-representational activism, how can a state or international agency define and protect the cultures of remote, invisible distinct peoples in a way that corresponds with the idea of a global community of self-determining peoples? Above all, how can it do so in a way consistent with the popular goal of cultural preservation? It is a challenge that, especially in its practical application in

---

[9] This problem is discussed with great clarity by Sally Engle Merry in *Human Rights and Gender Violence: Translating International Law into Local Justice* (University of Chicago Press, 2006).

indigenous peoples' initiatives, is mired in messy processes of legal and cultural negotiation, together with public lobbying and activism – all of which is fraught with possibilities for misunderstanding and contradiction.

More than this, it is a challenge that, in the interest of furthering our understanding of collective behavior, uncovers new, unfamiliar and emerging processes of identity formation. To begin with, the process of identity construction that occurs under the influence of multiculturalism in global governance makes it necessary to reverse the usual order in which the combined dynamics of collective identity and social justice claims are seen to emerge: it is now more than ever possible for identity to have a starting point in an invented category of belonging, which only acquires membership and attracts efforts toward cultivation of belonging and loyalty once it is institutionally established. With a starting point in the law of self-determination, identity choices and priorities can be given shape and substance and acquire followings in ideas – in particular ideas about categories of belonging – initially brought into being by legislators or committees of "experts," then popularized through the moral and conceptual persuasion of rights.

The invention of indigenism

The transformation of the term "indigenous peoples" from an abstraction in reports and initiatives sponsored by the International Labour Organization in the 1950s to a transnational social movement with universal recognition by the 1990s is a compelling example of the rights-based pathways toward the development of new categories of human belonging. Indigenous peoples, largely through the influence of discourse in the international public sphere, have come to represent a form of life with universal qualities: humanly shared, primordial political and social conditions and cultural virtues commonly seen to apply to all those who can claim original descent from territorially definable populations that were once subject to colonization, and who were more recently excluded from the processes of state building.[10]

Although there is no legal "gatekeeper" definition of indigenous peoples in international law, the most common reference point for understanding the concept "indigenous peoples" comes from a 1987 report by José Martínez Cobo, the "Study of the Problem of Discrimination against Indigenous Populations." Indigenous communities, peoples and nations are defined in the Cobo report as

those which, having a historical continuity with pre-invasion and pre-colonial societies that developed on their territories, consider themselves distinct from other sectors of the societies now prevailing in those territories, or parts of them. They form at present nondominant sectors of society and are determined to preserve, develop and transmit to future generations their ancestral territories and their ethnic identity, as the basis of their continued existence as peoples, in accordance with their own cultural patterns, social institutions and legal systems.[11]

The most important point to be gleaned from this official guideline is the combination of loose objective standards – historical continuity with a pre-colonial past in the context of "ancestral territories" – with subjective criteria: they "consider themselves" distinct and are collectively "determined" to pass on their heritage.

But the legal terminology associated with the common experience and inalienable rights of indigenous peoples long preceded the

---

[10] A simple and direct effort to provide guidance as to who they are at a formal level can also be found in Article 1 of ILO Convention 169 Concerning Indigenous and Tribal Peoples in Independent Countries (1989): "[P]eoples in independent countries … are regarded as indigenous on account of their descent from the populations which inhabited the country, or a geographical region to which the country belongs, at the time of conquest or colonization or the establishment of present state boundaries and who, irrespective of their legal status, regain some or all of their own social, economic, cultural and political institutions."

[11] José Martínez Cobo, *Study of the Problem of Discrimination against Indigenous Populations*, Vol. V (UN doc. E/CN.4/Sub.2/1986/7/Add.4) 48.

subjective self-identification and political mobilization around this term. The origin and growth in currency of the category "indigenous peoples" involved a dramatic shift from legal abstraction to a supra-state category of belonging, a term that acquired not only a "we" of collective self-recognition, but also the third party public recognition inherent in emerging standards in human rights law and a flourishing transnational social movement. Use and control of the term "indigenous" in the last half of the twentieth century changed hands from the bureaucratic elite that formally defined the concepts and priorities of international organizations to those representatives of societies marginal to nation states, who further redefined both the term and their sense of history to make "indigenous" a new source of political aspiration and strategy.

We can see distinct stages in the process by which the term "indigenous peoples," an abstract transnational category of belonging, acquired shape and legal substance, eventually to become an essential part of a popular global paradigm of human difference. Let us consider these in an approximate historical order, while paying due attention to the unevenness, overlapping and inconsistencies inherent in any timeline approach to conceptual/institutional transformations of this kind.

Non-recognition: a better sense of the widely ramifying consequences of the UN's applied sociological imagination can be gained by considering a situation prior to the rise of the indigenous peoples' movement, that of the League of Nations in the early twentieth century, in which a specific terminology of liberation was absent from international law. The most common reference point of the legal limits of this earlier regime of international law is the effort made by Levi General – better known by his chiefly title "Deskaheh" – to lobby the League of Nations Headquarters in Geneva in 1923 in protest against Canada's political interference in the Seneca's hereditary leadership. In the League there was no legal pathway for him to pursue his grievance, no term that identified those in his situation of occupation and marginalization by a nation-state. Instead, General put his name to a document titled "The Red Man's Appeal to Justice," using a language that today would generally be considered repugnant. Not surprisingly, Deskaheh's campaign for recognition and collective autonomy ended in failure, even though it eventually became a historical reference point for later, more successful assertions of aboriginal sovereignty.[12] This is a clear indication that in the early twentieth century the transnational conceptual typology of non-state peoples had not yet been developed, at least not in a way conducive to effective legal and public-outreach strategizing.

Conceptualization: the Spanish term *pueblos indígenas* was the focal point of an intellectual community in Mexico in the 1930s and 1940s.[13] It was perhaps a way to identify a status of prior occupancy in a context in which many claimed descent from Central American civilizations, and hence found pejorative connotations in the term *indios*. But it is unclear whether the literature produced in Spanish percolated through to the realm of global governance or whether the English term "indigenous peoples" was independently re-invented. In any event, the origin of "indigenous peoples" as a legal concept can be traced to the efforts of the International Labour Organization (ILO), the only League of Nations institution to have survived the restructuring of the global community in the aftermath of World War II. In 1941 the ILO sponsored a brief article in the Mexican-based journal *Revista América Indigén*, which announced ILO interest in improving the situation of

---

[12] R. Niezen, *The Origins of Indigenism: Human Rights and the Politics of Identity* (Berkeley and Los Angeles: University of California Press, 2003) 31–6; J. Rostkowski "Deskaheh's Shadow: Indians on the International Scene," *Native American Studies*, 1995, 9 (2): 1–4; J. Anaya, *Indigenous Peoples in International Law*, second edn (Oxford University Press, 2004).

[13] During the World War II era, the scholarly community in Latin America was already exchanging information and ideas about *pueblos indígenas*, particularly in the Mexico-based journal *Revista América Indígen*, which ran from 1941 to 1980.

indigenous workers.[14] A slow-to-emerge outcome of this goal was the 1952 International Labour Organization report entitled "Indigenous Peoples: Living and Working Conditions of Aboriginal Populations in Independent Countries," followed five years later with ILO Convention (No. 107) Concerning the Protection and Integration of Indigenous and other Tribal and Semi-Tribal Populations in Independent Countries. The principal objectives of this instrument were consistent with the then-current state-sponsored programs of assimilation: eradication of cultural differences, distinct status and, ultimately, the occupational exclusions and limited life opportunities of those peoples on the margins of states.[15] That is to say, indigenous peoples were not originally institutionally conceived as a category of people whose collective worth was defined by their distinct knowledge and traditions (not to mention their self-determination), but as a category of people conceptually marked off from the rest of humanity by a common condition of poverty, ignorance and marginalization, attributable not just to the negligence of states but in large measure to the *persistence* of tradition.

Legal reconstruction: the assimilationist orientation of the indigenous peoples' concept did not change significantly until self-identifying indigenous spokespeople began making claims and common cause on behalf of their distinct constituencies. In the late 1970s and early 1980s meetings sponsored by the UN Commission on Human Rights assembled delegates representing indigenous peoples under one roof (actually a rather architecturally impressive art-deco roof at the Palais des Nations in Geneva). And in 1982 the creation of the United Nations Working Group on Indigenous Populations inaugurated the regular meetings that became the focal point of the international movement of indigenous peoples until the final meeting in 2006, at which time it

---

[14] D.H. Blelloch, "The International Labour Organisation and the Indigenous Workers of the Americas," *Revista América Indígen*, 1941, 1: 35–7.

[15] See Anaya, *Indigenous Peoples*, for a discussion of the assimilative orientation and legal significance of ILO Convention no. 107.

was functionally replaced by the UN Permanent Forum on Indigenous Issues based at the UN headquarters in New York.

The advent of participation by indigenous leaders and organizations in UN meetings also provided impetus toward the development of new human rights instruments intended to reflect the experience and aspirations of indigenous peoples. In 1989 the ILO provided a legal corrective to its earlier assimilationist orientation toward indigenous peoples with the ratification of Convention (No. 169) Concerning Indigenous and Tribal Peoples in Independent Countries. This was the first international instrument oriented toward enhancing the ability of indigenous peoples to protect and develop their customs and institutions on their own terms, representing a paradigm shift that would not likely have occurred without the active participation of indigenous representatives in international meetings. In an overlapping initiative, from 1985 to 1993, the Working Group of the Sub-Commission on the Prevention of Discrimination and Protection of Minorities brought together a body of five international experts to collate and assess a massive collection of living and historical testimony of indigenous peoples from around the world, with the goal of developing a Declaration on the Rights of Indigenous Peoples, which was finally approved by the UN General Assembly in September 2007 (with the dissenting votes coming from those states with the most politically active indigenous organizations: the United States, Canada, Australia and New Zealand).

In UN meta-discourse, the importance of indigenous populations is partly numerical, providing an anchorage to the indigenous peoples' movement that has every appearance of factuality, even though the concept of "indigenous peoples" is ultimately based on the collective self-representation of those who attend international conferences, which makes meaningless the quantification of indigenous populations. Following the figures most commonly invoked in recent UN documents they comprise some 300 to 370 million original peoples from 5,000 to 6,000 distinct groups living in more than 70 countries. It is important to note (yet to my knowledge never noted) that these figures represent estimates of all those who could *potentially* invoke indigenous status, but does not include the all-important criterion of self-definition, the collective "determination" to preserve a distinct lifestyle. Without this information, we simply do not know how many people belong to indigenous communities; but legal-conceptual order calls for at least some form of numerical certainty, achieved in this case by invention and multimedia repetition.

The UN's efforts toward naturalization of the concept of "indigenous people" also extend into the realm of historical interpretation, in at least one instance by inserting the concept into a context in which it did not yet exist. A 1996 UN-sponsored working paper on the concept "indigenous people" by Erica-Irene Daes, discussing Article 22 of the Covenant of the League of Nations, replaces the paternalistic idea of "peoples not yet able to stand by themselves under the strenuous conditions of the modern world," which we actually find in Article 22, with the term "indigenous peoples" in her interpretation of it; and in so doing she gives the concept of indigenous peoples a legal history that extends into the early twentieth century, roughly thirty years before its actual appearance in ILO reports and legislation.[16] Daes' conceptual invention in part answers the need to overcome the disjuncture between the recent invention of indigenous peoples as a legal concept, with their primordial identity that reaches back into time immemorial or at the very least their "pre-invasion" history. With this sleight of hand – or perhaps more charitably, this subtle exercise of interpretive "presentism" – the pre-World War II cultural geography of global governance is rewritten in the form of a stark contrast between "civilization" and "indigenous peoples." This happens to be more descriptive of current

---

[16] E.I. Daes, "Working Paper by the Chairperson-Rapporteur, Mrs. Erica-Irene A. Daes, on the Concept of 'Indigenous People,'" United Nations Economic and Social Council, Commission on Human Rights (UN doc. E/CN.5/Sub.2/AC.4/1996/2) 6.

ideas, rather than the conceptual construction that then existed: a legal reinforcement of the mandate system and its mission of "tutelage" of those, broadly and vaguely conceived, under colonial rule.

The increasingly refined definition of indigenous peoples brings into relief a contrast with those who do not clearly fit the basic criterion of possessing distinct territories and connections to a pre-invasion past, but who remain distinct and non-dominant nevertheless. The concept of indigenous peoples has, from the beginning of International Labour Organization initiatives in the 1950s, been followed by a conceptual/legal blank space, an entity implicitly defined by reference to a condition of being "not-indigenous," that in one form or another, defies clear definition. At first the ILO used two inextricably linked terms: "indigenous peoples" and "tribal peoples" to designate those living without adequate access to the rights of citizenship and benefits of the state. "Tribal peoples" became a kind of catch-all category referring to those who (according to an explanatory document released by the UN in 2004) are "not 'indigenous' in the literal sense in the countries in which they live, but who nevertheless live in a similar situation," that is to say, a situation of marginalization, as experienced by Afro-descended peoples of Central and South America or tribal peoples in Africa like the San or Maasai.[17] Even though such peoples have difficulty establishing that they have lived in the region they inhabit longer than other population groups of their region, they do experience distinct challenges to prosperity and have durable attachments to their own customs and traditions. In practice, such peoples have referred to themselves as "indigenous" in order to participate in discussions taking place at the United Nations. A practical solution to the indigenous/tribal distinction, in the absence of specific UN-sponsored programs on behalf of tribal peoples, has been the self-representation of tribal peoples as

---

[17] United Nations, Department of Economic and Social Affairs, "'The Concept of Indigenous Peoples'; Background Paper Prepared by the Secretariat of the Permanent Forum on Indigenous Issues," UN doc. PFII/2004/WS.1/3, 2004a, 3.

indigenous peoples. And to this the UN has turned a blind eye, choosing not to be embroiled in the vexed process of defining categories of "peoples" to whom rights accrue, and instead allowing the terms "indigenous" and "tribal" to be "used as synonyms in the UN system when the peoples concerned identify themselves under the indigenous agenda."[18]

The category of the "non-indigenous" has recently manifested itself in the idea of "local communities," described in a UN report as those who live in "a rich complexity of non-indigenous traditional rural communities," who are unable to define themselves as indigenous, but who nevertheless "have accumulated knowledge, innovations and practices regarding the sustainable management and development of ... [their local resources] including useful environmental knowledge."[19] It remains to be seen whether this category will resonate with those living in conditions of marginalization without being able to claim indigenous status, and above all whether they will be able to use the narrow foothold in international law to reach an audience appreciative of their distinct knowledge.

Vernacularization: while ideas about indigenous rights were being shaped through legal standard-setting, they were also being cultivated in a wide range of formal and informal settings. The history of the concept of indigenous peoples thus offers clear examples of the processes of *vernacularization*. This usually refers to the translation of legal norms in local contexts in which participants in rights claims are unfamiliar with legal language and processes. In Sally Engle Merry's terms, it refers to the process by which human rights language is "extracted from the universal and adapted to national and local communities."[20]

---

[18] United Nations, "The Concept of Indigenous Peoples."

[19] United Nations, "'The Concept of Local Communities,' Background Paper Prepared by the Secretariat of the Permanent Forum on Indigenous Issues for the Expert Workshop on the Dissaggregation [*sic*] of Data", UN doc. PFII/2004/WS.1/3/Add.1., 2004b.

[20] S. Engle Merry, *Human Rights and Gender Violence: Translating International Law into Local Justice* (University of Chicago Press, 2006) 219.

The transformation of peasant political activism in Bolivia, from military cooption in the 1950s and 1960s to a national and transnational indigenous movement, is a clear example of this form of vernacularization, of national and local recognition and use of the new possibilities inherent in the international rights discourse. It exemplifies the process by which the term indigenous peoples was transformed from an abstract category of rights-bearers to a focal point of collective self-knowledge, multiplied many times into a widely recognized base of political identity. Universal suffrage in Bolivia in 1953 did not immediately result in political representation by the majority population of peasants in Bolivia. Autonomous peasant organizations failed to emerge past the centralized government control built into the mechanisms of a Peasant–Military Pact. The first autonomous peasant organizations to break through were either political parties, such as the Movimiento Indio Túpac Katari (the Túpac Katari Indian Movement) or trade unions like the Confederación Sindical Unica de Trabajadores Campesinos de Bolivia (the General Trade Union Confederation of Peasant Workers of Bolivia). The dominant ideology of the party movements was class oriented and dedicated to the interests of labor, which did not fit comfortably with trade union movements in the countryside based on *campesino* identity. The international indigenous discourse that emerged in the 1980s was a catalyst toward the culturalization of economic identity or ethnification of class discourse, which overcame this Marxist/*campesino* divide.[21] According to one succinct political analysis, it "permitted the discovery of a stage for the social massing of ethno-national discourse."[22] For this to occur the indigenous peoples concept had to be cultivated in village meetings

---

[21] A. García Linera, M. Chávez Léon and P. Costas Monje, *Sociología de los movimientos sociales en Bolivia: Estructuras de movilización, repertorios culturales y acción política* (La Paz: Plural, 2008) 168.

[22] "permitieron hallar un escenario de masificación social del discurso étnico-nacional." My translation. Linera *et al.*, *Sociología de los movimientos sociales en Bolivia*, 168.

and rallies, infused with history and local pride, to the point at which it became an integral part of national discourse. It was interpreted and actively promoted by intermediaries, particularly by trade union leaders and local politicians. It did not replace, but supplemented, existing concepts and institutional apparatuses. The national political discourse of indigenism (*indigenismo*) allowed Evo Morales to build on his qualifications as a trade union leader of cocoa growers (*cocaleros*) with the discourse of indigenous rights, combining the unifying themes of historical oppression, enduring rights to territory and the defence of cocoa growing with the international ideology and legitimacy of human rights in a political movement that propelled him to the presidency.

There is another, more literal sense in which vernacularization can occur: through a process of institutionally-mediated global popularization that can reach a point at which a concept becomes current in dominant languages. We recognize that a word has entered the vernacular when it is used widely and without equivocation or reflection on its meaning or history. Through just such a global cultivation of ideas, the term indigenous peoples has come to represent a distinct form of counter-modernity, a form of life full of possibility for human salvation, or at least the aversion of a global crisis of cultural extinction, having entered the realm, through bureaucratic conceptualization and quantification, of public consciousness. It now seems clear that at some point within the past several decades, through a mass of sympathetic media attention to indigenous lobbying and rights building, a threshold was crossed in which the term "indigenous" found its way into ordinary usage, becoming, in the popular language of public consciousness, a "household word." Internet searches of the term "indigenous peoples" using any server will produce hundreds of thousands, if not millions, of hits, with many sites oriented toward facilitating participation in UN initiatives. Journalists and media personalities communicating in any venue (including Jon Stewart in a 2007 interview in Comedy Central's *The Daily Show* with Bolivian President Evo Morales) are able to use the term "indigenous peoples" with confidence, knowing that they will not come across to their viewers, listeners or readers as ivory tower academics or legal specialists with obtuse vocabulation.

At the level of the organizations of global governance, the rapid development of indigenous representation and recognition is reflected in the rise in numbers of officially sanctioned nongovernmental organizations (NGOs), or more specifically indigenous peoples' organizations (IPOs). In 1985 there were eight indigenous nongovernmental organizations possessing consultative status with the United Nation's Economic and Social Council (ECOSOC); by 1995 this number had grown to fourteen, while in 2005 it had jumped exponentially to forty-two.[23] This degree of

---

[23] The organizations with consultative status with ECOSOC are as follows: Aboriginal and Torres Strait Islander Commission; The Aleut International Association; American Indian Law Alliance; Asian Indigenous and Tribal Peoples Network; Assembly of First Nations – National Indian Brotherhood; Association of Indigenous Peoples of the North, Siberia and Far East of the Russian Federation (RAIPON); Centre d'accompagnement des autochtones pygmées et minoritaires vulnérables; Cherokee Nation of New Jersey; Congress of Aboriginal Peoples; Coordinating Body of the Indigenous Organizations in the Amazon Basin; Cultural Survival; Foundation for Aboriginal and Islander Research Action Aboriginal Corporation; Foundation for the American Indian; Four Directions Council; Grand Council of the Crees – Eeyou Istchee; Indian Committee of Youth Organizations; Indian Movement "Tupaj Amaru"; Indian Council of South America; Indian Law Resource Centre; Indigenous and Peasant Coordinator of Communal Agroforestry (CICAFOC); Indigenous Peoples Survival Foundation; Indigenous Tourism Rights International; Indigenous World Association; Innu Council of Nitassinan (Innu Nation); International Indian Treaty Council; International Organization of Indigenous Resource Development; International Work Group for Indigenous Affairs; Inuit Circumpolar Conference; Métis National Council; Métis National Council of Women, Inc.; National Aboriginal and Islander Legal Services Secretariat; National Aboriginal Forestry Association; National Congress of American Indians; The National Indian Youth Council; Native American Rights Fund; Native Women's Association of Canada; Netherlands Centre for Indigenous Peoples (NCIV); Partnership for Indigenous Peoples Environment; Rigoberta Menchu Tum Foundation; Saami Council; Turtle Island Restoration Network; Union of British Columbia Indian Chiefs; World Council of Indigenous Peoples. The complete list of NGOs with ECOSOC consultative status, including the year in which the status was approved, can be found at: www.un.org/esa/coordination/ngo/pdf/INF_List.pdf.

representation and recognition of indigenous peoples in the institutions of global governance has developed recently and suddenly, with most new initiatives being established during the last two decades of the twentieth century.

The development of these programs and organizations should not just be considered from a perspective that emphasizes their efforts toward positive contributions to the well-being of indigenous communities, but can also be seen as attempts to control the actions of nation-states and large-scale industries. In their role as a counterweight to the globally powerful, indigenous peoples have in popular consciousness come to represent an alternative to the ecological and political abuses of modernity. And in practical terms, in their pursuit of local interests through universal rights and recognition, indigenous organizations have, intentionally or not, affiliated themselves with issues that bring together organizational coalitions of diverse interest groups. This has not only involved the development of regional blocs of indigenous organizations, but virtual global alliances of broad spectrum resistance. Examples include opposition to construction of large-scale hydroelectric facilities and other extractive industries, raising awareness of the rights abuses and displacements following from anti-terrorism campaigns (with a focus on the African Sahel), and resistance to the "biopiracy" of human genome research. Awareness of issues of specific concern to particular peoples is often expanded through multi-interest transnational coordination and information sharing.

Taken together, these global governance and NGO efforts are also associated with ideas that have come to apply generally to indigenous peoples. Collectively, indigenous peoples are seen as "victims of progress," marginalized by nation-states, removed from territories, excluded from possibilities for development, subject to state-sponsored programs of assimilation, resulting in interruption of the intergenerational transmission of their distinctive languages and cultural knowledge. Who better to illustrate this approach to defining the essence of indigenous peoples than Kofi Annan, who, as Secretary-General of the United Nations, was among the world's most effective communicators of the plight of the poor and powerless?

For far too long, the hopes and aspirations of indigenous peoples have been ignored. Their lands have been taken, their cultures denigrated or directly attacked, their languages and customs suppressed, their wisdom and traditional knowledge overlooked and their sustainable ways of developing natural resources dismissed. Some have even faced the threat of extinction. Indigenous peoples continue to suffer from prejudice and ... in many cases, they are trapped in the middle of conflicts, conscripted into armed forces, faced with summary executions and relocated from their lands. They are subject to extreme poverty, disease, environmental destruction and sometimes permanent displacement.[24]

The emphasis on the suffering and victimization of indigenous peoples has become a basic part of the legitimacy of indigenous initiatives as it percolates down to the many satellite agencies of the UN. A study of indigenous mental health sponsored by the World Health Organization, for example, describes the global pattern of suffering among indigenous peoples under the subheadings "depopulation," "violence," "dislocation" and "poverty."[25] According to a Web posting by the UN's International Fund for Agricultural Development, "in many countries, indigenous peoples are the most severely disadvantaged. They are often forced to live on the least productive terrain, denied rights to land, forests and other natural resources that they have managed sustainably for millennia, and marginalized by modern society."[26] A related statement by a

[24] K. Annan, interview in "*UNPFII Vol. 1 – Indigenous Peoples and the United Nations*," 2008, 6: 54.
[25] A. Cohen, "The Mental Health of Indigenous Peoples: An International Overview" (Geneva: Department of Mental Health, World Health Organization, 1999).
[26] International Fund for Agricultural Development, 2004, "International Day of the World's Indigenous People." www.ifad.org/media/events/2004/ip.htm. Accessed September 13, 2007.

coalition of prominent human rights NGOs is more direct in assigning blame to recalcitrant states: "when it comes to Indigenous Peoples, states have persistently failed to recognize and uphold [international human rights treaties]. The devastating consequence has been the profound impoverishment and marginalization of Indigenous women, men and children around the world and the denial of such basic rights as rights to food, health, and education and livelihood." [27]

Indigenous peoples suffer not only from global patterns of political isolation and repression; they are victims of developmental disadvantage, in part because they are not adequately included in the UN's own initiatives. In a joint statement released on the International Day of the World's Indigenous Peoples, Louise Arbour, then United Nations High Commissioner for Human Rights, and Rodolfo Stavenhagen, special rapporteur on the situation of human rights and fundamental freedoms of indigenous people, find "increasing evidence that indigenous peoples are largely overlooked in [the] global efforts [toward development]. They remain among the poorest of the poor, with little reference to them in the reports on implementation of the MDGs [Millennium Development Goals]." [28] Stavenhagen, interviewed for a public relations film sponsored by the United Nations Permanent Forum on Indigenous Issues, emphasized the disadvantaged circumstances of those who live

---

[27] Rights and Democracy, 2005, *Advancing the Human Rights of Indigenous Peoples: A Critical Challenge for the International Community.* Voices from a forum at the 61st Session of the United Nations Commission on Human Rights, April 13, 2005, presented by Amnesty International, la Fédération Internationale des Ligues des Droits de l'Homme, the Netherlands Centre for Indigenous Peoples (NCIV), Friends World Committee for Consultation (Quakers), and Rights and Democracy. www.ddrd.ca/site/publications/index.php?id=1430&sub section=catalogue. Accessed April 29, 2008.

[28] United Nations, "Message of Louise Arbour, United Nations High Commissioner for Human Rights and Rodolfo Stavenhagen, Special Rapporteur on the Situation of Human Rights and Fundamental Freedoms of Indigenous People, on the Occasion of the International Day of the World's Indigenous Peoples." Office of the High Commissioner for Human Rights, August 2007. www.unep.org/indigenous/pdfs/Statement-Louise-Arbour-Aug2007.pdf. Accessed May 3, 2008.

in isolation from the legal mechanisms of the state and the international order: "[T]hey are poor, they are isolated, they are socially excluded, discriminated against, marginalized, they live somewhere in the jungles, or somewhere in the swamps or in the mountains and have no access to lawyers or even to NGOs, and certainly not to the system of justice and the government and much less to international organizations."[29] Considered in isolation from other conceptions of indigenous peoples, this statement closely resembles the foundational ideas of the ILO in the 1950s – indigenous and tribal peoples are those who, through their isolation and ignorance, lack the benefits of the state – except that today the focal point of equitable inclusion is the mechanisms of empowerment through law.

Another notable feature of UN-sponsored vernacular discourse on indigenous peoples points in a very different direction, toward the cultural virtues of indigenous peoples, the need to protect their languages, knowledge and identities, and their potential contribution to human heritage. They are an answer to nostalgia for consensus on values handed down from one generation to the next in an unbroken chain that goes back beyond the inherited remembrance of origins. Their connection to traditional territories and respect for the environment, in particular, constitute a "fragile treasure currently under threat from the effects of rapid globalization."[30]

From the point of view of indigenous leaders, this idea is often expressed through a combination of environmental and spiritual stewardship. Carrie Dann, representing the Western Shoshone (who claim a homeland that encompasses most of Nevada, parts of Idaho and Utah

---

[29] R. Stavenhagen, interview in *"UNPFII Vol. 1 – Indigenous Peoples and the United Nations,"* 2008, 8: 38.

[30] UNESCO, 2006, "UNESCO and Indigenous Peoples: Partnership to Promote Cultural Diversity." http://unesdoc.unesco.org/images/0013/001356/135656M.pdf. Accessed September 10, 2007.

and a sizable part of the interior of southern California), expresses this idea in the UNPFII's 2008 publicity film with reference to a pan-Indian origin myth, in which the world is formed on the back of a turtle: "I am indigenous to this Turtle Island. Our teachings tell us that the Creator placed us here as caretakers of the land, the animals, all living things that were placed here with our responsibilities."[31] José Carlos Morales, representing the Brunka of Costa Rica in the same film, expresses much the same idea (in Spanish with English subtitles): "The most virgin and untouched flora and fauna of the planet – is on indigenous territory. We are the caretakers of the Earth, and want that this will serve humanity but without destroying the Earth!"[32] (The exclamation point is of course in the subtitled translation.)

Urgency is brought to bear on efforts to protect and preserve the cultural heritage of indigenous peoples because of the potential human benefits of their particular knowledge and inherent cultural virtue. Elsa Stamatopoulou, speaking on behalf of the Secretariat of the UNPFII, for example, links the place of indigenous people as environmental stewards with the survival of languages and biodiversity:

[W]e estimate that out of the approximately 6000 languages spoken in the world today, 4000 are spoken by indigenous peoples. And if one looks at the map of the world, one sees that the linguistic diversity in our world coincides with the biodiversity of our world. So we have to think of what it means. Indigenous issues, indigenous peoples are of global interest, we are all together in this humanity, because by protecting and being together with indigenous peoples we are protecting their cultural human heritage and the biodiversity of our world.[33]

---

[31] C. Dann, interview in "*UNPFII Vol. 1 – Indigenous Peoples and the United Nations*," 2008, 10: 33.

[32] J. C. Morales, interview in "*UNPFII Vol. 1 – Indigenous Peoples and the United Nations*," 2008, 11: 02.

[33] E. Stamatopoulou, interview in "*UNPFII Vol. 1 – Indigenous Peoples and the United Nations*," 2008, 13: 01.

This statement matter-of-factly avoids the romance and enchantment often associated with ideas of indigenous peoples and caretakers, but this does not mean that such ideas are not part of the UN's inspiration. Gro Harlem Bruntland, serving as Director-General of the World Health Organization, eloquently connected the idea of indigenous contributions to human heritage with the survival of possibilities for everyone to live more complete lives in an opening address to the 1999 International Consultation on the Health of Indigenous Peoples:

Indigenous peoples teach us about the values that have permitted humankind to live on this planet for many thousands of years without desecrating it. They teach us about holistic approaches to health that seek to strengthen the social networks of individuals and communities, while connecting them to the environment in which they live. And they teach us about the importance of a spiritual dimension to the healing process.

Indigenous Peoples, she concluded, "teach us how to live more correctly." [34]

The theme of indigenous knowledge as developing through (and expressing) a heightened connection to the supernatural was particularly evident in recent meetings of the Permanent Forum on Indigenous Issues, in which the public statements of delegates, even those with a focus on specific human rights violations, often invoke spiritual values, the interconnectedness of all beings, and the sacred, living nature of the earth. This of course makes more poignant the grievances of the powerless by connecting them to universal values, by associating the suffering of the few with the survival of humanity. And occasionally the focus turns exclusively to what might be called a cosmological claim, an effort to cultivate a shared belief in the imminent coming of a new heaven and

---

[34] In reaching this conclusion Bruntland is invoking a statement made by Wally N'Dow, Secretary-General of the 1996 United Nations Conference on Human Settlements. G.H. Brundtland, *International Consultation on the Health of Indigenous Peoples* (Geneva: World Health Organization, 1999) 1. www.who. int/director-general/speeches/1999/english/19991123_indigenous_people.html. Accessed July 2, 2010.

a new earth, a form of discourse that implicitly connects privileged spiritual knowledge with distinct rights.

Such was the substance of a speech given by Nicolas Lucas Tirum, a Mayan elder who was given a prominent place (quite literally, at the front podium next to the Chairperson and representatives of the Secretariat) in the eighth meeting of the Permanent Forum on Indigenous Issues in May 2009. The central subject of Tirum's message, stated plainly and directly in the opening line of his address, was the cosmological change to take place on December 21, in the year 2012, the 13th B'aqtun (a period of 5,200 years, each year consisting of 360 days) of the Mayan calendar, a new era in which self-respect and respect toward all beings in the universe will be realized; and from this change will follow an end to hatred and bloodshed and a renewal of the values of love, solidarity and brotherhood among humanity. (He later drew attention to the fact that the Kyoto Protocol is to be first formally evaluated in 2012, a time that corresponds perfectly with the transition from the 12th to the 13th B'aqtun.) But the close of the 12th B'aqtun, the period in which we are currently living, is a time in which the respect for Mother Earth – as mother of all living beings in a universe in which the elements are intimately connected – is being lost through a rationalist, utilitarian approach to science, politics and economic development, resulting in environmental deterioration, climate change, reduction of the world's biological and genetic patrimony and the loss of cultures and languages. In this time of disaster and imminent renewal, "it is urgent that universities and scientific institutes recognize the spiritual dimension of humanity, the connection and interconnection of all the elements of the universe" and open themselves to scientific pluralism (*pluralismo científico*), transform their monocultural visions and accept an approach to life that emphasizes the dignity, prosperity and respect of all peoples of the world.[35] At the same time, the millenarian cultures (*culturas milenarias*)

---

[35] "Es urgente que las universidades y los centros de investigación científica reconozcan la dimensión espiritual del ser humano, la conexión e interconexión

of the world, the indigenous peoples, are called upon to revive their traditions, to instruct their youth in traditional understandings of the cosmos. We (referring to his audience of some 500 indigenous delegates) should thoroughly study the knowledge that was bequeathed to us. The transition to the 13th B'aqtun calls for renewal of the spiritual strength that humanity has dismantled, to "nourish a process that advances life, balance, and harmony among all human beings and all beings of the universe." [36] His message was met with vigorous applause and the commendation by Chairperson Victoria Tauli-Corpuz, which she reiterated in her closing remarks the next day, noting that the elder's message was particularly important for the world's indigenous youth, above all in its call for a revival of their knowledge and traditions.

Such millenarian expectation, though not always quite so directly expressed, is a central theme of indigenous self-representation. In times of tumultuous change, the memory of a time and place in which one once lived secure in the illusion of permanence becomes a new reference point for the future self. There is comfort in the idea of the inevitable restoration of a life with a steady rhythm, predictable excitements and unnoticeable changes, without turmoil and danger, without loss and nostalgia. The most important impetus behind the formation of the international movement of indigenous peoples was the widespread perception that such loss and hope of renewal has a global dimension, that this is not an isolated experience but one that resonates with other "first peoples" from every hemisphere of the world, who come together with a combined energy replete with new possibilities for the future.

---

de todos los elementos del universo y el pluralismo científico." My translation. N.L. Tirum, "Mensaje de los Mayas de Ayer y de Hoy para el Futuro de la Humanidad: Un Compromiso Imperativo de los Estados y Gobiernos en el Marco del Trece B'aqtun." Unpublished presentation to the 8th meeting of the Permanent UN Forum on Indigenous Issues, New York, May 27, 2009, 2.

[36] "necesitamos alimentar un proceso que propone vida, equilibrio y armonía para todos los seres humanos y los demás seres del universo." My translation. Tirum, "Mensaje de los Mayas," 3.

Indigenous millenarianism is of course not the most common theme of NGO meetings at the United Nations headquarters, but it does point to a sacralization of public space that happens when the issues of greatest concern to a people are opened up (as they often see it) to the scrutiny of the world, when their few minutes before a microphone go out to (quite possibly) countless listeners and their carefully scripted speeches are accepted and taken in to the private inner workings of the United Nations to (so it is commonly understood) ultimately have an impact on the consciousness and consciences of the powerful. Following from these premises, the speeches often convey much more than information, more than affirmations of rights, more even than appeals to justice; they go on to express the most cherished hopes and aspirations and spiritual longings of those unaccustomed to being heard.

It would be misleading to interpret such expressions of hopeful futurism exclusively in terms of strategic cultural posturing. It is probably true that depicting a background of salvific exclusivism – in which a distinct category of people are the living representatives of a virtuous form of life uniquely adapted to the world, a corrective to an oppressively rationalist, destructive, hyper-industrial modernity and, more than this, the privileged bearers of the secret knowledge needed to interpret the coming apocalyptic transformation of the world – can be seen as a formulation of identity that favors the rights claims of specific peoples. If these peoples indeed represent right-living and the future realization of a perfect world, then their rights claims must be given priority, their grievances addressed, their territory defined and protected, and their status as distinct peoples recognized.

The global public discourse about indigenous peoples has therefore simplified and vernacularized two key definitional qualities attributed to them which, by their very nature, promote improbable understandings of the nature of suffering and collective virtue. An emphasis on oversimplified conceptions of victimization on the one hand, and cultural wisdom on the other – qualities that do not at all comfortably juxtapose – has resulted in distorted, unattainable standards of dignity and heroism among those who are subject to, and attempting to change, conditions of political abuse. Cumulatively, the dominant themes in the discourse on indigenous peoples in the international public sphere have produced a human impossibility: victims of institutionalized oppression, injustice and social injury who are at the same time held up as models of political and environmental responsibility.

The cultural contradictions of indigenism

The cultural and political fulfillments of indigenous peoples are increasingly sought through self-determination, more specifically a form of self-determination in which the choices involved in following one's political destiny are legally equal to those of other "peoples" in international law, but are in practice to be realized within the state. At the state level, indigenous peoples cannot be protected by (or from) the consistent application of a system of rights that applies to all citizens. They require a constitutionally distinct regime of rights. The international movement of indigenous peoples has thus ultimately become associated with many efforts by self-defining indigenous peoples to take control of their identity, and above all to control the legal foundations of their relationships with nation-states through their own assertions of indigenous "nationhood" or self-determination in the international public sphere.

Juxtaposing this focus on self-determination with the historical background of conceptual diplomacy brings out a dilemma that goes to the foundation of the indigenous rights movement: those peoples who are the bearers of distinct rights based on longstanding traditions and occupation of territory from time immemorial are, from a global perspective, only very recent inductees into the category of rights-bearers. Reliance on notions such as "tradition," "heritage" or "indigenous knowledge" encourages ignorance concerning the degree to which normative principles, processes and social roles, grouped under such rubrics, may in fact misrepresent actual past cultural practices and/or be out of step with the current practices, beliefs and values of those who are identified (and/or identify themselves) as belonging to indigenous nations. Indigenous peoples are perhaps the clearest example of those whose identities based upon distinctive languages, cultures and grievances are being researched, redefined and rearticulated, then communicated to an audience which is asked to provide affirmation and support. Ultimately, indigenous peoples were first the citizens of an *idea* before they became members of an international community with distinct rights.

The example of the indigenous peoples' movement shows that legal sociology can construct and popularize the very categories by which people arrange and act to defend themselves. This challenges the assumption that the taxonomy of human belonging straightforwardly gives names to existing social entities, something like the way ornithologists have given names to different bird species. It is largely through the language-transcending recognition of the category, "indigenous peoples" (or *pueblos indígenas, peuples indigènes, Indigene Völker,* etc.) and the institutional space created for it that leaders whose constituencies fit the UN's loose, largely tacit definitional criteria of socio-political disadvantage were able to represent themselves and their people as "indigenous" and give voice to their grievances. The indigenous peoples' movement began with an abstract category of human existence, and only later, largely through the efforts of professional intermediaries, acquired self-referencing peoples connected via transnational networks into a global community. A bureaucratically and legally conceptualized form of life was eventually taken hold of by its subjects as a source of rights and political leverage, ultimately becoming a state-transcending item in a new repertoire of possible political selves.

This would not be problematic if two of the basic features of the public understanding of the essence of indigeneity were not in contradiction with one another. In high-profile international institutions, use of the term "indigenous," or any other human category for that matter, linked without qualification to particular human traits, engenders stereotypes; and cumulatively these unqualified assertions have amounted to an image or set of attributes that mask some of the very real challenges faced by many of those who identify themselves (and/or who are so identified by others) as indigenous. The ennoblement of those seen to suffer, particularly those seen at the same time to inherently possess the highest environmental and political virtues, leaves no room for nuance or ambiguity. Following from the limited themes elaborated in the cultural representations of the international agencies, there are few public mechanisms for addressing the actual social and political crises that follow from removal and domination. The limits to political action in indigenous communities, even for those who inherited or had imposed on them enduring colonial forms of government, are in large measure built into the very discourse that defines indigenous peoples in the international public sphere – the publicly accepted discourse, imagery and poetry concerning what it means to be indigenous.

FIVE

Civilizing a divided world

Civilization in review

For all its well known historical complexity and moral corruption, the idea of civilization is another of the categories of culture to recently receive the imprimatur of authority from the institutions of global governance, not as noticeably or publicly, perhaps, as the indigenous peoples' movement, but with enough political resonance to make it one of the newest of the transnational "isms." That is to say, "civilization" has recently undergone a transition through UN meta-discourse to become "civilization*ism*," with an activist agenda. In the manner of many UN initiatives, this has occurred in a fairly straightforward way, with an unobjectionable emphasis on the importance of dialogue, understanding and alliance between civilizations as foundations of peace and global cooperation toward prosperity, followed by meetings (initially to make arrangements for more meetings), solicitation of expert opinions, inauguration of an International Year, and all the other familiar routines of international institutional urgency.

In contrast to the fast-paced, institutionalized recognition of the concept of indigenous peoples, the UN's conception of civilization faces some of the same difficulties in gaining traction with popular audiences as the efforts to garner support for long-term refugees discussed in Chapter 2, but for somewhat different reasons. It is difficult to make convincing arguments concerning the oppression and marginalization of civilizations. This is in part quite simply because civilizations are conceived as such grand, encompassing entities that it becomes difficult to demonstrate the connections between group belonging and tangible, communicable, sympathizable suffering. But in this chapter I want to argue that the problem goes further than this, that there are insurmountable contradictions built into the civilization concept, reflected in radically different popular ideas concerning their possibilities for dialogue and alliance. In one of its iterations the idea of civilization has a dissonant meaning in which the enduring idea of cultivated, purposeful human improvement – civilization as a universalist utopian vision – competes with the discredited residues of colonial hubris, in which civilization is a unique or uniquely superior possession of the colonizer. In another form, it more readily takes on a meaning associated with supra-state identity. Some – a limited few – can claim their own. In some publics, therefore, civilization is invested with pride, as the supra-state bearer of an illustrious history and with enduring potential for re-emergence into global prominence.

There are few words used in the study of human life on Earth with such an influence as "civilization." It ranks with "evolution" and "progress" as one of the moving forces of the nineteenth and early twentieth centuries, with enduring influence into the present. Yet the contrast between its impact in both interpreting and shaping history and its simple, modest origin could not be greater: the *Oxford English Dictionary* informs us that in the eighteenth century the term civilization was used quite simply in reference to the replacement of common law by civil law, or as Fernand Braudel puts it, "an act of justice or a judgment which turned a criminal trial into civil proceedings."[1] Nothing, at least nothing in the realm of legal concepts, could be simpler.

---

[1] F. Braudel, *A History of Civilizations*, trans. Richard Mayne (New York: Penguin, 1993) 3.

This usage was, as we all know, subsequently modified by adding onto civilization a sense of accomplishment, embodying the ideals of compassionate justice, extending the idea of a morally superior form of legal process to social order conceived on a grand scale, with progress and reason as guides to the actions and institutions of the state. And from this point it ideally served the purposes of colonialism and the assimilationist orientations of states attempting to secure cultural and constitutional uniformity. In the postcolonial era wide awareness of the harmful elements of civilization has made it indefensible among those publics whose background combines connections to colonial history with liberal ideals. Arguably, there is no other influential concept in the history of ideas more shifting, ambiguous and morally corruptible.

The ambiguity surrounding the term civilization begins with the fact that it embodies both a verbal noun form with a processual meaning – the movement toward civilization or process of becoming civilized – and a common noun form: the category of a politico-cultural "thing" that includes the Sumerian civilization, Chinese civilization, Western civilization, and so on. It combines meanings similar to those found in the words acculturation and culture, but with reference to something on a grander scale, involving agriculture, urbanization, literacy and bureaucracy.

Until the last half of the twentieth century, use of the word "civilization" as a process laden with positive connotations was the norm. There was a utopian element of inevitability to the march of history toward the perfect man and the perfect society built into nineteenth-century permutations of this idea, most clearly articulated in Herbert Spencer's idea of the "law of adaptation" in the "entire satisfaction of every desire, or perfect fulfillment of individual life."[2] More widely recognized is the fact that nineteenth-century permutations of the concept, centered on

---

[2] H. Spencer, *Social Statics* (New York: Robert Schalkenbach Foundation, 1995 [1850]) 389.

the process of improving those who lacked the attributes and advantages of civilization, served as justification for colonialism, imperialism and forced assimilation. There was often a philanthropic dimension to this use of the term, because it assumed (sometimes against Spencer's unfeeling approach to the survival of the fittest that argued for non-intervention in or destruction of societies unable to compete) that those who did not share in the benefits of civilized society could be transformed by the civilizing process, enabled to share in a movement of industriousness and universal prosperity. In this context, the verbal noun "civilization" was used in reference to the process by which those left behind by progress would be improved, "uplifted," educated into a higher level of being.

Nineteenth-century socio-evolutionism at the same time popularized the notion of civilization in the singular as a common noun, a category of object. Perhaps its most frequent use at this time was in reference to *the* civilization of Europe and North America, seen as distinct and superior, a single, incomparable accomplishment. This is the version of the concept that had a close affinity with the verbal form, that came to be connected to the idea of progress inherent in the dynamics of history, that, like its verbal permutation, served as a justification for conquest, colonialism and, in independent states, policies of forced assimilation directed at those distinct, supposedly inferior, peoples with rival claims to territory (in other words, those who were later to be identified as "indigenous peoples"). There was often an element of regretful fatalism associated with this singular approach to civilization. Lewis Henry Morgan described the overwhelming influence of civilization in his path-breaking ethnographic study *League of the Iroquois*, first published in 1851:

Our primitive inhabitants are environed with civilized life, the baleful and disastrous influence of which, when brought in contact with Indian life, is wholly irresistible. Civilization is aggressive, as well as progressive – a positive state of society, attacking every obstacle, overwhelming every lesser agency, and searching out and filling up every crevice, both in the moral and physical world; while Indian life is an unarmed condition, a negative state, without inherent vitality, without powers of resistance.[3]

Despite its sometimes baneful effects on the less powerful, however, civilization for many nineteenth-century scholars and moralists meant the achievement of an orderly society that had transcended the arbitrary powers of priests and kings through the systematic pathways of justice and scientific progress. It was, in other words, simultaneously a source of the destruction of the uncivilized and of their salvation.

Today, however, the connections between "civilization" and "improvement" seem to be less common than they once were, most likely because of the post-World War II era's sweeping rejection of colonialism and civilizing missions, which both encouraged and reflected the transformation of civilization into something to be engaged in through the exercise of state power. It has been transformed into a cultural/political given, a thing already extant, to be described and possibly understood and perhaps even communicated and negotiated with. This change can already be seen in the early twentieth century, when the moralistic concept of civilization, as something opposed to "savagery" or "barbarism," was supplemented and then largely replaced by a plural notion of civilizations as the most encompassing form of culture, as "culture writ large."[4] As such, it took on a form that can be described as a quasi-continental bloc, an encompassing category of culture that

---

[3] L.H. Morgan, *League of the Iroquois* (Secaucus: Citadel Press, 1962 [1851]) 444.
[4] A notable exception to the celebrationist view of civilization around the turn of the nineteenth and twentieth centuries came from the pen of Max Weber: "civilized man, placed in the midst of the continuous enrichment of culture by ideas, knowledge, and problems … catches only the most minute part of what the life of the spirit brings forth ever anew, and what he seizes is always something provisional and not definitive, and therefore death for him is a meaningless occurrence. And because death is meaningless, civilized life itself as such is meaningless." M. Weber, *From Max Weber: Essays in Sociology*, ed. H. Gerth and C. Wright Mills (London: Routledge & Kegan Paul, 1948) 140.

transcends the boundaries of nation-states to include a distinct portion of the globe.

In this usage, too, there is a fairly straightforward, identifiable origin. The idea of civilization as a geographically identifiable macro-culture can be attributed in large measure to Nikolai Jakovlevich Danilevsky, a nineteenth-century Russian jack-of-all-intellectual-trades: naturalist, economist, historian, philosopher and head of a prominent movement of Slavophiles, who pined for the values and institutions of the early Russian Empire and sought their restoration in a movement against the influence of Western Europe. This political/cultural nostalgia was buttressed by the idea of exclusive types of large-scale cultures, which developed according to natural laws. In 1869 Danilevsky published an article titled "Russia and Europe: A Look at the Cultural and Political Relations of the Slavic World to the Romano-German World," in which he took issue with the cosmopolitan ideal of the commonality of humanity and elaborated a conception of exclusive "cultural-historical types," of which he identified nine: Egyptian, Chinese, Assyro-Babylonian, Jewish, Greek, Roman, Muslim, Slavic and Romano German. His Pan-Slav loyalties were based on the argument that the "vast majority of the Slav tribes ... have built a huge, continuous state, which has already had an existence of a thousand years and is all the time growing in strength and power in spite of the storms which it has had to weather during its long historical life." [5] The hundreds of different nationalities within this mega-state vanish "before the preponderance of the Russian race," [6] whose political independence from the Western European Romano-Germans is indispensable. "[W]ithout the consciousness of Slav racial unity, as distinct from other races," Danilevsky proclaimed, "an independent culture is impossible; and without fruitful interaction between

---

[5] N.J. Danilevsky, "The Slav Role in World Civilization," in *Readings in Russian Civilization. Volume II: Imperial Russia, 1700–1917*, second edn, ed. Thomas Riha (Chicago: University of Chicago Press, 1969 [1869]) 384.

[6] Danilevsky, "The Slav Role in World Civilization," 384.

the Slav peoples, liberated from foreign powers and from their national divisions, diversity and richness of culture are impossible."[7] So here we find the beginnings of the "culture writ large" approach to civilization, in which strident Slavophilism was set against the political and cultural influence of Western Europe.

It was this basic approach that, stripped of its particular political agenda, was eventually sustained by a broader applicability to comparative history. "In the twentieth century," Braudel points out,

the plural of the word predominates, and is closest to our personal experience. Museums transport us in time, plunging us more or less completely into past civilizations. Actual travelling is more instructive still. To cross the Channel or the Rhine, to go south to the Mediterranean: these are clear and memorable experiences, all of which underline the plural nature of civilizations. Each, undeniably, is distinct.[8]

An influential version of this usage was articulated by British historian Arnold J. Toynbee in his epic survey of the history of civilizations, *The Study of History*, the first volumes of which appeared in the 1930s. For Toynbee, the most significant driving force of history was not to be found in nation-states or ethnic groups, but in very large cultural units such as the ancient Greco-Roman civilization, or the contemporary civilizations it has influenced, Western Europe and the "orthodox" civilization of Russia and the Balkans. The most significant unit for historical study was "neither a nation state nor (at the other end of the scale) mankind as a whole but a certain grouping of humanity which we have called a society [or civilization]."[9]

This "culture writ large" approach to human difference also found its way into (and was reinforced by) the nascent discipline of ethnology.

---

[7] Danilevsky, "The Slav Role in World Civilization," 388.
[8] Braudel, *A History of Civilizations*, 7.
[9] A.J. Toynbee, *A Study of History*, Vols. I–VI, abridged by D.C. Somervell (Oxford University Press, 1946) 11.

This might seem an odd place for it to have developed because of the discipline-shaping emphasis on cultural particulars in the early twentieth century, advocated by both British social anthropology and Boasian cultural anthropology in North America and supported by methodological requirements of long-term ethnographic research. French, German and American ethnological traditions of the early twentieth century, however, derived much of their impetus from the goal of defining distinct civilizations, the common mentalities or folk ideas that characterized entire continents or significant, distinct regions. Whether in the ethnological peregrinations of Leo Frobenius (discussed further below in this chapter), the ambitious scope of the Dakar Djibouti expedition led by Marcel Griaule (followed by his lifelong focus on the Dogon as the bearers of an essential African culture) or the sweeping culture-area approach of Alfred Kroeber, the idea of civilization as a grand cultural entity received scientific justification in ethnological projects.

The comparative approach to cultural distinctiveness has relatively recently been supplemented by a cultural *realpolitik* orientation to political crisis between civilizations. This is the conflict paradigm of Samuel P. Huntington, who, in the aftermath of the fall of the Berlin Wall and the breakup of the Soviet Union, declared boldly that "conflict between civilizations will be the latest phase in the evolution of conflict in the modern world."[10] The world according to this view is divided along the lines of grand cultural cleavages, each of which, within its area of influence, is capable of stridency, expansionism and strategic conflict. While civilizations do not have clear-cut boundaries or precise beginnings and endings, they are meaningful entities, attracting strong loyalties, emerging as "the most enduring of human associations."[11] Civilizations, as the highest level of cultural identity, will become the primary source

---

[10] S.P. Huntington, "The Clash of Civilizations?" *Foreign Affairs*, Summer, 1993: 22.

[11] S.P. Huntington, *The Clash of Civilizations and the Remaking of World Order* (New York: Simon & Schuster, 1996) 43.

of conflict in the post-Cold War era. It is not just the populist values of anti-colonialism, anti-racism and environmental security that are transcending nation-states to influence the behavior of states; chauvinism and xenophobia are more than ever before capable of forming at the supra-state level.

Huntington's most influential ideas involve a primordialist assumption of the naturalness of the abstract cultural entities that we refer to as civilization. It is sometimes difficult to tell if he is naturalizing a phenomenon that is inherently opaque and ideologically constructed, or simply interpreting and reacting to a global trend toward such naturalization and concretization of cultural opacity; alternatively he could well be doing both, and in the process contributing to the conceptual armature used by those who would make political use of civilization as a naturalized category. This is a multifaceted error that, as I intend to show, is unwittingly replicated by the United Nations' well intentioned civilization initiatives, even as they add to the complexity of the problem by explicitly reacting against Huntington's theory of inter-civilizational conflict.

It appears to be the idea of a world order shaped by attachments to supra-state entities, largely beyond the control of states, while providing guideposts for the ambitions of states that has inspired the concern of the UN agencies charged with the management of diversity. The way that civilization has been redefined in the process of meeting this challenge is another illustration of the intellectual tasks and diplomatic possibilities inherent in redefining categories of belonging.

Culture according to UNESCO

One of the most puzzling things about the UN's practice of legal sociology is the way it manages to create entities out of abstractions. Anthropologists have particular difficulty with this because of old assumptions about cultures as securely bounded entities, replaced by more current notions of flux and hybridity, neither of which seems amenable to understanding the creation of politically charged categories of belonging out of virtually nothing. With the civilization concept the process of concretization is particularly difficult because the supra-state nature of the concept means that few representatives of civilizations will be in a position to appear and declaim on behalf of their oppressed constituents. Without such grassroots participatory energies, how does a reinvigorated concept of civilization congeal as a cultural and political category out of the ether of ideas?

There is of course a history behind the UN's formulations of the concepts of culture and civilization; and, as with many institutionally supported ideas about human nature and belonging, the pivotal moment for the legal sociology enshrined in international law and global governance was the experience of German expansionism and the holocaust during World War II. In particular, the policy-driven destruction of peoples and groups in the Axis-occupied territories brought to the fore ideas or assumptions about what constitutes a people with a collective heritage. The experience of a major war that targeted non-combatants was consequential far beyond its immediate violence and suffering; it also had a durable influence on ideas about the essences of peoples and civilizations and on how these ideas were eventually put into effect.

While in practical terms the post-World War II regime of international law has restricted the definition of genocide to biological destruction of a targeted group, Raphael Lemkin's original formulation of genocide placed much more emphasis on non-violent strategies of human destruction, on what amounts to the purposeful dismantling of culture. In *Axis Rule in Occupied Europe*, in which he coined the term genocide, he applied the idea of a non-biological, at times intangible, destruction of targeted nationalities to specific policies enacted by Nazi Germany in its occupied territories.[12] The imposition of German control and the

---

[12] R. Lemkin, *Axis Rule in Occupied Europe: Laws of Occupation, Analysis of Government, Proposals for Redress*, second edn (Clark: The Lawbook Exchange,

systematic destruction of peoples followed an established geography, to which the invaders added their own prejudices and ambitions. This non-biological approach to genocide seems, in turn, to be inspired by Lemkin's juridical notion of *vandalism*, which as early as 1933 he proposed as a crime in international law. With this term he was referring to the purposeful destruction of what might be called "high culture," the works of art, literature and other forms of creativity that define the essence of a people, with the intention of destroying that people. Vandalism, Lemkin argued, takes the form of "systematic and organized destruction of works in the domains of the sciences, arts and letters, which constitute the unique genius and achievement of a collectivity." [13] It also refers to destruction of a people's capacity to produce such works in the future, such as through the "liquidation" of intellectuals or the closure of academic programs. This has implications that go far beyond the immediate survival of targeted groups. "The contribution of any particular collectivity to international culture," Lemkin proclaimed, "forms the wealth of all of humanity, even while exhibiting unique

2008 [1944]). Lemkin's key observation, which he associated with the term genocide, was that the imposition of German supremacy and the destruction of targeted groups and peoples was not an epiphenomenal accident of war but occurred through carefully calibrated designs, with specific policies applied to each people slated for elimination. He points out that in occupied Poland, for example, genocide took the form of the suppression of liberal arts studies, the systematic destruction of archives, libraries, museums and art galleries, and the imposition of a curfew, enforced very strictly against the Poles, unless they could show the authorities a ticket to one of the "gambling houses" that the Germans allowed to come into existence, all of which was intended to eliminate creativity and create an atmosphere of "moral debasement," with the intention of weakening the "spiritual resistance" of the national group.

[13] "[U]ne destruction organisée et systématique des œuvres, qui soit dans le domaine des sciences, soit dans celui des arts ou des lettres, sont le témoignage et la preuve de l'âme et du génie de cette collectivité." My translation. R. Lemkin, 1933, "Les actes constituant un danger général (interétatique) considérés comme délites du droit des gens." www.preventgenocide.org/fr/lemkin/madrid1933. htm. Accessed October 16, 2009.

characteristics. Thus, the destruction of a work of art of any nation must be regarded as an act of vandalism directed against world culture."[14]

Although Lemkin was primarily concerned with arguing for a new, robust regime of international law, he at the same time presented an implicit argument, to the effect that the essential qualities of human groups can be seen through the manner of their destruction at the hands of the criminal state. Whether or not this implicit exercise in legal sociology directly influenced the wording of the UNESCO Constitution, the idea of a world culture or an identifiable human heritage, which is the assembled product of the unique genius of peoples and civilizations, along with urgent drives to inventory and protect that heritage, were to become central dimensions of the organization's mandate. Cultural diversity, for UNESCO, has become "as necessary for humankind as biodiversity is for nature."[15]

In contrast with Lemkin's vision, there are no cultural criminals in the current system of international law. Consistent with the conceptual and legal avoidance of the term "cultural genocide" in global governance and international law, UNESCO's mandate has seemed positive to the point of utopianism – essentially the promotion of diversity, dialogue and human heritage as the foundations of global peace.[16] But if the

---

[14] "L'apport de toute collectivité particulière dans la culture internationale rentre dans le trésor de l'humanité entière, tout en gardant ses traits caractéristiques. Donc, la destruction d'une œuvre d'art de n'importe quelle nation doit être considérée comme acte de vandalisme dirigé contre la culture mondiale." My translation. R. Lemkin, "Les actes constituant un danger général (interétatique) considérés comme délites des droit des gens."

[15] *Universal Declaration on Cultural Diversity*, General Conference of UNESCO, Paris, November 2, 2001, Article 1.

[16] The notion of cultural genocide (an outgrowth of the non-biological forms of systematic destruction described by Lemkin) never did find its way into international law, except briefly in article 7 of the 1994 *Draft UN Declaration on the Rights of Indigenous Peoples* ("Indigenous peoples have the collective and individual right not to be subjected to ethnocide and cultural genocide"); but it was subsequently omitted, while leaving the substance of the protection intact in Article 8 of the 2007 Declaration ("Indigenous peoples and individuals have the right not to be subjected to forced assimilation or destruction of their culture").

most essential qualities of culture cannot be defined simply by criminal acts against it, how are we to recognize it, and in the process to recognize what it is to be human? In practical terms, the answer to this most difficult of questions follows directly from the state-centrism of world governance. In the realm of UNESCO cultural initiatives, states are characterized not so much as threats to the safety, prosperity and cultural expression of their citizens as they are the research assistants necessary for the identification and promotion of cultural difference.

The reporting role of states in the UNESCO system was given a greater sense of urgency with the burgeoning literature on globalization, which seems to have reached a critical mass around the turn of the millennium, sufficient at least for UNESCO's slowly moving gears to have shifted up. In the first decade of the twenty-first century the identification of globally shrinking cultural diversity was seen as an emergency – but not so much as a product of criminal government actions as of more abstract, agentless processes of cultural destruction through globalization. This led to a flurry of UNESCO initiatives, starting with the elaboration of new legal instruments: the 2001 Universal Declaration on Cultural Diversity, the 2003 Convention for the Safeguarding of the Intangible Cultural Heritage, and the 2007 Convention on the Protection and Promotion of the Diversity of Cultural Expressions. Each of these instruments in turn calls upon state members to produce their own memoranda- and report-based exercises in legal sociology. This activity was in practice not restricted to the reporting mechanisms built into the instruments themselves, but was part of the process of drafting the laws, as was particularly evident in the lead-up to the Intangible Heritage Convention, for which UNESCO sent questionnaires to state agencies (mostly ministries of culture), requesting definitions of "intangible cultural heritage." The replies provided by states are instructive, above all because they tend to add as much "tangibility" to their responses as seems possible. In an unofficial translation of Madagascar's submission, for example, intangible cultural heritage is partly defined as: "traditional and popular songs and dances, language, traditional oral literature, crafts and handicrafts, traditional games and sports," and, as a dangling appendage to this list, "art"; the Dominican Republic, for its part, seems not to have understood the question whatsoever when it included in its definition of *intangible* heritage: "all goods, including those submerged under water, material and non-material, movable and immovable, which have a special interest: historical, artistic, aesthetic, plastic, architectonic, urban, archeological, environmental, ecological, linguistic, sonorous, musical, audio-visual, filmic, scientific, techno-logical, testimonial, documental, literary, bibliographic, museographic, anthropological; and events, products and representations of popular culture"; whereas Spain more pointedly emphasized the popular basis of traditional culture "in its festive and popular aspects ... as is the case for the feasts of touristic interest," supported, logically enough, by Spain's Declaración de Fiestas de Interés Turístico (Declaration of Celebrations of Touristic Interest).[17] In keeping with what I assume would be popular expectations, flamenco dancing and bull fighting would thus constitute focal points of Spain's intangible cultural heritage.

The inherent charm of this oxymoronically acute naïveté should not distract our attention from the particular legal logic inherent in the global promotion of diversity: if the specific genius of peoples is to be preserved and made available to the world in the form of a collective human heritage, it must first be identified and inventoried. *Raison d'état* is in this sense not the practical logic behind the convenience of state governments but the place of states in the production of knowledge. The promotion of cultural diversity involves cooperation between glo-bal institutions and states in the exercise of national stereotyping, in defining culture or heritage through inventories of monuments and

---

[17] UNESCO, "Definitions for 'Intangible Cultural Heritage' (Replies to Questionnaires sent to National Commissions in February and August 2000)." www.unesco.org/culture/ich/doc/src/00078-EN.pdf. Accessed October 30, 2009.

the "intangible" artifacts of knowledge and ceremony. Culture in these terms consists of the most visible manifestations of performance with the widest popular appeal, the calendar events of mass participation and vicarious consumption.

To some extent UNESCO has recently begun to take into account the consensus of skepticism by anthropologists and other social researchers toward the once prevalent approach to culture as a fixed essence of a people, as in the preambular point to the 2007 Convention on the Protection and Promotion of the Diversity of Cultural Expressions, which states: "cultural diversity is strengthened by the free flow of ideas, and … is nurtured by constant exchanges and interaction between cultures." A 2008 report of the Intergovernmental Committee for this convention more directly addresses the challenge posed by flux-oriented approaches to culture: "'Promotion' [of culture] calls for perpetual regeneration of cultural expressions to ensure that they are not 'reified'." [18] Taken together this means that cultural reification is to be avoided by assigning to states – historically the quintessential promoters of truth-defying essentialism and assimilators of marginalized peoples embodying cultural and constitutional difference – the primary responsibility to define and protect cultural heritage; or, in legal language, the responsibility "to create and strengthen their means of cultural expression, including their cultural industries, whether nascent or established, at the local, national and international levels." [19]

In the hands of the UN the concept of civilization takes on some of these same tendencies toward artificial construction and concretization; but it encourages different kinds of institutional involvement than

---

[18] UNESCO, "Diversity of Cultural Expressions; Intergovernmental Committee for the Protection and Promotion of the Diversity of Cultural Expressions"; Paris, April 3, 2008, UNESCO doc. CE/08/1.EXT.IGC/3. http://unesdoc.unesco.org/images/0015/001598/159868E.pdf.
[19] UNESCO, *Convention on the Protection and Promotion of the Diversity of Cultural Expressions*, General Conference of UNESCO, October 20, 2005.

we see with the usual state reporting on diversity because it transcends the political and intellectual jurisdictions of states. States as research assistants tend not to collaborate among themselves, especially when it comes to representing their identities. And creating a tangible thing out of an abstraction is more difficult when states are no longer the exclusive, trusted custodians of information. Although states are centrally involved in the UN's civilization initiatives (as we will see below), there is a larger creative role for UN agencies in the identification of civilizations and implementing forums for dialogue between them. With an awareness of new possibilities for hatred and conflict on a larger scale than has ever been possible, the UN has initiated a high level, interagency approach to alliance and dialogue among civilizations, and in the process effectively re-conceptualized, and to some extent popularized, a global geography of culture.

The UN's civilizing mission

The practical origins of the UN's most recent civilization initiatives, like the conceptual foundations of indigenism, are surprisingly direct and identifiable. They appear to have been jump-started by an interview with Iranian President Mohammad Khatami by CNN foreign correspondent Christianne Amanpour on January 7, 1998 in which Khatami announced that Iran intended "to benefit from the achievements and experiences of all civilizations, Western and non-Western, and to hold dialogue with them."[20] He specified that this was to be a cultural, not a diplomatic initiative, that would involve primarily "thinkers and intellectuals."[21] This initiative was to circumvent or offset the failure of

---

[20] Transcript of CNN Interview with Iranian President Mohammad Khatami (January 7, 1998) in *Letters to Khatami: A Reply to the Iranian President's Call for a Dialogue Among Civilizations*, ed. A.J. Dennis (Bristol, IN: Wyndham Hall, 2001) 54.

[21] Khatami, in *Letters to Khatami*, 61.

efforts to establish diplomatic ties between Iran and the United States, in which, as Khatami explained, "the attitude of the U.S. after the victory of the revolution has not been ... civilized."[22]

Khatami's conception of civilization was amplified in a collection of his writings published by the Office of the President of the Islamic Republic of Iran in 1998. Here it is plain to see opinions consistent with those of Danilevsky, which draw a contrast between a prided grand heritage and the moral dissolution of the West, in this case more specifically the United States. Khatami's conception of the essence of his Persian heritage harkens back to its illustrious history: "Iran's glorious civilization was concurrent with the Greek city states and the Roman Empire. After the advent of Islam, the Iranians ardently embraced it. The blend of Iranian talents and the sublime Islamic teachings was a miracle"[23] Khatami's essentially theological approach to global order turns to the idea of an unchanging essence in the ordering of the universe: "The laws governing human existence are divine or natural traditions. It is possible that humans commit errors in the discovery of these laws, and later come to recognize their errors, but what changes here is the understanding of the laws, not the laws themselves."[24]

This approach finds its parallel in initiatives sponsored by the UN, absent explicit attachments or preferences toward any one civilization. UNESCO in particular seems to be broadly inspired by ideas of an innate "inner spark," the ultimate wellspring for the realization of human potential, the proper development of humanity, for basic needs that must be met to overcome the privations that stunt or cripple human growth. The idea that there is a human essence to be discovered, and that following from this there are general principles of human nature which can be recognized by everyone through intuitive recognition

---

[22] Khatami, in *Letters to Khatami*, 60.
[23] Khatami, in *Letters to Khatami*, 53.
[24] M. Khatami, *Islam, Liberty and Development* (Binghamton: Global Academic Publishing, 1998) 19.

of basic human qualities of virtue and goodness, has its origin in Medieval thought – and is an approach to moral universalism that essentially defines the post-World War II era of world governance. This can be seen especially clearly in the influence of Catholic Theologian Jacques Maritain on the 1947 UNESCO-sponsored Committee on the Theoretical Bases of Human Rights. Maritain influentially communicated to the Committee his conviction, drawn directly from the work of Medieval philosopher Saint Thomas Aquinas, that universal laws must reflect a human essence that has been brought into being by an immovable, perfect, superior intellect, that there exists a transcendent truth with its ultimate source in human nature, a truth that arises "from the simple fact that man is man, nothing else being taken into account." [25]

In Khatami's hands, this wellspring of civilizational being – this answer to the deepest of innate human needs – is not to be found in a Western science that is "impotent in addressing the metaphysical, philosophical, and mystical yearnings in humans." [26] Western civilization, with four centuries of history behind it, "is worn out and senile." [27] The signs are certainly there for all to see. The central question that remains for more thinking and scrutiny is "whether it has reached the end of its path." [28] The West is in decline, and in its place will arise the more richly pedigreed civilizations, such as Iran with its illustrious, "miraculous" Persian heritage.

Khatami's influence on civilizational initiatives in diplomatic circles seems to have been formative, with his presidency representing a new opportunity for progress toward peace in the Middle East. Following Khatami's interview with CNN and the Iranian presidential office's publication of his outline for an analysis of civilization and Iran's place

---

[25] J. Maritain, *The Rights of Man and Natural Law* (New York: Charles Scribner's Sons: 1943) 63.
[26] Khatami, *Islam, Liberty and Development*, 128.
[27] Khatami, *Islam, Liberty and Development*, 53.
[28] Khatami, *Islam, Liberty and Development*, 56.

in a rapidly changing world, the UN took up his proposal of dialogue between civilizations with alacrity.

The urgency with which the UN approached what became widely seen in diplomatic circles as a crisis surrounding the ideas associated with civilizations can be seen in the brisk pace of meetings intended to define the central problems and organize the work to be undertaken to achieve peace among civilizations. In November 1998, the UN General Assembly declared 2001 to be the United Nations Year of Dialogue among Civilizations, through a resolution emphasizing the "positive and mutually beneficial interaction among civilizations [that] has continued throughout human history despite impediments arising from intolerance, disputes and wars." The hemispheric romanticism of early ethnology finds its diplomatic parallel in this resolution's assertion that "civilizational achievements constitute the collective heritage of mankind, providing a source of inspiration and progress for humanity at large."[29]

On May 6, 1999 the Permanent Mission of the Islamic Republic of Iran, in collaboration with the School of International and Public Affairs, Columbia University, sponsored a panel discussion on "Dialogue among civilizations: a new paradigm" at the United Nations Headquarters in New York. Following this event, the inaugural meeting of the UN's Group of Eminent Persons on the Dialogue among Civilizations was convened in December 2000 in Vienna; and in August 2001 the Salzburg dialogue among civilizations took place, opened by UN Secretary General Kofi Annan, who described it as "a new paradigm of international relations."[30] Annan sketched out the main objectives of this unprecedented global effort toward ideological reform: "Without this dialogue taking place every day among all

[29] United Nations, "General Assembly Resolution 53/22, United Nations Year of Dialogue among Civilizations" (UN doc. A/RES/53/22, 16 November 1998) 1.
[30] United Nations, "United Nations Year of Dialogue among Civilizations: Report of the Secretary General" (UN doc. A/56/523, 2001a) 2.

nations – within and between civilizations, cultures and groups – no peace can be lasting and no prosperity can be secure."[31] He added a remark that seems prescient in the light of the 9/11 attacks that were to occur a short while later: "Where terrorism seeks to make our diversity the source of conflict, the dialogue can help make that same diversity the foundation for betterment and growth."[32] One outcome of this meeting was a document officially titled, in the arcane language of global bureaucracy, "Annex to the letter dated 27 September 2001 from the Permanent Representative of Austria to the United Nations addressed to the Secretary-General," but known more simply as the "Salzburg Reflections," a document that pithily captures the overarching purpose of the UN's civilization initiatives: "As the reality of a more interdependent world is pushing us ever closer together, we will have to improve our management of diversity."[33]

The objective of "managing diversity" was pursued by a wide range of states and organizations. In furtherance of the UN's "soft tool of diplomacy," events were held across the globe in such countries as Andorra, Austria, Canada, Costa Rica, Cuba, Egypt, Germany, Jordan, Latvia, Mali, Poland, Portugal, the Republic of Korea, Switzerland, Great Britain and Northern Ireland. The strange-bedfellows-effect of this initiative, consistent with the goal of dialogue across difference, is reflected in the fact that major support came from the governments of Austria, Iran, Ireland and Qatar.[34] A number of states took the project especially seriously. German federal ministries and representatives of civil society, for example, selected ninety projects to represent Germany's contribution, with the goal of fostering exchange of opinions among a wide range of social groups. These projects were undertaken by a vast array of

---

[31] UN, "United Nations Year of Dialogue among Civilizations," 3.
[32] UN, "United Nations Year of Dialogue among Civilizations," 4
[33] United Nations, "Letter Dated 27 September 2001 from the Permanent Representative of Austria to the United Nations Addressed to the Secretary-General" (UN doc. A/59/419, 2001b) 2.
[34] UN, "United Nations Year of Dialogue among Civilizations," 1–2.

civil society organizations, including large institutes, schools and small nongovernmental organizations.[35] The Government of Japan, for its part, sponsored the 2001 Global Youth Exchange Programme, in which forty young people from around the world were invited to Japan to exchange views on issues from a global perspective in a meeting that focused on the theme "dialogue among civilizations – from a century of conflict to a century of coexistence."[36] International organizations made their own contributions. The United Nations University, spearheading the academic institutional effort, organized a series of workshops, conferences and other events, including an essay contest for children, entitled "Dialogue Beyond Borders."[37]

A few years later, these initiatives were given renewed energy through a new rubric: the Alliance of Civilizations. The formative event behind this change of rubric and the resumption of efforts was the Madrid train bombings of March 11, 2004, which prompted renewed calls for efforts to counteract the purposeful ignorance and hatred being communicated globally by Muslim terrorist organizations. Launched in 2005 by Kofi Annan with the joint sponsorship of the Prime Ministers of Spain and Turkey, the Alliance of Civilizations was oriented toward the affirmation of "a broad consensus across nations, cultures and religions that all societies are bound together in their humanity and interdependent in their quest for stability, prosperity and peaceful co-existence."[38] There seemed to be a fairly broad agreement in all of these UN- and state-sponsored initiatives that dialogue among, and alliance between, civilizations was timely and that it presented a new paradigm which meets the requirements for the peaceful exchange of culture in our age.

[35] UN, "United Nations Year of Dialogue among Civilizations," 2.
[36] UN, "United Nations Year of Dialogue among Civilizations," 2.
[37] UN, "United Nations Year of Dialogue among Civilizations," 3.
[38] United Nations, *Alliance of Civilizations: Report of the High-Level Group, 13 November 2006* (New York: United Nations, 2006) 3–4.

Reconceiving civilization

Putting together the features conveyed in nearly a decade of meetings and reports, what does this redefined UN civilization concept amount to? What is the UN's model of civilization?

One of the structural oddities of the Dialogue between Civilizations and Alliance of Civilizations initiatives follows from the logical necessity of somehow appointing individuals to speak as representatives of civilizations. This calls for them to be either very influential, to somehow match the grandiosity of civilization as a social category – former heads of state, high ranking officials or Nobel Prize winners – or to be the most powerless – schoolchildren who, by their very being, represent the innocence of civilization and the capacity to learn from and be tolerant of difference. One does not find peasants, street sweepers or taxi drivers representing civilization. Those given the task of intellectually framing the discussion are elevated, given the title "High Level Group," in an apparent effort not just to acknowledge their status, but also to make them worthy of their august subject matter.

It is the intellectual output of this High Level Group that has become the primary source of ideas in the UN concerning the nature of civilization. Most prominently, it embodies everything good about scriptural religion. It includes the tolerant side of Christianity, Islam, Judaism, Hinduism and Buddhism. The way that religious influence on civilization is understood tends to emphasize its qualities of tolerance and peace. Again in Khatami's terms, Islam, in its very essence, "seeks dialogue, understanding and peace with all nations." [39] This is a message that seems to have been picked up on as a possible source of counter-terrorist influence, and is therefore reflected more widely in the UN literature. Violent insurgencies and terrorism are undertaken only in the *name* of civilization, corrupting and misusing its inherent goodness

---

[39] Khatami, in *Letters to Khatami*, 56.

for personal and political ends. Civilization is inherently tolerant. It cultivates difference while recognizing the value of difference in others. And bringing these peaceable qualities of civilization to the fore is a new, untested strategy of global diplomacy.

Consistent with this foundational premise, the strategic focus of the UN's civilization initiatives is public persuasion. Educational and publicity-oriented efforts are dedicated to highlight the inherent peacefulness of civilization, above all to bridge a supposed divide or diminish an escalation of misunderstanding between Islamic civilization and the West. One approach to this issue sharply questions the validity of Huntington's "clash of civilizations" hypothesis by pointing to the particular nature of the crises in the Muslim world and the specific measures that can be taken to overcome them. This is reflected in Kofi Annan's hope that "the dialogue among civilizations [will] become a means to lessen the fear of diversity and serve as a tool in the ongoing struggle against terrorism."[40] "Over the past few years," Annan states, "wars, occupation and acts of terror have exacerbated mutual suspicion and fear within and among societies. Some political leaders and sectors of the media, as well as radical groups have exploited this environment, painting mirror images of a world made up of mutually exclusive cultures, religions, or civilizations, historically distinct and destined for confrontation."[41] Annan's view was seconded by Mohammad Khatami in a 2006 address to the United Nations University, in which he declared that the interests of peace lie in a "paradigm of 'dialog' rather than 'altercation' and moving along the lines of 'dialog among cultures and civilizations' instead of clash between them and trying to resolve the problems the world currently has, through launching intra- and inter-civilizational dialog."[42]

---

[40] United Nations, "United Nations Year of Dialogue among Civilizations," 4.

[41] United Nations, "Alliance of Civilizations," 3.

[42] M. Khatami, "Dialogue Among Civilizations: A Necessity for Living in Peace and Non-Violence, Bridging the Development Gap among Nations, and Building a Global Citizenship" (U. Thant Distinguished Lecture, United Nations

The terrorism of jihadists, according to this perspective, is limited to a small number of fanatics; the Taliban of Afghanistan are politically and militarily defeated, exercising power through the only avenue left to them, through the illegitimate violence of suicide attacks; the violent protests and assertions of difference among Muslim immigrants in Europe is in large measure an outcome of social marginalization and economic desperation; and the Palestinian/Israeli conflict is historically vexed, but with remaining possibilities for movement toward a solution.

Beyond these specific conflicts, the global community sees an obligation to counteract the overarching assumption of a new world order marked by an increased potential for conflict between civilizations. The UN initiatives are based on the idea that it is through a global effort to multiply opportunities for encounter between people of different civilizations, which allow the creativity, order and peacefulness of civilization to speak for itself in a dialogue of recognition and tolerance, that we have the best chance of making the world more secure in the new millennium.

Civilizational utopianism

UN initiatives in furtherance of peace among civilizations are part of a wider transformation in the intellectual culture of global governance: in a reversal of the expectations of some social theorists and intellectual historians, the political utopia is making a comeback, encouraged perhaps by social conditions which combine great collective promise with great insecurity. In this approach, the possibilities inherent in the growth of knowledge and its new technologies, the market economy, the participatory values of democracy and/or the instrumental effectiveness

University, Tokyo, August 25, 2006), www.unu.edu/uthant_lectures/index.htm. Accessed November 19, 2007.

of bureaucratic organization find their reflection in visions of a future world united by civilizational completion and global transformation.[43]

In Germany after the dismantling of the Berlin Wall in the fall of 1989, for example, a debate ensued surrounding the viability or risks of utopian thinking, particularly in the light of the failed Soviet experiment. There were some commentators and opinion makers who proclaimed the "end of the utopian age," which had robbed Europe of its innocence.[44] But, even in the face of criticism that pointed to the catastrophic realities that followed from radical political idealism, others continued to hold out hope that utopian thinking could be made consistent with the demands of reasoned social reform on a global scale.[45] Out of this debate there has emerged a thriving literature, largely inspired by the model of practical cosmopolitanism elaborated in Kant's essay "On Perpetual Peace," that sought to promote the idea that yearning after a utopian ideal can still be consistent with reality (*realitätsgerecht*) and can provide an important source of inspiration for innovative practical action.[46]

One contemporary outcome of this revitalized socio/political futurism is wider acceptance of the premise that the ideal and the real have an important source of connection in the instrumental potential of the utopian imagination. There is a new potential for governance without government to solve the world's most pressing problems: uncontrolled

---

[43] The discussion of the revival of civilizational utopianism that follows includes a recontextualization of material that appears in R. Niezen, "Postcolonialism and the Utopian Imagination," in *Postcolonial Theory and the Arab-Israeli Conflict*, ed. Philip Salzman and Donna Robinson (New York: Routledge, 2008).

[44] See, for example, R. Maresch and F. Rötzer (eds.), *Renaissance der Utopie: Zukunftsfiguren des 21. Jahrhunderts* (Frankfurt am Main: Suhrkamp, 2004); and H. Wilke, *Heterotopia: Studien zur Krisis der Ordnung moderner Gesellschaften* (Frankfurt am Main: Suhrkamp, 2003).

[45] R. Saage, *Politische Utopien der Neuzeit*, second edn (Bochum: Winkler, 2000).

[46] An example is Harten's utopian perspective on education. See H.-C. Harten, "Utopie," in *Historisches Wörterbuch der Pädagogik*, ed. Dietrich Brenner and Jürgen Oelkers (Weinheim and Basel: Beltz, 2004).

conflict, structural injustice, hunger, poverty, disease, environmental degradation, and terrorism. For Dieter Senghaas, for example, it is now possible to cultivate and construct a global political culture that would promote tolerance and facilitate conflict resolution among competing peoples, and thus dampen and ultimately eliminate propensities to conflict based on narrow national or ethnic attachments.[47] Global peace is no longer an abstract possibility but has achieved concrete potential through the increasingly common experience of economic, social, political and cultural homogeneity and interdependence. It is therefore possible to design a new architecture or a world order of global peace that "civilizes" those peoples and regions still given to deep, unresolved animosities and violent conflict. This is not a utopian project in the sense that it is based on chimerical assumptions of an ideal, transcendental reality. There is, for Senghaas, a real possibility for constructing a global regime based on functional and moral interdependence, which solves, to an extent never before achieved, the problem of collective violent conflict.

Such instrumental, practical hopes for a future that has overcome the ills of narrow national-mindedness and rampant animosities are not limited to planners and bureaucrats but are also taken up by those whose intellectual starting point is in postcolonial critiques of cultural/political imperialism. Peace planning on a global scale can begin by situating conflict in the imperialist imagination of the Occident, and then moving toward an ideal of consensual, state-free, non-coercive social reform. Or the oppressive nature of cityscapes, extending out from the dark corners of technocratic capitalism, can be overcome by the renewed humanism of cities brought down to human scale, inspired by a universal commitment to community values.

The recognition of planetary social integration as an unavoidable condition of an ideal future introduces a civilizing dimension to the

---

[47] D. Senghaas, *Zum irdischen Frieden* (Frankfurt am Main: Suhrkamp, 2004).

utopian imagination (the verb form of civilization). The possibility of implementing innovative regimes of global governance and conflict resolution requires using tools of persuasion to establish universal legitimacy, overcoming antediluvian forms of structural animosity and more recent manifestations of strident ethnic attachments and nationalism. Even the ancient idea of applying the utopian imagination to the design of cities has taken on a global dimension that calls for networks of insurgency to overcome inevitable resistance.[48]

From this perspective, it is not the existence of a condition of globalization that is summoning a revival of the utopian imagination, but the fact of its incompletion, the existence and persistence of uncomfortable human differences – and ultimately popular ideas about those differences – that interpose themselves between present experience and the possibilities of the future. Whenever the utopian imagination takes on a universal dimension together with efforts to remain consistent with reality, it faces the challenge of imposing itself on the unenlightened, of civilizing those who are attached to countervailing values and practices. How does one bring peace to those who remain firmly attached to their hatreds? How is it possible to realize a vision of a humanized world when there are so many who resist the ideas and programs of a community-friendly counter-modernity? How are those with far-seeing vision to deal with atavistic traditional thinking and behavior that does not aim beyond the concerns of kinsmen? What is one to do with the refusers and apostates who cannot see past their own narrow interests, who repudiate the value of a better world order and decline to cooperate in its realization?

This means that the UN's civilization initiatives contain the same germ of verbal activism that grew out of the evolutionary version of the nineteenth century. No matter what form a focused global vision of the

---

[48] See D. Harvey, *Spaces of Hope* (Berkeley and Los Angeles: University of California Press, 2000).

future takes, it will always face the problem of the unconverted who stand in the way of its realization. Having renounced argument through sanctions, it is called upon to use ideological armature, to change the thinking of those who refuse agreement. Acting on the UN's ideals of civilization involves a global effort of public persuasion.

There is irony here in the fact that the advocates of particular civilizations are among those who stand in the way of the realization of a cosmopolitan alliance of peaceable civilizations. The nature of reawakened cultural belonging, even at the most encompassing level of abstraction, inclines toward pride of belonging and exclusivism. It is an intellectual ingredient of ambitious state politics, with possibilities for use and misuse, but little room for the dilutions that occur through global imaginings, except perhaps to mask its unpleasant flavors. The UN conception of civilization attempts to transform grandiose visions of cultural/historical belonging into vehicles of tolerance, simply by conceiving of them as inherently tolerant. And in so doing it replicates the tendency toward conceptual indulgence by strident states and civilizations themselves.

Ethnographic enchantment

Ethnography is usually associated with a long-term approach to research that focuses on minutia, or what Malinowski called the "imponderabilia of actual life and of typical behaviour." [49] But the cultural romance of civilization that acts on a grand vision is also part of the history of ethnography; and even though it may seem an impossible task to produce an account of an entity like "Slavonic," "Muslim" or "African" society based on the individual-encounter, I-was-there model of field research (certainly not one that would today readily win support from granting

---

[49] B. Malinowski, *Argonauts of the Western Pacific* (Prospect Heights: Waveland, 1984 [1922]) 20.

agencies), this is precisely the kind of venture we find in the background of the "culture writ large" approach to human diversity. The significance of this observation for the concept of civilization, particularly for its affinity with radical hope and re-enchantment, comes out most clearly when we compare a model of tightly focused ethnography, that provided by Audrey Richards (a student of Malinowski), with the results of Leo Frobenius' numerous research journeys to Africa, acting upon what he felt to be a distinctly German understanding of the essence of pre-modern human experience.

British social anthropologist Audrey Richards, whose principal field research was done in the early 1930s, established her career with a detailed study of a specific ritual, or set of rituals: the Bemba girl's *chisungu* initiation ceremony. Richards did note and include in her analysis the outward features of a *chisungu*, its "extravagant burlesque," the crowded concourse with thronging dancers and noisy singing which, through its sensory lavishness, emphasizes the elements of an oral constitution: it repeats, proclaims, reaffirms and ultimately teaches the lessons of womanhood.[50]

But there is another, quieter way that these lessons are conveyed, through the device of a carefully rehearsed public pronouncement, in which the Bemba girl on the last night of her initiation ceremony handles meticulously constructed pottery figurines (*mbusa*) and rehearses the songs associated with each. This is a stage in the ceremonial cycle which Richards described as both magic and "legal acts involving the girl in a public assumption of her new duties."[51] The majority of the figurines, she found, referred symbolically to the obligations of husband and wife, which among the Bemba were complicated by a fundamental contradiction: matrilineal descent in a society marked by the domination of men

---

[50] A.I. Richards, *Chisungu: A Girl's Initiation Ceremony among the Bemba of Zambia* (New York: Routledge 1982 [1956]) 168.

[51] Richards, *Chisungu*, 162

in public and domestic life. The *mbusa* figurines were therefore a kind of constitutional mnemonic device that represented moral attitudes and obligations in quotable form. This interpretation is, in the manner of the early British social anthropologists, anecdotally supported:

> On an occasion when a young married woman was tempted to go off to a beer-drink and leave her baby unguarded in the hut behind, an older woman suddenly shouted to her the song associated with the house *mbusa* ... This song calls to mind the moral tale of the mother who leaves her baby alone in the house so that it falls into the fire and gets burnt. The girl in question looked irritated and impatient, and then shrugged her shoulders, gave up her project and went inside her house.[52]

The exactitude exercised in the construction of the *mbusa* and the performance of their associated songs can thus be understood though the connection between symbols and the guides to behavior which make up the foundation of Bemba social life.

So far Richards' functionalist interpretation of the *chisungu* is reasonably straightforward (consistent with the notorious analytical oversimplicity of her mentor, Malinowski). But she complicates her analysis in two ways. First, she attributes to the ceremony a psychological function which takes the interpretation beyond the functionalist emphasis (established through the influence of Durkheim and Van Gennep) on the reinforcement of group ties that excludes the effects of practices and institutions on the individual. The ceremony, Richards tells us, provides the girl with confidence in the assumption of her new duties, and contributes to her sense of security.

Second, and more interesting, is Richards' analysis of symbolism. She posits that the principal reason for the complex design of the *mbusa* figurines is that they, and their associated songs, have secondary, "secret" meanings that are eventually learned and understood by the most

---

[52] Richards, *Chisungu*, 163.

intelligent women through subsequent repetitions, questions, answers and guesses; and what is more, these more sophisticated interpretations of the symbols can change with the times. There is both a great degree of legitimacy and a highly flexible quality in the formal expressions of public morality. The "function" of symbols must therefore be open to shifting emotions, multiple interpretations and changes in social effect, the very things that separate the *chisungu* ceremony from a formal legal contract. Even in the most pragmatic approach to ritual, defined by the analysis of "function," there is room for a kind of enchantment, evident in Richards' description of the combination of security and flexibility in a ceremony that allows women, who are institutionally dominated by men, to live confidently and with dignity.

As with all perceptions of an end to magic in the world, it is the loss of these qualities that is the focus of her regret. More than any social anthropologist of her time, she seemed explicitly aware of the fact that she was the first and the last to systematically record a ceremony that epitomises a distinct way of life. She reveals this in the first lines of a short preface to *Chisungu*: "I watched the ceremony described in this book in 1931, while I was doing field-work among the Bemba ... I never witnessed another ceremony of the same kind. Twenty years later, when I published my account, such ceremonies seemed to be dying out in Africa; this book is therefore a record of what may now be quite extinct." [53] So far, this only tells us matter-of-factly that the Bemba's *chisungu* and other ceremonies like it in Africa are things of the past; but what are the consequences of this loss? She only hints at an answer: "[W]hen I did some work on the Copper Belt in Northern Rhodesia in 1934 I was asked to stay at Nkana mine in order to organize a chisungu ceremony there because the girls in urban areas were so very badly behaved – an invitation I did not feel capable of accepting." [54] So the loss of ritual has

[53] Richards, *Chisungu*, xiii
[54] Richards, *Chisungu*, xiii.

immediate consequences for the young women who lack the guidance of an initiation ceremony and the rich, symbol-laden knowledge it communicates. There is no general statement here about human enrichment through diversity; nothing about the color and comfort of ritual providing a more meaningful life. Richards has a single-minded focus on describing the *chisungu* on its own terms, as the subject matter of a kind of sympathetic science. In this context nostalgia is almost redundant; it is easy enough to understand what the world has lost from the mere description of it before the full effects of colonial dislocation.

Only when we move to another level of abstraction – the study of culture in the context of a wider form of life or "civilization" – does it become easier to find unabashed cultural longing. When, in his 1991 book *The Idea of Wilderness*, Max Oelschlaeger writes, "The Paleolithic Mind likely envisaged nature as alive and responsive, nurturing humankind much as a mother nourishes her baby at her breast," he is tapping into a wellspring of ideas about human difference, in particular a contrast between the lifeways of industrial modernity and of societies that have maintained a connection to an age of spiritual and technological simplicity.[55] Such primordialism is a form of the utopian imagination in which the future is to be transformed by a return to the virtues of the distant past, which can overcome the hubris of modernity through recovery of the wisdom once possessed by all humans, above all through the possibility of reanimating those intimate forms of society that existed before the imposition of conditions of social suffering, environmental pathology and cultural amnesia – all the ruin that occurred first by the expansion of colonial empires and later by new forms of global imperialism.

Ethnographic projects motivated and methodologically guided by cultural romanticism were for the most part overshadowed by the

---

[55] M. Oelschlaeger, *The Idea of Wilderness: From Prehistory to the Age of Ecology* (New Haven and London: Yale University Press, 1991) 16.

professionalization of anthropology in the early twentieth century on both sides of the Atlantic, but their influence has still been as great or greater on the popular imagination. Those who dedicated themselves to depictions of the picturesque found ready audiences. A search for a distinct, spiritually elevated African soul was undertaken, for example, by the German ethnologist Leo Frobenius, who spent some forty years (between his various professional duties in Frankfurt, including a directorship of the municipal ethnological museum) visiting various regions of sub-Saharan Africa, cumulatively traversing the continent in search of its common inner essence, its spiritually elevating mysteries. Frobenius was a publicly visible and popular figure, dubbed "the returner home" (*der Heimkehrer*), and celebrated throughout Germany as an embodiment of adventure and exoticism. For his part, he did what he could to encourage this, such as by celebrating his 65th birthday and the 40th anniversary of the Museum where he was director by riding a camel through the streets of Frankfurt. The ultimate source of his popularity seems to have been a combination of high adventure and omnivorous cultural romanticism, ideally in combination. His descriptions of the arduousness of his adventures, for example, were almost always accompanied by his self-proclaimed drive for discovery, above all a single-minded search for the cultural essence of Africa:

[Once] when I was wounded with a poison arrow in my shin, I cauterized the wound with a burning cigar. What appeared to me to be more important, however, was my love for Africa that drove me on and left me to forget my torments. I loved everything African and was filled with respect for these people and their culture. And so I set about on the quest for the sense [of it] and developed my conception of the soul and spirit of culture. This was for me not only something abstract; I felt myself to be connected with the Africans in our hearts.[56]

---

[56] "Als mich ein Giftpfeil ins Schienbein getroffen hatte, brannte ich die Wunde mit meiner glühenden Zigarre aus. Was mir aber wichtiger erscheint, das ist meine Liebe zu Afrika, die mich antrieb und mich die Strapazen vergessen ließ. Ich

He found a rich seam in the mute Paleolithic artistry of rock paintings from Eritrea, which he sent back to the Frankfurt museum in copious quantities, and which spoke to him of "extraordinary peoples [*Erstaunlichen*], those with a pious sense of profundity." [57] Such artifacts, for Frobenius, represented an alternative way of life, and, by extension, provided answers to social and intellectual life that were carved in stone, a record of human perfection that can serve those of a later epoch as an alternative to a rigid, life-suppressing state order.

This is a position that was to sit uncomfortably with his membership in the National Socialist Party and his participation in the ethnological projects of the Third Reich.[58] But this dark aspect of his biography becomes clearer when we consider the Nazis' own version of anti-rationalism and cultural romance. For Frobenius, delving into prehistory answered the need for a change in our feeling toward life (*Lebensgefühl*); and of course much the same could be said for what the National Socialists had to offer their members.

In autobiographically recounting his impressions after some two years of travel in central Africa in 1906, he was prompted to wax eloquent about the qualities he found common throughout equatorial Africa, an impression of the essence (*Wesens*) of all of Africa, which he described as the "old, authentically African, warm blooded culture," in which "everything was permeated with the same smell of rising hut

liebte alles Afrikanische und war erfüllt von Ehrfurcht vor diesem Menschen und ihrer Kultur. So machte ich mich denn auf die Suche nach dem Sinn, entwickelte meine Vorstellungen von der Seele und dem Geist der Kultur. Das war aber für mich nicht nur etwas Abstraktes, ich fühlte mich den Afrikanern von Herzen verbunden." My translation. Leo Frobenius, cited in H.-J. Heinrichs, *Die fremde Welt, das bin ich; Leo Frobenius: Ethnologe, Forschungsreisender, Abenteurer* (Wuppertal: Peter Hammer Verlag, 1998) 66.

[57] L. Frobenius, *Erlebte Erdteile: Ergebnisse eines Deutschen Forscherlebens*, Vol. I (Frankfurt am Main: Frankfurter Societäts-Druckerei 1925) 34.

[58] See S. Ehl, "Ein Afrikaner erobert die Mainmetropole. Leo Frobenius in Frankfurt (1924–1938)," in *Lebenslust und Fremdenfurcht: Ethnologie im Dritten Reich*, ed. T. Hauschild (Frankfurt am Main: Suhrkamp, 1995) 121–140.

fires, sweat- and fat-soaked hides and animal glands. Everything is herbal, strong, and tectonic."[59] In Frobenius' version of civilizational romanticism, cultural qualities common to Africa, genuinely experienced, have the capacity to mitigate or counteract the stultifying effects of rational, industrial modernity.

This grand-vision approach to ethnology is an embodiment of the morally ambiguous nature of global or civilizational cultural projects, offering lessons – or, better, cautions – that apply equally to the conceptual inventions and research paradigms of international agencies: when one begins with a foundational premise of ritual as counter-modernism, the focus shifts from the initiate to the *observer* as the beneficiary of symbolic knowledge. Who else is the potential bearer of both the accumulated mass of historical knowledge of the disenchanted West and the recorder of those ethnographic observations and experience, seen as antidotes to the loss of magic from the world? The Africans become unwitting agents of a change in the way *we* (the author and his sympathetic readers) feel, providing a new sense of who *we* are, giving *us* a sense of secure identity. We who were once deprived of sensory experience are enlightened through contact with our deepest, innermost human spirit, as preserved and expressed by the Africans in the sights, sounds and smells of village life. Cultural romance thrives on the sweeping panorama of assembled fragments, recorded for their pleasing qualities, cobbled together in an ethnography of peripatetic superficiality. The symbolism that stands out for public consumption is that which succeeds in offering poignant contrast with the haste, individualism, routinization, rigid order and centralized power of an imagined modernity.

---

[59] "alte, echt afrikanische, warmblütige Kultur … Alles strömt den gleichen Duft schwelender Hüttenfeuer, schweiß- und fettgetränkter Felle und tierischer Drüsen aus. Alles ist herb, streng, tektonish." My translation. L. Frobenius, *Kulturgeschichte Afrikas: Prolegomena zu einer historischen Gestaltlehre* (Wuppertal: Peter Hammer Verlag and Frankfurt: Frobenius-Institut, 1993) 15–16.

It is in the very nature of re-enchantment that the reality it creates is distanced and abstracted from the detailed, specific, routine nature of ritual, above all from what might loosely be referred to as the legal content of ritual. Enchantment is created by stripping away the constitutional dimensions of ritual practice (of the kind described by Richards), and by turning instead toward an imagined inner essence (of the kind imagined by Frobenius), common to a people, a civilization or humanity, discernible in the ululations of song, the poetry of motion, the heat and dust and pressing crowds of a performance that for a moment breaks down the barriers of human understanding across difference. It is there to be discovered in cultural encounter, but of a particular kind: in contexts in which the deep meaning of words and motions, particular to a people and giving personal sense to their behavior, is not understood by an observer whose interpretation of what is witnessed and experienced turns instead toward a grandiose vision of human perfectibility. The re-enchantment of ritual practice begins when one abandons reflection on meaning-in-context and turns instead toward meaning-for-betterment.

This means that the civilizational imagination is not (or no longer) principally ethnographic in the sense of being formed by the observations and interpretations of an alien observer, but presupposes the cultivation of a supra-national public, drawn to the attractions of belonging to a higher entity, a greater culture, and a richer history than the narrow confines of a birthplace. The idea of civilization evokes something one can belong to (often in opposition to the West, which is understood as having a history that makes it an illegitimate focus of loyalty) as an esteem-building supplement to whatever bonds of group membership an individual might already have, but with the advantage of requiring no obligations, other than a modicum of intellectual loyalty. Seen from this perspective, civilization seems to include the idea of membership in a faith, but at the same time transcending it. This becomes clear when we piece together the ideas expressed previously by Muhammad Khatami. Persian civilization has been transformed by the advent of Islam, but remains residual in the illustrious Muslim heritage of Iran.

Civilization is contiguous with religion in the sense that it is founded on belief – not in the form of a divine revelation but in its approach to history. The hopeful vision of the future that comes from the utopian imagination provides a motivation and ready-made filter for the interpretation of the past. The level of abstraction with which culture is described and modified by global institutions is such that the xenophobic civilizationism associated with nostalgia can simply be edited out, made more appealing to the consumers of culture and activist engagement, separated from ambition and channeled instead to the colors and comforts of innocent political communities. The knowledge-base of civilization is, in Marc Bloch's terms, "a vast symphony of frauds," in which people take liberties with their heritage because of their attachments to it.[60] The central criterion of the truth for those who see themselves as belonging to a civilization becomes the *feeling* produced by a piece of information or an idea. History, for the devotees of a civilization, is assembled from fragments of affirmation.

Ultimately history can become therapeutic in the sense that it serves as a source of recovery from a loss of dignity. The troubling aspect of therapeutic history is not just epistemological, not just its wilful contrarience toward the self-critical search for knowledge, but its potential to provide the intellectual armature to those responsible for abuses of power. It is a kind of naked hegemony that surrounds plain falsehoods with moral defences. It is usually tolerated when expressed by the powerless, but, unaccountably, has been overlooked as the foundation of ideas among those who declaim on behalf of civilizations.

---

[60] M. Bloch, *Apologie pour l'histoire ou métier d'historien* (Paris: Armand Colin, 1993 [1949]) 98.

Contradictions of conceptual diplomacy

One of the destabilizing features of the concept of civilization follows from the intergenerational persistence of meaning, from the fact that there are limits to the human capacity for conceptual flexibility and reconfiguration. This can be seen in a tendency for the early singular form of civilization to intrude on the plural form, with the conviction that *a* civilization has achieved mastery over other forms of life through its unique control over the powers of technology, bureaucracy and moral rectitude. It presses forward on this agenda through an energized verbal form: those who enjoy the benefits of a superior civilization have an obligation to *civilize* others, to engage in the work of improving and uplifting those living a meagre existence on its margins.

Although the UN's Dialogue and Alliance efforts are premised on a rejection of Huntington's theory of inter-civilizational conflict, they simultaneously create an institutional reality for the hemispheric align-ments that Huntington postulates. While oriented toward dialogue, alliance, understanding and peace, the UN's efforts could well breathe into life the artificial divisions associated with civilization. The genera-tive capacity of legal sociology at the highest level of global governance is such that acting upon dusted off, xenophobically inspired definitions of the concept – even with the positive goal of combating terrorism through broad initiatives of understanding and cooperation – gives it a greater degree of institutional reality, legitimacy and potential for political action. While well intentioned, the UN's guiding perspective on the diplomatic uses of cultural communication reveals either a fun-damental contradiction or a concession that is fatal to the Alliance of Civilizations initiatives. If (contra Huntington and his predecessors) the world is not, in fact, divided into historically distinct civilizations, then what is the nature of the dialogue and alliance between civiliza-tions that the UN is sponsoring? Clearly, dialogue and alliance between entities that do not really exist, or that exist only as opaque reference points for broad categories of identity, cannot be expected to be diplomatically useful or meaningful. Yet if the UN were to explicitly concede (mainly to Huntington) that the world is truly divided this way, but that it is initiating dialogue to promote conditions for mutual understanding and peace between historically rival civilizations, it would run the risk of overlooking the Janus face of continentally conceived culture; it could at the same time inadvertently reinforce a form of identity construction that can serve the purposes of state-sponsored chauvinism and expansionism.

Let us apply this insight to the example most often invoked in official UN discourse. An effective argument can be made that each of the numerous conflicts in the Muslim world is set within a specific context and has particular causes and that these do not amount to a generalized conflict between civilizations. But to make this argument in the context of an inter-civilizational forum is starkly contradictory. Separating the idea of civilization as a venue of exclusively positive expressions of cultural creativity and cooperation from the reality of state-sponsored ambitions of regional domination is contrary to the most important painful lessons of modern history. If the significant conflicts involving Muslim populations really do have specific causes and possible solutions, and if the Huntingtonian idea of inter-civilizational conflict is fundamentally illusory and potentially supportive of illegitimate state policies, then the only reasonable approach to an initiative of inter-civilizational discourse would be to seek to dismantle it and find alternative, crisis-specific venues for dialogue, mutual understanding and peace. At one level, UN dialogue between civilizations brings into sharper reality a phenomenon that, at another level, it sees as ideologically strident and politically dangerous.

Legal enchantment is of course not limited to the conceptual constructs of civilization. It has, if anything, a more central place in the ideas produced around the concept of indigenous peoples. Beliefs about prehistoric population movements and occupation of territory, for example, are increasingly (or so it seems) in conflict with professional opinion based on archaeological research. Ideas of indigenous (read "innate") environmental harmony and sagacity are at odds with a critical anthropology that multiplies the instances of Paleolithic and contemporary indigenous environmental abuses and paints a complex picture of human experiences of the environment. At the same time there can be little doubt that for self-proclaimed indigenous peoples, auto-history, with all its distortions and fraudulence, can produce feelings of affirmation and re-dignification.

Although the indigenous peoples' movement is based on a terminology of identity that in some ways parallels the international reconstruction of civilization, it embraces a very different constituency. Indigenous peoples' forums are intended to establish a place in the international public sphere for those distinct societies marginalized by nation-states, sometimes offering them moral leverage in the "politics of indignation." But civilization forums potentially also give voice to states with supra-state cultural orientations and ambitions. How might one effectively make a rights claim or express a grievance on behalf of a civilization? The concept serves mainly as an abstraction to explain (or explain away) the sources of intractable human conflict that have not been successfully dealt with through specific, result-oriented avenues of diplomacy.

There is at the same time a sense in which the initiatives on behalf of indigenous peoples (discussed in Chapter 4) and of civilization do not comfortably juxtapose. As soon as a culture-bearing entity is conceptualized, described and defined, it becomes endowed with a capacity to attract ambitions, often over and against the ambitions of others. Notably absent from the invitation lists of meetings on civilization are those who represent peoples or communities on the margins of nation-states. The new way of conceptualizing civilization is not intended to provide legal or strategic leverage for oppressed or marginalized minority communities within nation-states. This produces an implicit division of the world, with corresponding exclusive global governance initiatives, into those who are "civilized" and those who are "ethnic," "indigenous," or, failing all else, "local communities," thereby bringing back into life an old paradigm (albeit with a greater measure of post-colonial sensibility and cultural romanticism) that once divided the world into those following the pathway of progress and those who are its inevitable victims.

This does not mean that there is no room for dialogue outside the usual pathways of diplomacy between peoples suffering from intracta-ble conflict. There is, on the contrary, a literature dealing with the topic that demonstrates the potential effectiveness of loosely structured dia-logue among those whose peoples are in intractable armed conflicts.[61] Programs that have brought together Israeli and Palestinian youth are models of this kind of effort.[62] But diplomacy in all its forms, includ-ing that of schoolchildren engaged in dialogue across difference, most readily succeeds when there is candor and specificity about the sources of conflict. There is less possibility for durable success when dialogue is built around categories of belonging that are generalized, unspe-cific and opaque, inviting a fill-in-the-blanks process of self-and-other stereotyping.

When a legally conceived category of belonging goes wrong, there is no simple, direct way to correct it because the languages and institu-tions of law and diplomacy tend to instrumentally reinforce the con-cepts they invoke. Because of this, UN discourse does not recognize, and has no new answer for, the enduring tendency for states to exercise

---

[61] See, for example, L. Ellinor and G. Gerard, *Dialogue: Rediscovering the Transforming Power of Conversation* (New York: John Wiley & Sons, 1998); M. Hewstone and R. Brown (eds.), *Contact and Conflict in Intergroup Encounters* (Oxford and New York: Blackwell, 1986); H. Saunders, *A Public Peace Process: Sustained Dialogue to Transform Racial and Ethnic Conflicts* (New York: St. Martin's Press, 1999).

[62] M. Abu-Nimer, *Dialogue, Conflict Resolution and Change: Arab-Jewish Encounters in Israel* (Albany: SUNY Press, 1999).

expansionist ambition by appealing to hemispheric or civilizational ideals.

Today the civilizational dialogue of the international public sphere promotes the ideas of peace and progress within distinct hemispheric realms. Tomorrow, there may be a new source of intellectual/diplomatic urgency with cosmopolitan intent – or none at all. Even though the UN's civilization initiatives may change beyond recognition or fall into oblivion, there is a central lesson to be found in them: the conceptual germs of legal ideas about social belonging, properly cultivated in the language of rights, have a remarkable capacity to come to life.

But in the last several chapters we have seen that not all categories of people that the UN chooses to define and represent will inevitably spring into global prominence and become a gathering point of claims and identities. Those defined as tribal peoples did not form themselves into a legal identity but amalgamated with the indigenous peoples' movement. "Local communities" is probably too generic and insipid a concept to capture the imaginations either of self-appointed representatives or of rights advocates, not to mention the public. And even the term "civilization" has its limitations, mainly because of the success of a postcolonial discourse that has given it a pejorative connotation when applied to the Occident, with salvific implications reserved for those seeking an ambitious re-conceptualization of their modernity- and state-transcending history. The influence of legal sociology is not limited to those categories that "take," that stir the imaginations of rights defenders and their audiences, but extends to those whose common qualities include invisibility, uncertainty and public indifference.

SIX

Reconciliation

The human rights confessional

A reconfiguration of the moral order of difference through international law can be clearly seen in the two interrelated ways that the worst abuses of states are recognized and remedied: in state-sponsored apologies and forums of truth and reconciliation. One of the most unusual features of the global rights regime is a moral/legal development in which the act of apology and the truth and reconciliation commission have together become the most significant and legitimate methods by which the collective harm wrought by the state is acknowledged and remedied. Public apologies and truth and reconciliation commissions have become like confessionals for states. As expressed by Desmond Tutu, the state apology becomes an expression of love: "[A]s a nation we are saying, we are sorry, we have opened the wounds of your suffering and sought to cleanse them; this reparation is a balm, an ointment, being poured over the wounds to assist in their healing" [1] Expressing essentially the same point more prosaically, anthropologist R.A. Wilson points out that in South Africa, "national legal discourse did not contain the language with which to undertake its own rehabilitation, and the liminality of the TRC

---

[1] D. Tutu, *No Future Without Forgiveness* (New York: Doubleday, 1999) 61.

allowed it to plagiarize from a religious idiom."[2] This suggests something odd about the processes of apology and of truth and reconciliation: there is a widely shared expectation that misguided states, through their personnel, should express deep human feelings of personal regret and desire for absolution. There is no manifestation of genocidal violence or other form of systemic political abuse so severe that it overrides the legitimacy of public contrition inscribed in international law. Their most important feature is that they *are* public, that the sins of the state are exposed to the light of day.

One of the central goals of apology and testimony in these human rights remedies is the conceptual reform or "re-education" of the citizen-bases of those states identified as having committed human rights violations in their recent history. In some circumstances the rights-affirming ideas associated with apology and truth and reconciliation are inconsistent with durable prejudices and propaganda for which the state is being held responsible. This introduces a tension between the judgments and moral content of human rights as expressed in the state's language of contrition and the misguided ideas once tolerated or cultivated by the state, which may still be held by a significant segment of the citizenry. The central significance of the apology and truth and reconciliation commission (TRC) as human rights remedies lies in the fact that they call upon states to take an active part in the persuasion of its domestic publics, to undertake efforts to bring popular opinion more in line with the moral universals of human rights. Human rights do not just use persuasion as a direct source of shame against the perpetrators of rights violations, but as an active instrument of their rehabilitation.

In this chapter I also intend to highlight a basic disjuncture between the absolutes of persuasion and the multifaceted reality of suffering at

[2] R.A. Wilson, "Reconciliation and Revenge in Post-Apartheid South Africa: Rethinking Legal Pluralism and Human Rights," *Current Anthropology*, 2000, 41 (1): 75–87, 80.

the hands of the state. The use of persuasion as an inherent feature of human rights remedy introduces a tension between the effort to achieve clarity and directness in communicating with publics and the complexities and ambiguities of collective remembered experience. The need to simplify and communicate broadly can produce a sense of isolation, of shouting into the wind, among those whose experience is distorted by or left out of the new narrative of the state. If organized campaigns of public persuasion call for consistency and simplicity intended to maximize the reach of ideas ("message discipline" in campaign-speak), we can expect this to be no different in the state's organized efforts to rewrite its own history and promote a new regime of tolerance and human rights-recognition – often at the expense of informed opinion and ultimately the very goals of truth and reconciliation.

The interconnected phenomena of apology, confession, forgiveness and reconciliation are emotionally charged aspects of a quintessentially Christian approach to peacemaking, to the restoration of harmony in community as a foundation for a more universal ideal of a fraternity of co-religionists. When someone apologizes for wrongdoing, they are ideally acknowledging responsibility for harm, self-avowedly the agent of another's suffering; but at the same time their personal responsibility and loss of honor is diminished by the Christian idea of sin as an essential aspect of human nature. An apology is therefore a deeply personal act, involving not only contrition, but above all self-revelation, in which a willingness to expose one's frailty – that is to say, one's basic humanity – is an act of integrity and strength.

Recourse to public apology clothes the state in the mantle of the human spirit. This means that states, like individuals, are involved in processes of moral correction and self-development, but – and this is significant in ways we cannot yet imagine – without the biological limits of mortality. In their roles as protectors of diversity, states have acquired more sharply defined personalities. The processes of power-sharing and the increased moral accountability of states is making them more significant as moral and political actors than ever before by raising their profile as the reference points of new rights regimes and, through their cumulative responses to rights and cooperative arrangements with minorities, endowing them more than ever before with distinct personalities.

Formal public apologies for human rights abuse are politically acceptable because at some level they take place in, and come to represent, the *aftermath* of revolution, not necessarily in terms of constitutional rebuilding from the ground up, but of irrevocable transformation in the moral foundations of the exercise of state power. There is not necessarily a change of heart in those who hold the most responsibility for the moral wrong of states, but most importantly a change of government and of personnel that produces, together with policy reform, an impression of contrition and effort toward moral correction.

Although criminal procedures and TRCs are both founded on testimony, there are two basic and consequential differences between them: first, in criminal proceedings, testimony is a means toward arriving at an ideally fair, reasonable, fact-based judgment, whereas in the TRC, the most important judgment lies *at the beginning* of the process. It is that cumulative, slow to build, popular judgment that establishes the historical truth of state-sponsored violence toward its own citizens on a grand scale. Once this has been settled with admissions of responsibility and regret by high-level state officials, the process of gathering testimony en masse, ultimately to rewrite the historical narrative of the nation, can begin.

Second, once underway truth and reconciliation commissions are ideally non-adversarial. Unlike criminal proceeding, there is usually a diminished standard of proof, no systematic effort to root out falsehoods, no cross-examination, little ferreting out of facts and no presumption of innocence until proven guilty. Instead they are based on testimony, plain and simple. Among those represented as the survivors of abuses of power, the central criterion of the truth is sincerity. But for those seen collectively or individually as the perpetrators of abuse, public forums are deaf to denial, wanting only to hear confession and contrition. This is related to the goal of constructing a new narrative of the state, one infused with personal accounts of injustice and suffering, usually with a more implicit assumption that their root causes have already been overcome by reform.

A truth and reconciliation commission is quintessentially legal and bureaucratic, an outcome of judicial process run by appointed officials according to rule-based procedures; and yet in its most essential elements – in terms of the expectations of the people it assembles and the information it gathers – it is inefficient, redundant, emotional, and even spiritual. It becomes a venue for the articulation of memories pulled past the obstacles of repression, inhibition and avoidance of re-experienced emotional pain. It brings together in one time and place the opposite extremes of institutional pedantry and narrative performance.

The perpetrators of the sins of states are those whose personal responsibility is clouded by the ethics of obedience, by the fact that the state (in an earlier incarnation) holds responsibility for the characterization of targeted others as inconvenient and somehow collectively defective and hence in need of improvement or elimination, and for the institutionally guided vision of sacrifice for an ultimate good. One of the most heartbreaking lessons of history is that humans are capable of any act of evil when they find themselves in the condition of being "untouchable," with the ambitions and promises of incumbent power as a moral justification, in which all is condoned in the loyal service of the state. Unprovoked violence does not require direct orders. There are always some willing to betray, besiege, torture and kill in conditions of public anonymity through information-silence or the dismissive wave-of-the-hand immunity of official denial.

And then regime change happens, and with it comes a moral crisis.[3] At one level this is straightforwardly a personal crisis for the erstwhile perpetrators of organized violence. It follows from the shattered illusion of permanence in the present, from acting on the comforts of immunity without thinking that power might change, that one might have to face one's former victims without the protection of the state. How does one live with one's neighbors as a former perpetrator against them of some of the worst imaginable crimes? Such was the dilemma of "Harry," a former ZANU-PF thug who worked with his gang in support of Robert Mugabe's bid for re-election as President of Zimbabwe by torturing and killing Mugabe's political rivals. Seven weeks after the establishment of a coalition government Harry told a reporter for the London *Times*, "Maybe one morning, I will wake up murdered … I know other people won't forget what happened." [4] He was sweating and shaking when he attended a reconciliation workshop sponsored by the Catholic Commission for Justice and Peace to admit to his acts of torture and killing, ostensibly in the interest of being able to look into the eyes of his neighbors and live in harmony.

But the crisis brought about by the aftermath of state-sponsored violence is not just personal, not just a matter of the safety and survival of perpetrators, but is more significant in its implications for the rule of law and ultimately the stability of the state. If Harry's neighbors were

---

[3] To my knowledge the only truth commission to be sponsored by a state regime that was itself responsible for widespread human rights violations (resulting in the TRC mentioned later in this paragraph) was the 1983 Zimbabwe Commission of Inquiry into the Matabeleland Disturbances, instituted to investigate crimes committed by the army during a specific violent incident during Mugabe's rule. The four commissioners assigned to this Inquiry did produce a report, but, contrary to the purposes and expectations of truth commissions, it was never made publicly available and never leaked from inside the government. See P. Hayner, *Unspeakable Truths: Confronting State Terror and Atrocity* (New York: Routledge, 2001) 55.

[4] J. Raath, "Mugabe Torturers Confess as Church Starts Quest for Reconciliation," *The Times*, April 17, 2009, www.timesonline.co.uk/tol/news/world/africa/article6108799.ece. Accessed April 19, 2009.

to act on the hatreds accumulated over years of political abuse – years marked by pain, loss of loved ones, and fear – outside of any public process, then violent reprisals would almost inevitably result. Revenge in these circumstances would be understandable, perhaps even elicit sympathy, but at the same time it would create an inescapable cycle of vengeance as the primary vehicle for justice.

The institution of the truth and reconciliation commission – with more than forty having taken place worldwide since the late 1970s it is now safe to call it an institution – is a mechanism through which it is possible to see the transmission of values from the constructions of international law to local settings, sometimes described formally as *international norm diffusion*. Ideas inscribed in international law about the right conduct of states are only the beginning. We can also find in them the influence of widely held assumptions and expectations about suffering and what it is to be a victim, about wrongdoing and what it is to be a perpetrator, along with how one must approach reconciliation through expressions of guilt, atonement and forgiveness. We also often find in these venues expressions of ideas about human belonging, the importance of identity and its manner of expression. The TRC is but one of the means by which such concepts and values are exchanged between global institutions and representatives of oppressed minorities or "traditional" societies. Their ultimate goal is public persuasion, to reach past the active or residual propaganda defences of states to create a new, convincing, broadly accepted narrative of the state, one that is more closely aligned with international norms than its predecessor.

It would be wrong to assume that the rights violations that give rise to state-sponsored apologies and TRCs are experienced exclusively in that part of the world sometimes vaguely referred to as the "South" – often shorthand for a stereotypical political geography of dysfunction and abuse of power. One of the most recent state-sponsored admissions of and apologies for human rights abuse has occurred (and is occurring at the time of writing, with a mandate until 2014) in Canada, in response to the legacy of Indian residential schools, of which (again at the time of writing) some 80,000 living people have had experience. It is on this example that I now concentrate my attention.

The violence of assimilation

During childhood there are moments in which one is forced to enter into the world beyond the shelter of family, in which one confronts the emotions of insecurity and fear through encounter with unpredictable forces, occasionally experiencing painful ordeals and injury. This is a normal part of establishing personal autonomy in preparation for the responsibilities of adulthood. But for some children in circumstances of endemic violence, insecurity becomes the norm, and the need for responsibility is imposed before they have had the chance to explore the world through imagination and play. We easily recognize those who are said to have never had a childhood, for whom the need to cope with survival, with premature responsibility for those still less autonomous, with bereavement and separation, for whom the struggle for life cuts short their innocence, forcing change on them, both in their circumstances and in their personalities, making them strikingly different from those the same age who have been sheltered by functioning families, endowing them with a kind of precocious, melancholy maturity.

The experience of those children who have lived through conditions of institutionalized violence and insecurity raises an issue concerning the legacy of trauma that commonly resulted from the residential school experience, an issue now gaining prominence in Canada through the establishment of a truth and reconciliation commission. What qualities of the residential schools do former inmates point to that could have resulted in their failure to cope in later adulthood? What qualities of the violence that took place in residential schools made it act, dramatically, durably and consistently, upon people's mental health and the security of their identities? I hope that beginning by examining these questions in some detail, particularly from the perspectives of those identified as the victims or subjects of human rights abuse, will inform an issue of more immediate concern to this book: what are the implications of human rights remedy for identity and group membership? Or, expressed another way, what is the nature of the legal sociology inherent in coming to terms with human rights abuse on a large scale?

To begin to address these questions it is first necessary to understand the nature of the wrong that has given rise to contrition, formal apology, testimony and reform. Let me then describe the residential school experience, as collated through testimony assembled over a period of some twenty years from research projects in northern Quebec, Ontario and Manitoba given directly to me or via public venues by those who describe themselves as school "survivors." My exposure to this topic was especially concentrated in Cross Lake, an aboriginal reserve community in northern Manitoba. Here I was witness to a community's response to the remedy of state apology – a reticent, circumscribed apology at first, but one that nevertheless opened the floodgates of memory and heightened awareness of collective trauma, providing an illustration of the reach of human rights ideals into local settings, into the reformulations of history and identity of marginalized communities subject to abuses of power.

Forced assimilation is a form of violence particularly destructive of what we recognize as the normalcy of childhood. State-sponsored programs of cultural assimilation are today associated with lasting, insidious forms of post-traumatic mental illness, resulting above all from of the forced removal of children from the security of families, communities and identities. On a nearly global scale, there is an apparent correlation between the common historical experiences of repressive state formation – not just through violence toward those on the margins but through their removal from territory and from intergenerational transmission of knowledge – and the contemporary experiences of intergenerational trauma.

The violence that was once part of everyday life in Indian residential schools was brought home to me with particular poignancy in a community meeting in Cross Lake in 1998, not long after the Canadian government issued its Statement of Reconciliation, announced a reformed aboriginal policy titled Gathering Strength, established the Aboriginal Healing Foundation, and dedicated $350 million to support community-based healing initiatives in acknowledgment of the harm caused by the residential school program. The meeting was sponsored by a speaker from a reservation community in Saskatchewan on a tour to many aboriginal reserve communities throughout Canada. This was a two-day event replete with stories of abuse at the hands of those who were supposed to be educators and caretakers, of suffering in the aftermath of the school experience, of loneliness, addictions, and an inability to refrain from abnormal sexuality. It was, as the following excerpt from the meeting shows, painfully forthright in its account of institutional violence:

[The] guy that sexually abused me, I remember leaving his room at three and four o'clock in the morning, just hitting my head on the pillow, just falling asleep and all of a sudden there they are with the lights on. Get up. Time to clean up. Wash up. Go do your chores. Then set off for school. But I never went to school to go learn anything. I wanted to, but I was so tired … that I fell asleep in [the] classroom … Then when we got to the school, we were abused there again by the teachers who didn't understand that we were up half the night being sexually abused.[5]

The model for this gathering seemed to be that of the Pentecostal revival meeting (a Church, not coincidentally, growing quickly in Canada's aboriginal population), with an atmosphere of extravagantly

---

[5] Statement presented in a public meeting, Cross Lake, Manitoba, October 8, 1998, recorded and transcribed by the author. Also cited in R. Niezen, *Spirit Wars: Native North American Religions in the Age of Nation Building* (Berkeley and Los Angeles: University of California Press, 2000) 77–8.

open confessional, tearful expressions of pain, regret, repentance and attestations of sobriety and healing.

On the first day of the meeting I sat next to an elder from my "neighborhood" in the southwest part of the village who listened quietly, showing little emotion. The next day we returned to the same seats we had sat in the day before. While we were waiting for the meeting to start he leaned toward me and said, "I want to show you something." He reached into a canvas game bag and brought out an object that looked vaguely like a dead cuttlefish, a whip made from strands of nylon cord knotted together at one end. He then told me the story behind this object, about how in residential school he had been punished (I assume for a minor offence like wetting his bed) by being tied down and strapped. "This is what the priest used to beat me with," he said. He had gone home and made the replica the previous evening after listening to a day of testimony and being reminded of his own experience, which he had for many years pushed from his memory and about which he had never spoken.

Such memories following from the violence of removal of children from their families and communities in policies of forced assimilation pervade the testimony and academic reporting of the experiences and legacy of the residential school system, not only in Canada but in many parts of the world. I have argued elsewhere that such experiences constitute a source of common identity in the transnational movement of indigenous peoples, bringing together people from every quarter of the globe who can point to globally similar patterns in their troubled relationships with settler states and similar histories of institutionalized policies of cultural assimilation.[6] The Cross Lake elder's construction of an artifact based on his experience is a tangible representation of this kind of testimony, which more commonly takes the form of artifacts of

---

[6] R. Niezen, *The Origins of Indigenism: Human Rights and the Politics of Identity* (Berkeley and Los Angeles: University of California Press, 2003).

discourse, efforts to record for posterity the interlocutor's memories of suffering by translating subjectivity into a formal record.

One of the themes repeated through such testimony is the pain experienced by children of separation from family, of being subjected to physical control directed toward the interruption of affect. In testimony recorded in the aftermath of the 1998 policy reform an elderly Cree woman remembered her experience in Cross Lake's St. Joseph's residential school:

I had a little brother who had taken ill. He had tuberculosis. He [wasn't allowed to] stay in bed, and he had to carry out chores like the others ... He came down one time and sat at the boys' table. And I was sitting on the other side of the room, and I took a look his way and smiled at him, and the sister hit me for smiling at my own brother ... Later my brother [died] from his sickness.[7]

The denial of love, almost more than the physical punishment that sometimes accompanied it, seemed to last in the memory as a source of trauma. Somehow the cumulative effect of such acts of separation was to make it clear to the children that nobody in their lives was capable of caring for them, that the institutional rejection of their family and everything connected with it, coupled with their own rejection of the values being imposed on them, made them utterly alone. This is reminiscent of techniques sometimes used to make prisoners bond with their captors, adding finality to all other forms of control by making it clear to captives that they have no other source of solidarity, no worth as a person apart from the esteem of their captors.

This means that for those children in residential school who did not find a source of belonging through the school and Church, the

---

[7] Interview conducted and translated from Cree by Don Settee, Cross Lake, 1999. I am grateful to the Cross Lake First Nation for making available to me the testimony of elders intended to record for posterity their residential school experience.

experience often had far-reaching effects on identity and self-esteem. Rejection of the ideas and institutional rules of those with absolute power over them could lead to an impasse which left individuals with a durable and profound sense of loneliness. They experienced prolonged denial of the basic psychological needs of love, play and identity affirmation. They were commonly left with a feeling of rejection, not only by a family that they no longer saw, a family that was not there to protect them, but by school authorities who were often the most direct source of insecurity, and by other students, organized into their own protective hierarchy, with its own potential for brutality.

The children incarcerated in residential schools were as fully and completely powerless as it is possible for humans to be. They were powerless, not just through the condition of physical and legal incapacity shared by all children, but through the combination of essential qualities that defined the residential school system. Residential schools are perfect examples of the phenomenon referred to by Erving Goffman in *Asylums* as "total institutions."[8] Rules and patterns of behavior under sanction of Church and school were not questioned as outcomes of human design, but became quite simply the way things were. True, there were many instances of "ordinary resistance" engaged in by incarcerated children, from the innocuous, such as stealing food or secretly speaking their own forbidden languages, to the consequential, such as arson. But the completeness of control (an unambiguous manifestation of the phenomenon referred to by Foucault as bio-power), the exclusion of competing values and the absence of any other source of affect and affirmation than those in authority, made it difficult for child inmates to see the basic configuration of power that so completely controlled them.

Besides the immediate qualities of the institutions, the children were powerless because of their lack of effective advocacy networks outside

[8] E. Goffman, *Asylums: Essays on the Social Situation of Mental Patients and Other Inmates* (Piscataway: Aldine Transaction, 2007).

the residential school system. Again, exceptions come immediately to mind; there were instances in which families and communities, informed of the abuses taking place in schools, hid their children from school authorities or intervened directly to remove children; but the residential school system was reinforced by the laws and enforcement agencies of the state, and during the period in the mid-twentieth century when the residential school system was in full swing, the incarcerated children came from communities that had been marginalized, slated for the extinguishment of their distinct rights and identities. This meant that the children in residential schools were often denied the support of their families and communities, who in any case were legally and politically marginalized, having been systematically denied access to any formal system of advocacy such as we might find today in nongovernmental organizations or ombudsmen. This powerlessness not only had implications for the self-image and self-esteem of school inmates; it was also inconsistent with the basic goals of education. The residential school program was destined to fail, simply because of the stark contradiction inherent in the objectives of instilling the values of democratic citizenship and individual autonomy through authoritarian transmission of ideas and control of every aspect of children's lives.

To fully understand the distinct psycho-social consequences of the residential school experience, we must also consider the common circumstances of students upon their release from school, going beyond the immediate sources of trauma in individuals, to take into view the troubled dynamics of efforts by former school inmates to reintegrate into families and communities. Under these circumstances we find the more insidious effects of forced assimilation, which separates individuals from families and communities, even as they are brought together in spatial proximity. The experiences of social disconnection, maladaptation and loneliness resulting from institutionalized cultural deprogramming clearly compound the mental health challenges faced by former inmates of residential schools.

It was not just the immediate traumas of abuse in the institutional setting that marked the subsequent life trajectories of those who had been inmates, but also the dissonance and disconnect experienced by youth who had been systematically de-cultured and de-languaged and then released into social circumstances for which they were unprepared (or perhaps more accurately, "de-prepared"). For many this entailed a process of reintegration and delayed learning, or possibly a rejection of the language and way of life of members of older generations who maintained attachments to a traditional lifestyle.

From such problems of reintegration into families and communities follow the consequences of the school experience on subsequent generations, on those who experience what might be called intergenerational trauma, whose parents were influenced in their parenting by forced separation from any positive form of family intimacy, and more significantly by incarceration within an abusive institutional model of child education and domestic routine. Diminished capacities of communication and nurturing within families have had consequences for the offspring of survivors that are often as significant as the immediate traumas of abuse in residential school.

The intergenerational effects of the residential school experience were seen by some survivors to be manifested in the breakdown of nurturing and cultural transmission within the immediate families of those who had been raised in the institutional setting of residential schools.[9] "I found I was always yelling at my kids," a former school inmate from Port Alberni, British Columbia, once told me, and then speculated that in his

[9] Although not an official entry in the DSM-IV diagnosis manual, Brasfield describes a pattern of disorder, referred to by some clinicians as "residential school syndrome," as shorthand for the manifestations of mental illness among those with a personal history of incarceration in residential schools. Understandably enough, residential school syndrome involves what Brasfield finds to be a "quite striking avoidance of anything that might be reminiscent of the Indian residential school experience." Other markers of this disorder include: "diminished interest and participation in aboriginal cultural activities and markedly deficient

parenting he could not prevent himself from imitating the severe forms of discipline he experienced in the Alberni Indian Residential School.[10] Many children incarcerated throughout their youth were named and identified mainly by the numbers with which they were assigned upon their arrival, raised in conditions of suffocating routine and order, without examples of affection or affirmation, without the techniques of nurturing and discipline necessary to raise their own families. Fred Kelly, another residential school survivor from Port Alberni, sees this as a central, common aspect of the residential school experience that lasted well past the immediate traumas and humiliations of childhood: "We were deprived of the care, love, and guidance of our parents during our most critical years of childhood. The time we could have learned the critical parenting skills and values was lost to the generations that attended residential schools, the effects of which still haunt us and will continue to have impacts upon our people and communities."[11] As an example, he draws on the most important of his own family relationships: "I was not able to hug or kiss my mother until she was seventy-three, the final year of her life."[12] The institution, with all its strict routines and sobriety, provided a pathological model for family life, which subsequent generations have either replicated in emotional inhibition, in the interruption of almost the entire gamut of intergenerational communication, and/or rejected utterly through life choices marked by lassitude, punctuated by

knowledge of traditional culture and skills. Often there is a markedly increased arousal including sleep difficulties, anger management difficulties and impaired concentration. As might be the case for anyone attending a boarding school with inadequate parenting, parenting skills are often deficient. Strikingly, there is a persistent tendency to abuse alcohol or sedative medication drugs, often starting at a very young age." C. Brasfield, "Residential School Syndrome," *B.C. Medical Journal*, 2001, 43 (2): 79.

[10] Cited in Niezen, *Spirit Wars*, 84.

[11] F. Kelly, "Confessions of a Born Again Pagan," in *From Truth to Reconciliation: Transforming the Legacy of Residential Schools*, ed. Marlene Brant Castellano, Linda Archibald and Mike DeGagné (Ottawa: Aboriginal Healing Foundation, 2008) 24.

[12] Kelly, "Confessions of a Born Again Pagan," 25.

abandon and recklessness, and ultimately leading to the breakdown of domestic patterns of caring and responsibility. This is associated with widely recognized forms of abuse and neglect, which in turn become tangible signs to impressionable young people of the precariousness of belonging and intimacy, yet another dimension of the breakdown of intergenerational continuity. That is to say, collective manifestations of trauma, historically traceable to common experiences of institutional violence, can themselves become sources of chronic insecurity and trauma in subsequent generations.

But the repertoires of identity to be found in the legacies of state-sponsored projects of assimilation also include models of recovery. The following narrative, for example, includes a self-conscious rejection of the abuse, neglect and self-destructiveness of the narrator's own parents and other close kin:

It was a beautiful day. Summer day. I could hear a little baby crying from a distance. And I though, "oh, jeez, what the hell's that?" So I kept walking and pretty soon it was close, this crying, it was close. And I saw my mom and dad's house and it was all broken up. The windows were broken. And that noise was coming from inside that house. And I saw my little brother sitting in the floor there with pampers soggy. Back then we didn't have running water; we had a barrel of water. They spilled all that, and they knocked over the stove so it was just black all over. People were passed out all over the place ... And I thought there that I would never drink alcohol in my life, that I would never put my family through what my mom and dad did to our family.[13]

Taken together, the narratives that emerged in the new spirit of openness to memory and self-examination following the Canadian government's first steps toward acknowledgment and apology present an account of the experiences and consequences of residential education that are multifaceted and deeply inscribed in the psyches of those who suffered

[13] Interview in Cross Lake, 30 October 1999.

from them. As instruments of assimilation, residential schools have left a complex legacy fraught with the ambiguities of memory and the intergenerational consequences of trauma. There is nothing in the pictorial record to tell us of their effects, aside perhaps from the sadness that so often comes through in the eyes of the children – again an intangible. They were both catastrophic and insidious in their consequences. Reliant on remembrance, the ruins they created quickly became overgrown. By being hidden from view, the legacies of residential schools insinuate themselves into the intangibility of memory, revealed only through an accumulated mass of testimony, story upon story, until the exceptionalism of personal experience shapes itself into a perceptible pattern.

Herein lies an obstacle to the understanding and correction of institutional violence: the public audience of testimony is called upon to be patient, to be persuaded not by a shocking iconic image conveyed in a millisecond, but by the slow, imaginative power of narrative; and not just one narrative but enough to reveal the structural outlines of a national policy and its instruments. Experience tends to be homogenized through testimony that privileges the "sayable," above all that emphasizes the suffering resulting from stark emotional trauma and personal injury.[14] This is not so much because those giving testimony are unable to express complex emotion or to collectively represent variety of experience as it is due to the preferences and limited attentiveness of public audiences, the consumers of testimony.

This limitation of public knowledge prevents the depiction of the complex, multifaceted nature of residential school experiences. The social and psychological consequences of assimilation are fraught with

---

[14] Fiona Ross makes a similar observation in her study of women's testimony to the commission in South Africa. Truth commissions, she finds, foreground "certain forms of violence in the public record, [rendering] some kinds of pain more visible while displacing other forms of experience and expression." F. Ross, *Bearing Witness: Women and the Truth and Reconciliation Commission in South Africa* (London: Pluto, 2003) 162.

paradox and ambiguity, challenging even to specialists. But the nature of testimony is such that witnesses tend to be limited to accounts of personal harm; and the nature of public audiences is such that the patterns they are called upon to see and to act on readily become imperceptible, not enough to overcome the competing, widely accepted values of order, cleanliness, transmission of faith, and the preparation of uncivilized people for the values of citizenship, not enough to overcome the denial of narrated experience as individual and exceptional; and quite possibly not even enough to provoke indignation on a scale that sets in motion or legitimizes the mechanisms of redress and reconciliation.

A change of spirit

Residential schools for Indians were established through an official relationship between the federal government and Christian missions in 1892, following the recommendations of the Davin Report, which found promise in the well-established US model of Indian boarding schools.[15] A 1958 workshop sponsored by the Oblate Fathers in Canada titled "Residential Education for Indian Acculturation" reveals the thinking behind a nationwide effort to "civilize the poor ignorant dwellers of the North American forests."[16] One contributor to this workshop, P.A. Renaud, OMI, sketched out several then-existing approaches to bringing about "education for acculturation," pointing to the proven effectiveness of "[isolating] the child as much as possible from his native background, ideally twenty four hours a day and twelve months of the year, to prevent 'exposure' to Indian culture,"[17] though he argued that

---

[15] See Niezen, *Spirit Wars*, for a comparative history of US boarding schools and residential schools in Canada.

[16] Oblate Fathers in Canada, "Residential Education for Indian Acculturation, Workshop I: General Principles" (Ottawa, 1958, Deschâtelets Residence library, doc. no. 8D1/21) 4.

[17] P.A. Renaud, "Education for Acculturation," in Oblate Fathers in Canada, "Residential Education for Indian Acculturation," 34.

this was "artificial" and "divorced from the cultural stream of the community" and indicated a preference for first educating parents, "to raise their children the 'Canadian way' ... so that their children be readier for the Canadian school than they themselves were."[18] The legacy of residential schools in Canada makes plain that the method of total isolation was seen by many missionaries and government officials as the preferred "prescription" for "success and thoroughness" in Indian education. This was the origin of a crisis subsequently interpreted in human rights terms, a crisis that called for remedies of compensation and resources for healing, and more symbolically of official recognition of wrongdoing and atonement for it.

The official relationship between the federal government and the Churches ended with a policy change in 1969, as the assimilationist orientation to aboriginal education lost legitimacy and the era of Indian residential education progressively came to an end. With the school closures that took place in the 1970s and 1980s came an accumulating mass of testimony, which in turn fueled an increasingly vocal base of activists, pointing to nationwide patterns of abuse that took place in the residential schools.

Much of the pressure behind the most recent truth and reconciliation commission in Canada came from journalists who in the 1980s and 1990s seized on the issue of Indian residential schools in Canada as especially worthy of public attention. The apogee of such rights-abuse journalism can arguably be found in Geoffrey York's *The Dispossessed*, based on some seven years of experience in the 1980s as the Winnipeg bureau-chief for the *Globe and Mail*. First published in 1989, this book was prominent among exposés that challenged and disturbed a public inclined toward complacent assumptions of benevolent state-sponsored multiculturalism. It accomplished this by presenting (in the words of the back dust jacket reviews) an "angry primer" on native issues, a

---

[18] Renaud, "Education for Acculturation," 36.

"litany of pain and suffering" that no Canadian could read "without a sense of shame." Among the harrowing material presented by York is the finding that in Edmonton "as many as 80 per cent of the Indians had been sexually abused at church-run schools" and that this abuse had become self-perpetuating, with victims becoming abusers, to the point at which "research has found that 75 to 94 percent of the [adult] residents have been sexually abused in their childhood." [19] By academic standards such "facts" reported by York are poorly documented (the "research" in question is simply invoked as such, without citation) and improbable as an overall picture of life in Canada's reserve communities. It simplified and magnified a crisis, with the explicit goal of provoking a "sense of shame" and calls to action. And in this sense it succeeded: the effect of such reporting on public opinion was far greater than painstaking, attuned-to-subtlety-and-complexity scholarship.

In 1991 four aboriginal and three non-aboriginal commissioners were appointed to investigate the issues surrounding Canada's Indian policy and advise the government on their findings. The commission's report, released in 1996, makes a sweeping condemnation of nearly every aspect of Canada's aboriginal policy, as in an introductory statement by the commissioners:

Successive governments have tried – sometimes intentionally, sometimes in ignorance – to absorb Aboriginal people into Canadian society, thus eliminating them as distinct peoples. Policies pursued over the decades have undermined – and almost erased – Aboriginal cultures and identities. This is assimilation. It is a denial of the principles of peace, harmony and justice for which this country stands – and it has failed. Aboriginal peoples remain proudly different.[20]

---

[19] G. York, *The Dispossessed: Life and Death in Native Canada* (London: Vintage, 1990) 30.

[20] Canada, Royal Commission on Aboriginal Peoples, *People to People, Nation to Nation: Highlights from the Report of the Royal Commission on Aboriginal Peoples* (Ottawa: Minister of Supply and Services Canada, 1996), www.ainc-inac. gc.ca/ap/pubs/rpt/rpt-eng.asp. Accessed November 13, 2009.

Through much of the five-volume, 4,000-page Royal Commission report, assimilation policies were described and discredited, while the need for aboriginal self-determination (including a since-forgotten recommendation of the establishment of a national aboriginal parliament) was given standing as a pathway toward healing and political reconciliation.

Modes of repentance and of suffering

With the schools no longer in operation, the remaining pathways for action went in the direction of atonement and healing. The pressure was applied first to the Churches, and they were the first to respond, albeit to their own congregations. The United Church of Canada issued an apology in 1986, followed by the Oblate Missionaries of Mary Immaculate in 1991, the Anglican Church in 1993, and the Presbyterian Church in 1994.[21] For the Churches, there is a ready-made pathway for contrition, with a well-established idiom of self-revelation, even self-abasement, encouraged by the promise of forgiveness. The Anglican apology delivered by Archbishop Michael Peers to the National Native Convocation provides an example:

I am sorry, more than I can say, that we were part of a system which took you and your children from home and family.

I am sorry, more than I can say, that we tried to remake you in our image, taking from you your language and the signs of your identity.

I am sorry, more than I can say, that in our schools so many were abused physically, sexually, culturally and emotionally.

On behalf of the Anglican Church of Canada, I present our apology.[22]

---

[21] Aboriginal Healing Foundation, *1999 Annual Report*, Ottawa (www.ahf.ca/about-us/annual-reports, accessed August 30 2009) 7.

[22] Anglican Church of Canada's Apology to Native People. A message from the Primate, Archbishop Michael Peers, to the National Native Convocation Minaki, Ontario, Friday, August 6, 1993. www.anglican.ca/rs/apology/apology.htm. Accessed September 15, 2009.

The federal government response was slower to take shape, and less effusive once it did. The accumulation of evidence and activism, and above all the Report of the Royal Commission on Aboriginal Peoples, led in 1998 to the Gathering Strength aboriginal policy reformulation and an accompanying Statement of Reconciliation:

The Government of Canada acknowledges the role it played in the development and administration of these schools. Particularly to those individuals who experienced the tragedy of sexual and physical abuse at residential schools, and who have carried this burden believing that in some way they must be responsible, we wish to emphasize that what you experienced was not your fault and should never have happened. To those of you who suffered this tragedy at residential schools, we are deeply sorry.[23]

This Statement, as many critics were quick to point out, fell short of an apology for the residential schools, but only expressed regret for the most serious harm caused by the schools.

When, on February 15, 2008, Australian Prime Minister Kevin Rudd offered an apology for the Stolen Generations – those aboriginal people who were fostered to non-aboriginal families in a policy of cultural erasure with similar goals of assimilation to those of residential schools – during his inaugural address, the contrast with Canada's response to the residential school legacy was highlighted:

For the pain, suffering and hurt of these Stolen Generations, their descendants and for their families left behind, we say sorry. To the mothers and the fathers, the brothers and the sisters, for the breaking up of families and communities, we say sorry. And for the indignity and degradation thus inflicted on a proud people and a proud culture, we say sorry. We the

[23] Indian and Northern Affairs Canada, "Notes for an Address by the Honourable Jane Stewart, Minister of Indian Affairs and Northern Development, on the occasion of the unveiling of *Gathering Strength – Canada's Aboriginal Action Plan,*" Ottawa, Ontario, January 7, 1998. www.ainc-inac.gc.ca/ai/rqpi/apo/js_spea-eng.asp. Accessed August 30, 2009.

Parliament of Australia respectfully request that this apology be received in the spirit in which it is offered as part of the healing of the nation.[24]

Again, a groundswell of activism, inspired in part by the Rudd apology, combined with the facts of successful litigation and the negotiation of the Indian Residential Schools Settlement Agreement (of which more will be said immediately below) provided the impetus to Canadian Prime Minister Steven Harper's delivery on July 11, 2008 of a Statement of Apology for residential schools, which includes the following:

While some former students have spoken positively about their experiences at residential schools, these stories are far overshadowed by tragic accounts of the emotional, physical and sexual abuse and neglect of helpless children, and their separation from powerless families and communities. The legacy of Indian residential schools has contributed to social problems that continue to exist in many communities today. We now recognize that, in separating children from their families, we undermined the ability of many to adequately parent their own children and sowed the seeds for generations to follow, and we apologize for having done this.[25]

The expectations attached to this apology had been clarified by years of activism. To be accepted by its mass audience, including residential school survivors, the apology had to be delivered by the prime minister in an appropriately dignified setting (it was delivered in parliament). It had to be presented personally and with sincerity ("coming from the heart") to those who represented the aboriginal leadership and those who had experienced a residential school. (The Grand Chief of the Assembly of First Nations, Phil Fontaine, represented both, but other survivors were also in attendance.) Above all it was called upon to be

---

[24] The full text of Australian Prime Minister Kevin Rudd's apology is widely posted on the Internet, including: *Montreal Gazette*, "Rudd's Apology," February 15, 2008, www.canada.com/montrealgazette/story.html?id=d4818512-c8b3-4a14-81df-19b5f0c7a190. Accessed April 20, 2009.

[25] Text of Prime Minister Harper's apology, Wednesday, June 11, 2008, www.fns.bc.ca/pdf/TextofApology.pdf. Accessed April 25, 2009.

specifically directed to the schools and to include candid mention of their broad effects (which it did).

Another expectation is not quite as apparent: in the course of manifesting a sincere expression of regret and a promise of no return to discredited policies, the official apology is expected to reconfigure the past, to construct a binary of perpetrator and victim in which (at least for the immediate formal purposes of establishing contrition) the state alone takes responsibility for harm, and to radically simplify the changing history and the structural conditions behind institutional abuse. The state-sponsored apology, we should keep in mind, is a public act that conveys much more than the heightened emotion of political contrition, and more even than a good-faith portrayal of the nature and extent of officially sanctioned torture and genocide. The public apology usually contains a sub-text concerning the essential nature of victimhood and suffering. In this aspect of the apology we can see the outlines of a powerfully conveyed theory of social suffering. Professional academics, no matter how willing and capable they might be in communicating their ideas to a broad audience, are no match for the kind of attention received by state representatives pronouncing words of contrition.

The Canadian government was also called upon to act in response to the pressures of litigation. The Indian Residential Schools Settlement Agreement, negotiated between the federal government and the Assembly of First Nations, Inuit representatives, lawyers for former residential school students and the Anglican, Presbyterian, United and Catholic Churches, was announced in 2006 and, following court approval, came into effect in September 2007. In essence the Settlement Agreement was forced upon the government by the specter of a mass of successful and costly litigations by former residential school students, which had already begun and was poised to bankrupt the Churches. Litigation added conclusively to evidence of harm by government that had occurred on such a large scale that it effectively called for a human rights remedy.

The federal response to the legacy of residential schools as laid out in the Settlement Agreement began with two processes designed to address individual claims. A Common Experience Payment (CEP) provides a lump sum to former school residents following a simple formula based on the number of years they attended school. But there were those who were subject to abuse more than others, who had strong cause for litigation. The Independent Assessment Process (IAP) was established to deal with the claims of those former students who reported experiencing "sexual and serious physical abuse, as well as other wrongful acts that caused serious psychological consequences to the claimant";[26] in other words, those who might under other circumstances have pursued a successful lawsuit against the government and/or a Church. The IAP became a venue for a kind of non-adversarial, streamlined civil suit adjudicated by an independent panel, with no cross-examination of witnesses, concluding with an assessment of the nature of the abuse and the amount of compensation to be awarded, following similar criteria (based principally on loss of opportunity and income) to those used in civil proceedings.

The Settlement Agreement also calls for a truth and reconciliation commission.[27] Even in its planning stage, the TRC can be seen as part of a global tendency toward identity affirmation through legal venues. This is especially clear from the kinds of activity set in motion by the commission. In August 2009, newly appointed commission chair, Murray Sinclair, emphasized to the media the importance of an array of culturally affirmative activities – such as healing sessions, talking circles and displays of aboriginal art and dance – as some of the ways that

---

[26] Indian and Northern Affairs Canada, "The Adjudication Secretariat," www.irsad-sapi.gc.ca/ab-ap-eng.asp. Accessed August 30, 2009.

[27] The official court notice of the TRC presents it in the context of "Money for programmes for former students and their families for healing, truth, reconciliation, and commemoration of the residential schools and the abuses suffered: $125 million for healing; $60 million to research, document, and preserve the experiences of the survivors; and $20 million for national and community commemorative projects." www.residentialschoolsettlement.ca/summary_notice.pdf. Accessed November 13, 2009.

testimony should be expressed, even before the site of the commission had been decided. "We're not going to be sitting there at a table at the front of a band hall or at the front of a room asking for people to come forward and stand in front of a microphone and tell their story," he told a reporter for the *Globe and Mail*.[28]

As it happened, the first national gathering of the TRC, held in Winnipeg from 16 to 19 July 2010, placed greater emphasis on aboriginal cultural affirmation than anyone seems to have anticipated. In the video-recorded "talking circle," in which a microphone (or "talking stick") was passed clockwise from speaker to speaker, those in the circle or in the audience who emotionally broke down in the midst of the at times harrowing, sorrowful testimony were offered the consoling effects of burning sage, fanned by eagle feathers, and water blessed in a morning ceremony by women from the Three Fires Midewiwin Lodge, an Anishinabe medicine society. Blankets placed in the centre of the circle were used to collect tear-soaked tissues, later (the moderators explained) to be burned in a sacred fire, returned in gratitude to the Creator. The talking circle was surrounded on all sides by other forms of affirmative representation: drumming, pipe and water ceremonies held at sunrise each morning; small venues such as Inuit sewing demonstrations, games, and throat singing; Métis fiddling and sash weaving; a tent cryptically labeled "emotional and cultural supports" (with no one there able to explain the meaning of "cultural supports" aside from the mere presence of a half-dozen elders of various aboriginal origins, the living repositories of collective knowledge and experience); daily sweat lodge ceremonies; and on the last day a pow-wow, followed by a fireworks display, to close the event. The new narrative of indigenous history in Canada is also to be expressed in commemorative projects, including a research center and a proposed exhibit in the Canadian Museum for Human Rights, under construction in Winnipeg. The common denominator of these efforts is tangibility.

[28] B. Curry, "Residential Schools Inquiry to Move West," *The Globe and Mail*, August 27, 2009, A4.

The suffering of those subject to rights abuse is to be made manifest as a reference point for the political emergence of the oppressed and, more implicitly, for a state identity that situates injustice in the past.

Unlike the formative Truth and Reconciliation Commission in South Africa, which called upon perpetrators of violence to appear, testify and express contrition, those responsible for violence in residential schools are not the focus of Canada's TRC. The few surviving priests and nuns responsible for abuse in the schools are advanced in age, mostly in their eighties or nineties, and are not being actively prosecuted or required to testify to the Commission. This means that instead of focusing on narratives of wrongdoing and contrition, there will be an emphasis in the TRC on aboriginal testimony and activity directed toward the inscription of memory, self-revelation and re-dignification.

In response to a question about the possible value of such efforts toward truth and reconciliation, an Oblate priest drew upon his experience in a reserve in which there was a confirmed history of sexual abuse from a fellow priest:

[V]ery indirectly, I heard rumors, rumors, rumors that something was wrong and you could sense something, but what exactly, I didn't know. Until the day that the RCMP made an official investigation and charges were laid … Then the trial took place and went on and on and the priest ended up pleading guilty to a certain number of charges and was remanded for sentencing. And when the time came for sentencing a woman came to me and said, "I was the only one of the mothers of the victims who attended every part of the trial. And tomorrow I'm going to be at the sentencing." I asked her what was so important for her in all that, why did she have to go to every part of the trial? And she told me that it was not out of a spirit of revenge, but for her it was very important that the truth be known, that justice be served, and that the individual face the consequences of his actions … The next day, on my way to the corner grocery, someone called to me – he was drinking – and he said "tomorrow there's a priest who's going to be sentenced and we're happy. And it's only a question of time before the same thing happens to all of them." And the same day, at another part of the village, I was shouted at pretty much the same way … [Then] the trial was over. In the days that followed I went back to the grocery store and someone I knew to be one of the victims called to me: "Hey J, Hi! How's it going?" I said hello but was very surprised at the warmth of the greeting. While taking a walk in the reserve, I came to a place where there was another person I knew well and who I knew was among the victims and he shouted, "Hey, J, How's it going? What ya doin'?" And I was again very surprised to be greeted so warmly while we were right in the midst of the sentencing. Two or three days later [the mother of some of the victims] came to see me. And she said, "I went to the sentencing. It wasn't easy. Before the opening of the session we were all in a waiting room and someone said 'X is going to jail and we're happy, and the other priests are going to go to jail and we're happy'." And she said, "It's not true. He's going to prison because he did something wrong and its just." ... And I'm absolutely certain that the change of attitude was because of what this woman said, because she gave them a chance to reconsider and to be aware of the differences between people and situations. To get away from generalizations ... She had three children who had been abused by this priest and two of them committed suicide.[29]

[29] "Il y a eu un prêtre qui m'a précédé, et éventuellement a été condamné pour des abus sexuels envers des garçons sur la réserve. Il n'a jamais été dans les pensionnats, mais il a ... abusé des enfants. Et c'est moi qui l'ai remplacé. Quand je l'ai remplacé, j'ai été un an dans la communauté, et c'était certainement un tabou absolu, car je n'ai jamais entendu parler de rien, avec aucune allusion avec rien ... Après trois ans ... un Oblat s'est rendu disponible pour venir travailler en milieu amérindien, et ... on lui a confié cette communauté-slà ... Et lui, au bout de la deuxième année, s'était fait apostrophé par une famille, il faisait le tour des familles, par une famille, comme quoi c'était terrible qu'un prêtre aille dans cette maison alors que des enfants avaient été abusés. Et cela a été la première fois qu'on a eu un écho direct de cette réalité-là, et c'était possible qu'il y avait une prise de conscience communautaire et que le tabou était en train d'être brisé. Après cela, de façon très indirecte, j'ai des ouïes dire, des ouïes dire, des ouïes dire qu'il y avait quelques anomalies et on sentait qu'il y avait quelque chose, mais quoi exactement on ne le savait pas. Jusqu'au jour où la GRC a fait une enquête officielle et les accusations officielles ont été posées. Et à partir du moment où les accusations officielles ont été posées, le confrère qui était là a vécu pendant quelques années beaucoup, beaucoup, beaucoup d'hostilité. Parce que le tabou étant brisé, on pouvait manifester ce qui était secret, et il a été l'objet d'hostilité de la part de plusieurs personnes. D'autres personnes ont conservé quand même une très, très, très bonne relation avec lui, mais on sentait dans le village une certaine animosité ... Au bout de 6 ans, moi je suis revenu prendre charge de la pastorale de cette communauté-là ... [A]u moment où ce que le procès s'est déroulé et remis, repris, remis, repris, le prêtre en question a fini par plaider coupable sur un certain nombre de chefs d'accusation et cela a été remis pour le prononcé de la sentence à une date ultérieure. Quand est venu le temps du prononcé de la

In the context of a discussion about truth and reconciliation, this narrative makes the point that criminal prosecution alone is inadequate when it comes to overcoming the legacy of collective harm, that healing takes place through efforts to understand – above all to personalize – the wrong in a struggle against categorical hate.

For the victims, the processes of truth-searching and self-revelation in the aftermath of violence are not without risk, as is evident in the prominent display of the number of a twenty-four-hour crisis line on the federal government's website for the Independent Assessment Process, together

sentence, une dame vient me voir et me dit: 'je suis la seule des mères des victimes à avoir assisté à toutes les étapes du procès. Et demain, je vais aller pour le prononcé de la sentence'. Et je lui ai fait dire qu'est-ce que pour elle était important là-dedans, qu'est-ce qui avait été important pour elle d'aller à toutes les étapes du procès. Elle me disait qu'elle n'avait pas d'esprit de vengeance, mais que pour elle c'était très important que la vérité soit établie, que la justice puisse se prononcer, que l'individu puisse vivre les conséquences de ses actes … La veille, en allant au dépanneur, quelqu'un m'a apostrophé, la personne était un peu en boisson, elle me dit: 'Demain, il y a un prêtre qui va être condamné, puis on est bien contents. Puis c'est seulement une question de temps pour que tous les prêtres subissent le même sort'. Et la journée même, à un autre endroit, je me fais apostropher à peu près de la même façon. Alors je me suis dit, avec le prononcé de la sentence, l'agressivité va être à son paroxysme pendant quelques semaines. Le procès a lieu. Dans les journées qui suivent, je retourne au dépanneur, quelqu'un que je sais pertinemment associé aux victimes m'interpelle: 'Hey, J., salut! Comment ça va?' Je réponds au salut, mais je suis quand même très surpris d'une salutation aussi chaleureuse. En prenant une marche sur la réserve, j'arrive à un autre endroit, et une personne que je connais bien et que je sais aussi reliée intimement aux victimes et me lance un cri: 'Hey, Jacques, comment ça va? Qu'est-ce que tu fais?' Et je suis encore une fois très surpris d'être salué de façon si chaleureuse alors qu'on est dans le contexte immédiat de la condamnation de l'individu au pénitencier. Et deux ou trois jours après, la dame en question revient me voir. Et elle me dit: 'Je suis allée au prononcé de la sentence. C'est pas facile. Avant l'ouverture de l'audience, on était tous dans une salle commune et quelques uns ont dit X va être condamné, puis on est bien contents, puis les autres prêtres aussi vont être condamnés pis on est bien contents'. Puis elle a dit: 'J'ai dit, ça c'est pas vrai. Celui qui va être condamné, c'est parce qu'il a fait des choses, et c'est juste.' … Et moi je suis absolument certain que le changement d'attitude était dû au témoignage que cette dame avait donné, parce qu'elle leur avait permis de faire une prise de conscience dans la différentiation des personnes et dans la différentiation des situations. Sortir des généralisations … Elle avait eu trois enfants qui avaient été abusés par ce prêtre-là, dont deux s'étaient suicidés." My translation. Interview by Marie-Pierre Gadoua, Montreal, August 12, 2009.

with the warning: "Important. This web site deals with subject matter that may cause some readers to trigger (suffer trauma caused by remembering or reliving past abuse). The Government of Canada recognizes the need for safety measures to minimize the risk associated with triggering."[30] Raising awareness of the distinct circumstances of an oppressed minority or distinct people is one thing, but promoting healing through venues of public testimony is something else altogether. If the individual therapeutic process of recovery from trauma can be vexed, durable and even fraught with personal danger, how much more complicated must be the process of public disclosure, commonly understood by the hackneyed expressions, "raising buried memories" and "opening old wounds"? What might be the consequences that follow from public expressions of deep psychological pain resulting from widely shared traumatic experience, perpetrated by those who belong to an identifiable category of people?

Such concerns are ultimately related to wider considerations of the pathways of identity construction in the context of public self-representation. The problem here is not limited to the reinforcement of negative stereotypes of Indian insobriety and self-destruction; it also applies more broadly to the cultivation of distant sympathy toward those who are seen to suffer. Luc Boltanski's *Distant Suffering* makes the important observation that the politics of pity readily creates exemplary models of sufferers, going beyond the focus on a single unfortunate or a particular situation to somehow capture a common plurality, "to constitute a kind of procession or imaginary *demonstration* of unfortunates brought together on the basis of both their singularity and what they have in common."[31] Paul Antze and Michael Lambek argue along similar lines, pointing to the connections between memory and identity politics and to the tendency

---

[30] Indian Residential Schools Secretariat, www.irsad-sapi.gc.ca/index-eng.asp. Accessed August 31, 2009.
[31] L. Boltanski, *Distant Suffering: Morality, Media and Politics* (Cambridge University Press, 1999) 12.

for memories of violent acts against individuals to become "emblems of a victimized identity." [32] Media images that depict victimization from warfare, forced removal and the imposition of starvation have a tendency to remain long past an immediate crisis, to publicly define the essence of a people. Not only prejudice but compassion too thrives on a tendency to generalize, to implicitly extend the feelings provoked by a single compelling instance to a wider category – a people, a nation, a gender or a race.

Revolt of the accused

We have seen that for those narrating their experiences of state-sponsored abuse, the truth and reconciliation commission sets in motion a dynamic tension between the symbols of assertive identity and the essentialisms of victimhood; but toward those seen to be the perpetrators of abuse there is less room for nuance or ambiguity. Their place is to publicly represent a counterpoint to the awakening of a people by embodying the forces of suffering and repression. The public testimony and media coverage leading up to and through the process of truth and reconciliation commissions encourage a simplified dualism of victim and perpetrator. The prescribed, narrative nature of human rights remedy is such that the contest between those who recount memories of suffering and those who, by the nature of their social membership, stand accused of perpetrating abuse, is ultimately one-sided.

It is in the nature of public perceptions of institutional violence that the complex history of the relationships implicated in violence will be simplified in a way that emphasizes the starkest injustice, the most brutal sadism, and the most poignant suffering. Pascal Bruckner makes this point succinctly when he writes, "we manifestly prefer the aesthetic of crime to the ethic of compromise." [33] Even though the

---

[32] P. Antze and M. Lambek (eds.), *Tense Past: Cultural Essays in Trauma and Memory* (New York: Routledge, 1996) vii.

[33] "Nous préférons manifestement l'esthétique du crime à l'éthique du compromis." My translation. P. Bruckner, *La tyrannie de la pénitence: essai sur le masochisme occidental* (Paris: Bernard Grasset, 2006) 95.

TRC may wish to achieve balance by giving voice to "positive" stories, the ultimate, cumulative effect of testimony is inevitably one in which the worst abuses become emblematic of the wrongs of states and the deepest torment becomes emblematic of the experience of their victims.

In a series of interviews with priests of the Missionary Oblates of Mary Immaculate, an Order historically responsible for operating fifty of the fifty-eight Catholic Indian residential schools in Canada, I was surprised to find a consistent sense of injustice toward the government-mandated response to the legacy of residential schools, expressed diplomatically by some and with unconcealed disdain by others.[34] The priests seem to be engaged a kind of sterile revolt with no outlet, no one to listen to them sympathetically and write stories about them or lobby in other ways on their behalf. Instead they expressed the idea (though not in these words) that they are all being tarred with the same brush and in the process the contributions of the Order to the welfare of the Indians were being forgotten.

Their common approach to the legacy of residential schools contains little of the contrition that one might expect in response to the narratives of school abuse and the suffering of survivors. For one thing, the priests seemed to share the view that the schools were historically inevitable. In recounting the history of the Oblate missions, such a feeling of inevitability was certainly attributable to those responsible for the establishing residential schools for aboriginal people in the early twentieth century. And who could blame them? "There was simply a changing North, a changing situation with all the influx of immigrants coming in … The Bishops and the priests would say, 'how are they going to live?'" Clearly the way forward was education. And with families living

---

[34] A total of nine interviews with Oblate priests were conducted by me and/or by my Research Assistant Marie-Pierre Gadoua in Montreal, Ottawa, St. Albert, Winnipeg, and Rome. I am grateful to Marie-Pierre Gadoua for making these interviews possible and providing me with comprehensive documentation of the Oblate involvement in residential schools, which served as an important background and supplement to these interviews.

scattered on the land, "the only way was residential schools so that at least they would have a full year of schooling." [35]

Those who earlier in their missionary careers had been assigned responsibility for a school wanted to talk about the positive, such as how "they [the students] developed, they grew, and they liked the place. They enjoyed it. In fact they were sad when we closed it down when I left." [36] Even in recalling a situation in which a nun was applying excessive discipline – implicitly something that in the course of things was almost bound to happen – there is a positive lesson to be learned about the importance of leadership, of early intervention for the welfare of the children:

[T]here was this sister that really didn't fit in. She was heavy handed. And when I tried to talk to her, she couldn't change. So at Christmas ... I brought in a lay person and I made arrangements to have somebody else come in that was more of an educator ... I would tell the sisters, "look, those girls are not happy. Why should they be here, and why are we here, if they're not happy? The least we can do is make them happy while they're learning." But somehow her makeup didn't allow her to work well with the kids. If I hadn't changed her, I could've had a whole bunch of lawsuits on my hands later on. [37]

According to some priests, the unrecognized contribution of the Church extends to its response to the unfolding awareness of abuse in the schools. Bishop Douglas Crosby, who delivered the Oblate apology of 1991 on the occasion of the annual Lac Ste. Anne Pilgrimage north of Edmonton, Alberta (an established event participated in by tens of thousands of piously Catholic aboriginal people), recently expressed disappointment about the press response to the event:

Toward the end of the session, a woman spoke up, "I want to say something," she announced. "I went to residential school." All the cameras turned toward her; all the tape recorders pointed in her direction ... The woman continued, "I want to thank the Oblates for the work they did at the schools." As she explained why she thought the Oblates deserved thanks,

---

[35] Interview in St. Albert, Alberta conducted by R. Niezen, September 10, 2009.
[36] Interview in St. Albert, Alberta conducted by R. Niezen, September 10, 2009.
[37] Interview in St. Albert, Alberta conducted by R. Niezen, September 10, 2009.

the cameras were turned off, the microphones put away … It was not the story the media wanted to cover then – or now.[38]

The Independent Assessment Process was a source of particular disappointment for one Oblate priest, who, in preparing the Church responses to accusations mediated by the IAP, found that the government had not thoroughly checked the backgrounds to claims, that former students had made accusations against priests or nuns who had not been assigned to the school in which alleged incidents took place, or alleged that incidents occurred at a time when, according to Church records, the school had not yet been opened or even not yet constructed. The IAP, he said, has "proven to be a contemptible process, in which the former residential school students arrive with an absolute presumption of credibility and the priests and nuns with a no less absolute presumption of guilt."[39] In a written invective against the Independent Assessment Process, he makes the argument (with key words set in bold font to follow the IAP [Independent Assessment Process] acronym) that, under this government-mandated judicial process, former residential school students know they can:

Increase the	Amount by	Piling up
Invented	Atrocities	Preferably
Including	Anal	Penetration …
Shame on Canada for having		
Implemented this	Aberrant	Pastiche of Justice
which leaves		
Innocent people	"Alleged	Perpetrators."[40]

[38] Bishop Douglas Crosby, OMI, "A Reflection on the Oblate Apology," unpublished presentation to St. Joseph's Parish, Ottawa, March 19, 2009.

[39] "s'est avéré un processus ignoble, où les anciens pensionnaires arrivaient là avec une absolue présomption de crédibilité, et les religieux et les religieuses avec une non moins absolue présomption de culpabilité." My translation. Interview with Father Jacques L'Heureux conducted by Ronald Niezen and Marie-Pierre Gadoua, Ottawa, August 14, 2009.

[40] Jacques L'Heureux, "IAP (Independent Assessment Process)," unpublished document, October 14, 2007, 1.

He made no effort to conceal his sense of betrayal by the Canadian government in its approach to compensation: "In time of war people pimping their mother or sister to prostitution for a bite or a cigarette were called 'crosseurs' in plain French. Canada is doing exactly that to their former [Church] partners in order to obtain a release from former Indian Schools' residents." [41]

The inherent nature of human rights remedy accounts for the priests' reaction to the provisions of the *Settlement Agreement*. Theirs is a reaction against a legal process in which the key findings and judgments have been mostly made at the beginning, in which they are, individually and as a religious order, given little opportunity to be heard, to contribute to the reconstruction of state history and national identity. In their revolt against judgment before process, the priests have tended to resist the common trajectories of testimony, emphasizing instead the mistruths, manipulations and public misconceptions that resulted from the various state-sponsored proceedings.

Given their loyalty to a brotherhood that is the foundation of their lives, there was only so far that the priests were willing to go in terms of enduring the pain of collective self-examination. Although some acknowledged the Church's well-intentioned errors in the manner of educating native students, none were prepared to acknowledge the stark contradiction between the values that stimulated assimilation efforts – ideals of a global community of peace, brotherhood and sisterhood, love, learning, progress – and the approaches commonly used to hasten these ideals – intolerance, institutional regimentation and brutality. Although the Oblates represent only one of the Church organizations formerly responsible for residential schools, the responses of the priests to the remedies set in motion by the government of Canada indicate that there is a long way to go before the encounter between dissonant identities and histories produces anything like a consistent narrative of the residential school

[41] L'Heureux, "IAP (Independent Assessment Process)," 2.

experience, not to mention reconciliation between those commonly collectively identified as perpetrators and those seen as their victims.

The social construction of penitence

The ultimate compulsion behind soft power is its influence on the powerful in their efforts to maintain control of the authority and apparatuses of the state. Responding to this compulsion, states are able to (re) define themselves and come into prominence as moral actors through the mechanisms intended to overcome their tendencies to harm or destroy their own citizens. The openness to the reformulation of history that has become a central part of the global pattern of response to the most significant human rights violations is an opportunity for both states and for the collective subjects of state-sanctioned oppression to be re-imagined and to re-imagine themselves.

The literature on human rights remedy acknowledges this construction of state identity, but sees it taking different forms and assigns widely varying values to it. To Pascal Bruckner, the sole possible outcome of the reconfigurations of penitence is debasement, in which our sorrow alone sets us apart and "enthrones us in the new aristocracy of reprobates." [42] Those who advocate for the legitimacy of human rights, naturally enough, see things differently. Rudi Teitel, with a focus on the criminal mechanisms of transitional justice, makes a point that applies more broadly to rights remedies:

investigation into wrongdoing by an overthrown authoritarian government is a form of collective public ritual that constructs a shared past. It is a way of defining and setting limits on the history of state-sponsored violence. Through the process of bringing charges and hearing evidence, a successor regime is able to control the direction of historical investigation, to establish the facts of the previous state's transgressions and

[42] Bruckner, *La tyrannie de la pénitence*, 136.

to denounce them in a convincing way that destroys the legitimacy of authoritarian rule.[43]

And for Martha Minnow, there is hope to be found in the basic idea that "public power – through prosecutions, reparations, and commissions of inquiry – can locate the violations on maps of human comprehensibility, deter future violations of human dignity, and ensure that the ambitions of the agents of violence do not succeed." [44]

Largely through the broad legitimacy of the soft power mechanisms of human rights, there is more room than ever before in national and international forums for the kind of civil society that combines the pursuit of justice with the affect and esteem building of social inclusion. R.A. Wilson points out that "truth commissions are transient politico-religious-legal institutions which have much greater symbolic potential than dry, rule-bound, technically obsessive courts of law";[45] and this makes them particularly well suited to the expression of emerging forms of group identity. For many of those who have suffered historical inequities (and their sympathizers), there is a growing commitment to the value and possibility of redress, to the re-conceptualization and re-humanization of the origin myths of the state, to the idea that systemic injustices can and should be corrected to the point at which there is a regular, fair distribution of the benefits of national and international society, above all while promoting local self-determination and cultural autonomy. Considered broadly, state-sponsored efforts toward the elimination of distinct languages and ways of life have led to a globally common counter-movement toward the rediscovery and revitalization of the collective self.

---

[43] R. Teitel, *Transitional Justice* (Oxford University Press, 2000) 49–50.
[44] M. Minnow, "The Hope for Healing: What can Truth Commissions Do?" in *Truth v. Justice: The Morality of Truth Commisions*, ed. R. Rotberg and D. Thompson (Princeton University Press, 2000) 235.
[45] Wilson, "Reconciliation and Revenge in Post-Apartheid South Africa," 80.

SEVEN

Juridification

Legal intensification and substitution

This book has shown that one of the most significant global transformations that we can now see occurring is the development of new forms of legal sociability, expressed above all through identities that coalesce around legal claims and processes. Courts, legislatures and treaties are becoming more significant than ever before as mediators of human belonging, at levels both within and beyond the nation-state. This change goes largely unnoticed because the identity-awakening that accompanies legal process has to do with the discovery of an inner essence, something that is believed to have always been there but has only been waiting for the right conditions to be discovered. And the emergence of something that has always existed might well make for an epiphany and a new confidence in living, but it does not constitute a revolution noticeable by those on the lookout for such things. Or perhaps the revolution is quiet because of the scale of the entities in which it is occurring: marginalized peoples and interest groups, sometimes brought together in common cause, bringing about change through slow accretions, not the possessors of power from which a sudden shift of behavior produces cataclysms or reverberations that find their way into history.

Rights and rights-oriented institutions are more than ever before being used to underwrite assertions of identity and belonging. The

United Nations, with its global recognition and high prestige, has the capacity to bring to life social categories it has itself invented or fundamentally transformed. Social entities can be brought into being through the long-term magical properties of words, expressed through the incantations of public advocacy and lobbying.

One agency in particular, the Human Rights Council (Human Rights Commission), is a source of ideas with wider appeal (though perhaps with less intense conviction) than any universal scriptural faith; and this ideological influence makes it a point of reference for both local aspirations of rights and recognition and for universal ideals of cultural ecumenicalism. As the international movement of indigenous peoples shows most clearly, words chosen by an international institution contain not just a potential for the abuses of ideological power and hegemonic constraint, but also have more positive strategic, constructive (and constructivist) meaning. Liberation with reference to historical injustice and social integrity is often to be found in the conceptual tools of philanthropic legalism, which, with a surprising degree of autonomy, is able to produce new categories in a global repertoire of rights-based identity.

All pathways for securing the defenses of a community through claims of rights considered in this book lead in the direction of juridification, the formalization and uniformization of concepts, categories and defense strategies of social membership and survival. Juridification most commonly refers to the increased concentration and/or extended social reach of rules, norms and procedures based in bureaucratic institutions and legislative enactment. One form of juridification involves *legal intensification*, a widened jurisdiction of legal institutions and increased recourse to formal processes within societies in which law already preponderates in bureaucratic procedure, dispute resolution and governance. This can be distinguished from what I call *legal substitution*, the processes by which formal law is introduced to or becomes dominant in societies or communities that have previously relied more exclusively on informal, customary institutions and procedures.

Until recently, much of the discussion of juridification has occurred in the realm of legal intensification as part of analyses of social change in capitalist society. One of the leading contributions to this topic is Jürgen Habermas' *The Theory of Communicative Action*, which includes an extended analysis of legal reification (*Verrechtlichung*) in capitalist societies. For Habermas, juridification in the modern welfare state has taken two basic forms:

1. an increased recourse to the medium of law, connected to the continuous growth in positive law; and
2. epochal shifts toward juridification characterized by new legal institutions, along with corresponding changes to the "legal consciousness of everyday practice." [1]

An example of such a "juridification wave" might be the construction of the European Union's legal integration, in which a concentration of legislatively or judicially enacted rules have created what some legal scholars have argued is a radical convergence of the norms, rules and institutions of European states. [2]

The sense in which juridification has been taken up in legal anthropology has more to do with an extension of the accessibility, legitimacy and frequency of use of formal legal institutions and procedures in communities or groups that simultaneously have recourse to informal mechanisms of dispute resolution. Without specific reference to the terms "juridification" or "legalism," this is a problem with a long pedigree, constituting an essential aspect of the Great Divide that was long assumed to have separated moderns from pre-moderns. It was, for

---

[1] J. Habermas, *The Theory of Communicative Action*, Vol. II, trans. Thomas McCarthy (Boston: Beacon, 1987) 367.
[2] See P. Legrand, "European Legal Systems are Not Converging," *International and Comparative Law Quarterly*, 1996, 45 (1): 52–81.

example, central to Henry Maine's *Ancient Law*, first published in 1861, which took a broadly comparative approach to the institutional evolution of human societies through the transition in laws, with a focus on the emergence of legal relationships (and hence civilized society) in ancient Rome. Maine's universal legal history is strikingly parallel to the etymological origin of the term "civilization" (see Chapter 5) in that he associates the origin of civil law in ancient society more generally with a universal design of human progress. Civilization, for Maine, meant a replacement of collective legal processes and obligations, marked by moral stagnation and the arbitrary domination of households by the *pater familias*, with an increase in freedom and "civility" through individual, contractual relationships. He famously characterized this transition in one compact sentence: "The movement of the progressive societies has hitherto been a movement *from Status to Contract*."[3] Not coincidentally, this is a movement that has occurred in its purest form but once, in the West (needless to say), with all other societies in some form or other languishing in the thralldom of "status."

Max Weber's account of "disenchantment" (*Entzauberung*) and his parallel analysis of the growing influence of legal rationalism and its operational superiority over social orders based on religious or traditional authority is perhaps the most influential benchmark in the intellectual history of analyses of the phenomenon of juridification.[4] Bruno Latour helps us to situate Weber in relation to Maine when he writes, "It is not only out of arrogance that Westerners think they are radically different from others, it is also out of despair, and by way of self-punishment."[5] In Weber there is none of the confident faith in the

---

[3] H. Maine, *Ancient Law* (London: Dent; New York: Dutton, 1917 [1861]) 100.
[4] See J. Habermas, *The Theory of Communicative Action*, Vol. I, trans. Thomas McCarthy (Boston: Beacon, 1984) for a critical discussion of Weber's account of the legitimacy of rational legal structures.
[5] B. Latour, *We Have Never Been Modern*, trans. Catherine Porter (Cambridge, MA: Harvard University Press, 1993) 114.

trajectory of human history that we find in Maine. The servants of the state, whose domination resides in "legal statute and functional 'competence' based on rationally created *rules*," are agents of a modernity that is technologically superior but fails to provide a necessary sense of life's "meaning."[6] The extended reach of bureaucracy and law, together with scientific rationalism, are responsible for both the increased applied power of knowledge and the spiritual decay associated with disenchantment. Capitalist society is unique in the extent to which it produces technological, managerial mastery of the world, led by agents whom he characterized as "specialists without spirit, sensualists without heart."[7] Disenchantment, according to Weber, "means that principally there are no mysterious incalculable forces that come into play, but rather that one can, in principle, master all things by calculation. This means that the world is disenchanted. One need no longer have recourse to magical means in order to master or implore the spirits, as did the savage, for whom such mysterious forces existed. Technical means and calculations perform the service."[8] And capitalist society is exceptionally capable of dominating other forms of society, which implies (as with Maine) a convergence theory of human history, with structural conditions leading humanity to one basic, bureaucratic/legal/scientific/disenchanted and hence lonely and meaningless form of existence.

This book has shown that, whether optimistic (as with Maine) or pessimistic (as with Weber) in its view of the emerging social order, the simple model of juridification based on an assumption of a universal history of legal substitution and legal intensification is incorrect (or at the very least incomplete) in two principal ways. First, the oft-assumed connection between legalism and individualism through a loosening of

---

[6] M. Weber, *From Max Weber: Essays in Sociology*, ed. Hans Gerth and C. Wright Mills (London: Routledge & Kegan Paul, 1948) 79.

[7] M. Weber, *The Protestant Ethic and the Spirit of Capitalism*, trans. Stephen Kalberg (Los Angeles: Roxbury Publishers, 2002 [1904–5]) 182.

[8] Weber, *From Max Weber*, 139.

local attachments and collective obligations is doubtful. Juridification is not resulting in a loss of identity and dissolution of community boundaries, but on the contrary provides the foundation for their protection and reinforcement. Juridification in this sense focuses attention on the ways that dissident actors are making use of legal engagements with formal organizations and state structures for the promotion of distinct collective rights and identities, even in circumstances of political disillusionment.

Second, an increase in the influence of legal process is not leading us toward a disenchanted world, but is providing a new basis for the expression of radical hope, the virtues of confession and absolution, and belief in (or accommodation of belief in) supernatural agency. The idea of law as based on systematic, orderly, rational principles and procedures is so deeply rooted that it takes a stretch of the imagination to see what is actually before us: courts and legislatures can be venues for the expression spiritual longing; and the institutions of global governance can act as guardians of sacred knowledge, even to the point of sponsoring millenarian expectations. International agencies are responsible not only for a multiplication of laws, but a hankering after a world without them, in which the spiritual knowledge of enlightened ancestors has been restored. The after-image of the world we have lost continues to glow in the very legal processes that Weber associated with disenchantment.

The virtues of the oppressed

Publics yearn not just to care, but to care passionately; yet they tend to be skeptical and reserved in arriving at their judgments and commitments. Because of this tension, the dual claims of injustice and collective virtue are amplified and simplified for popular audiences. Experienced intermediaries between rights claimants and the consumers of rights appeals know the "buttons," the words and images most likely to move and mobilize publics. Message discipline calls for clarity in the depictions of the subjects of rights, particularly depictions of their collective essences and the injustices they face. An appealing claim will usually have a base of suffering and horror, and sometimes also of cultural color and intimacy, sufficient to overcome tendencies toward public complacency and to lend advantage in the competition with rival claims and representations of victimization.

This means that through the public mechanisms of human rights and humanitarian intervention an entirely new process has developed by which law influences the range of human expression. This process of formalization acts not by imposing or extending the reach of official order, but by arranging the priorities of legal protection in accordance with the preferences of popular audiences. The influence of popular will as a source of leverage in bringing about the rights compliance of states means that the arguments and artifices of persuasion have gone far beyond the confines of courts and legislatures, to appeal to and involve abstract mass audiences more intensively and on a wider scale than ever before.

We can see the preferences of publics at work in the priorities of humanitarian intervention, the causes that are selected (or overlooked) as priorities by NGOs and agencies of global governance. There is little predictability to the directions taken by public audiences in the focal points of their attention; but this should not prevent us from making some (of necessity preliminary) observations about their prevalent tendencies and the implications of their choices for the effectiveness of the protections of rights.

The influence of public preferences in rights claims is clearest in the international movement of indigenous peoples. This category of human existence has come to represent in the popular imagination a form of counter-modernity, somehow removed from the ills of rationalism and disenchantment, even as their representatives and helpers make strategic use of legal instruments and venues. The romantic imaginings of international agencies has created space for the formal organization and legal defenses of those who have come to represent pre-modern ways of life. Those who make claims on behalf of indigenous peoples have benefited from a long history of popular ennoblement of those who live in conditions of simplicity and harmony with their environment. Here the qualities that seem to resonate most with popular audiences have to do with the preservation of cultural virtues threatened by the reach of environmentally destructive modernity. There is a utopian dimension to the sources of appeal that give impetus to indigenous rights claims, which hearken to a world of cultural color, intimacy and innocence that can only be recovered by protecting those who remain as its living representatives.

Publics tend to be attracted to appeals that emphasize the innocence and unblemished virtue of the sufferers of injustice. The quintessential intervention-worthy subjects that meet this basic criterion are children, as evidenced by the images of abuse of Palestinian youth by settlers that sparked the indignation of the Israeli public. Whatever the faults of their political community, children are guaranteed by their limited capacities as children to have no part in them. Their indisputed innocence commingles with nurturing sentiments and a vague awareness that they are the living inheritors of the ways the world is made better today.

It is probably easier to identify the causes that have difficulty gaining traction with popular audiences. Consumers of injustice, in exercising moral judgments and prioritizing their commitments, see only what is before them (or presented to them). They have a limited capacity to make historical abstractions or see the structural conditions behind the pathologies of the dispossessed. This has important implications for the informal mechanisms of soft power. A community that is no longer represented as innocent becomes less deserving of sympathy. The structural violence at the origin of their moral failings is often abstract, difficult to depict, not as immediate as testimonies of violence and victimization. The public does not readily see the chain of responsibility leading to structural conditions put in place though the exercise of power, largely because it is excluded from view. There are no mitigating circumstances in public judgments, and certainly not enough cumulative power of indignation to provide leverage for the informal mechanisms of human rights in addressing complex structural conditions of political abuse. Ultimately soft power is corrupted by the fact that the most influential publics want more than anything else to be motivated by distant love – not a form of love that is based on insight and forgiveness, but that, like infatuation, prohibits recognition of fault in the beloved.

Every legal system has its particular form of ineffectiveness, its own structural defects, problems it cannot solve, areas of human experience into which it cannot reach. The central weakness of the human rights system follows from conditions of invisibility to publics. Human rights do not favor camouflage, but lend advantage to displays of difference and the ability to stimulate ideals of the future variety of human experience. Public involvement in the expectations and tastes of social justice therefore mask the long-term consequences of illegitimate domination and political abuse. Distant empathy tends to romantically attribute superior virtue to the oppressed, leaving less room for compassion toward those who are broken in spirit. It calls for oppression to be tangible and accompanied by moral rectitude and cultural virtue. Where these expectations are not or cannot be met, the public gaze tends to focus narrowly, voyeuristically and judgmentally on the pathologies and dysfunctions of the excluded. They become known – and in the feedback loop of identity, know themselves – for their inclinations to self-destruction, addictions, family violence and misdirected hatreds. Those who, following a breach of justice, are unable to capture the fractured attentions of potentially sympathetic, indignant, distant others, are left without remedy. The informal workings of human rights, or soft law more generally, exclude those who don't suffer enough, or in the right way.

More than anything else, a condition of chronic dependency makes a human population invisible to, or rejected by, publics. From the point of view of information consumers, it matters little how that condition came into being, whether through the human removals that make room for mega-project development or the displacements and destruction of war; those who are chronically dependent on private charity, transfer payments from the state or international aid do not suffer in ways that readily provoke sympathy. On the surface, they represent lethargy, depression, addictions and inward-turning violence – all the predictable vices of imposed idleness. Their chronic insecurity and mental torment and the political abuse at the root of their displacement are often historically distant and abstract. Their connections to the cataclysms that created their condition are not immediate, recognizable and correctable.

It would be an over-simplification to infer from this that a kind of evolutionary logic is built into the mechanisms of public mediation in collective rights, as though those with the most colorful plumage of rights and culture will be advantaged in transmitting their form of life to future generations. People do collectively manage, sometimes miraculously, to survive marginal conditions of existence. But in terms of the fulfillment of the universalizing project of human rights, those living in conditions of invisibility represent a fundamental structural shortcoming.

Institutional essentialism

Juridification does not entail a logically and empirically elegant substitution of one form of society with another. Modernity theory often assumes a process of social transformation in which the efficiency and regularity of rule-based organization, and above all its capacity for large-scale, long-term enterprises, would eventually make it the sole basis for social existence, out-competing kin-based or "tribal" organizations;

but the qualities of culture and politics that are most rapidly becoming universalized are the strategies by which people maintain their collective distinctiveness. These include legal defenses of a community, which require clear definition of what that rights-bearing community is and what specific individuals have membership in it. Claims to distinct collective rights call for a clear understanding of a legal boundary that defines those who are to be the beneficiaries of those rights and those who are not. And claims based more particularly on culture call for a selection and identification of the most important features of distinct heritage. The preservation of human cultural heritage as a global project presupposes the pursuit of legal definitions of culture and creation of inventories of the most cherished products of culturally-transmitted ingenuity.

The agencies of global governance are primary producers or gathering places of ideas about human belonging. I have used the term *conceptual diplomacy* to describe the fulcrum for this process in agencies of global governance, but it can be seen at work more broadly in almost any influential agency with a mandate in the promotion of rights. Conceptual diplomacy aims at producing a hidden-in-plain-sight, purloined letter effect, through the creation and promotion of ideas about self and others that are concealed from view through their currency. Such is the nature of legally elaborated social categories, developed in the absence of social formations, and only subsequently translated into social identification, action, claims and popular recognition. Identity choices and priorities can be given shape and substance and acquire followings in categories initially developed in the abstract by experts, and then incrementally become an unquestioned part of the world in which we live, largely through the cumulative powers of public persuasion.

It is easy to see how ideas that originate in bureaucracies can become welded to peoples' aspirations, institutionalized, juridified, and consequently impossible to challenge, rethink and reform with the usual academic processes of intellectual exchange and criticism. The institutions of human governance act on their ambitions, not by imposing a universal social blueprint, not, as some states have been inclined to do, by coordinating policies of assimilation aimed at correcting those awkward ways of life that refuse absorption, but by restricting the range of choice one has to be human, by unintentionally and selectively eliminating awkward forms of nonconformity, and ultimately allowing, even promoting, a paradoxically limited range of cultural practice and of techniques for the defense of difference, ultimately adjusted and expressed to suit popular inclinations.

I have tried to show that this process can occur hegemonically when ideas of social membership, and occasionally even the very categories of belonging widely identified as distinct and rights-bearing, are quite simply brought into being, constructed in a literal sense, not so much by those who are claimants of rights and identities in the first instance, but by groups of experts, usually with no claims of membership in the categories they produce. The management of diversity has become a universal project. World governance initiatives toward collective justice reveal a paradox in which strategies for cultural protection are increasingly reliant upon globally uniform strategies of defense, acted on within a limited repertoire of recognized forms of human existence and cultural expression.

Juridification from below

Given conditions of freedom to form politically oriented nongovernmental organizations, with access to receptive media outlets (now facilitated by the Internet) and to multiple legal forums, people whose grievances correspond with social concepts generated in international institutions are sometimes able to generate headline-worthy rights campaigns. Under these circumstances, international law and bureaucracies, propelled by global popular legitimacy, are able to prioritize causes and define human groups and their corresponding conditions of injustice, around which people are able to identify themselves, articulate their essential qualities and form politically active communities or organizations. Whether strategically oriented or not, such naturalization of categories of identity has become a side-effect of global governance conceptualizations of rights-bearing groups, peoples and cultures. The categories of belonging initiated through creative development and application of social categories in international law and diplomacy have brought about new conditions for the assertion of the rights and integrity of distinct societies. Global conceptions of belonging highlight the distinctiveness and rights of minority peoples who – often supported by transnational networks – take up the most politically useful ethnonyms and legal constructions sponsored by states and global institutions in campaigns of justice. The pursuit of cultural justice involves a process by which the collective victims of political abuse are bracketed off by cultural markers, identified as having a distinct form of spiritual agency and represented to an unknown audience as a people in need of special protection from those who would destroy them – or apology and redress from those who once tried, without complete success.

We are witness therefore to the increasing significance of a form of juridification in which the artifacts and performances of tradition become invested with legal significance. A group of Ainu singing and drumming outside a Tokyo subway station, for example, are not just performing for a public audience but are at the same time making a claim of distinct rights. Their performance is an assertion of cultural virtue and simultaneously an appeal for recognition as a distinct people. Even material artifacts exported to distant consumers of rights and culture – such as the canoe paddled by Crees and Inuits in the canals of Amsterdam – can become infused with legal meaning. The products and performances of traditional knowledge have become inseparable from rights claims, enacted through cultural performance and affirmed by public approval.

Anthropologists have largely overlooked the influence of publics in this kind of transnational exchange, possibly because doing so would involve reflecting on a largely anonymous, unknowable collectivity in a discipline that emphasizes the rich detail of direct social interaction. But there can be no question that public lobbying and pursuit of recognition are associated with social and political processes that add salience to cultural identifications and political boundaries. This is encouraged in part because claimants of collective rights are almost pre-formed lobbying entities, ready for collaboration with transnational NGOs with pre-set identity attachments, communications networks and political objectives. On the receiving end of these efforts, the publics, with their potential for sympathetic indignation, can be seen as major sources of energy that set the soft power of human rights and social justice movements in motion.

To reach the widest possible sympathetic audience, advocates are called upon to strategically depict the reality of oppression, to give, in its crassest form, a *telenovela* version of virtue and oppression. There is no analytical distance that transcends the need for emphasis on the innocence in the oppressed. In human rights campaigning, the complex, often sordid reality of broken societies is either edited out or misrepresented. Even scholars whose professional identity is based on a commitment to truth have commonly become inured to the call for strategic distortion. The perceived need for strategic essentialism has introduced a moral tension to many academic projects: to present and analyze the complexity of what one learns, or to edit and advocate. There are greater rewards inherent in taking sides than in acting on impersonal, abstract, uncertain principles of knowledge production through the discomforts of critical thought. There is understandably a preference for knowledge that is in the short term empowering, resonant with publics and useful in the pursuit of justice, with little thought given to the longer term consequences – for both knowledge and rights – of calculated misrepresentation. The academy, in other words, is implicated in the structural violence inherent in distorted appeals to popular will as an avenue to cultural justice.

The foregoing brings into question the practice, most evident in "activist" anthropology, of attempting to persuade publics with reference to their pre-existing hopes and prejudices. In doing so, one allows oneself to be limited by a persistent assumption of the public's limited capacity for growth, learning and (self-)critical thinking. This means that, rather than pandering to publics, the task of scholarship should be to make the language of rights and representation more nuanced. In the long term, an effective engagement is not one that carefully calibrates the tools of outreach and capitulates to opinion or that salves the academic conscience by presenting misleading, de-contextualized truths in the supposed interest of a greater good. If social change is the common goal of engaged research and the human rights movement, then both should consider informing – even openly challenging – the basic values and ideas held by publics, by those who are, after all, the ultimate sources of both the effectiveness and the paralyzing contradictions of the quest for cultural justice.

Re-enchantment

Contrary to the Weberian model in which juridification and disenchantment occur in tandem, we have seen that *re-enchantment* can be an essential feature of juridification through the claims of culture. Human rights are also influenced by affect; and bureaucracies, particularly those that include participatory public venues, can be places of re-enchantment. If we take at face value the ideas produced by agencies of global governance – especially the awkward style in which these ideas are expressed: in a steady flow of run-of-the-mill, functional bureaucratic language, punctuated by flourishes of hyperbolic pedantry – we would fail to appreciate the actual extent of their influence. Re-enchantment has entered the realm of global governance and can be seen in the guiding values behind the management of diversity.

Legal forums are of course not the only venues for this hopeful futurism. Counter-modernists, such as those advocating on behalf of New Social Movements, whose starting point is one form or another of cultural degenerationism analogous to that of Herder's deistically inspired celebration of early, stateless forms of life, are not well disposed toward processes of juridification. Their ideal is a form of existence that asserts its dignity and survival in a realm that is fundamentally disengaged from legal formalism. Even if particular communities or individuals have fleeting contact with the forums of international agencies, states and nongovernmental organizations, these do not influence the innermost qualities of their being, above all the intimate knowledge of the rhythms of life in the forests, steppes and savannahs, a timeless intergenerational realm of myth, a form of consciousness based in symbolism and metaphor that remains resistant to the formalities and punctualities of modern life. Despite their active connections with ancestral knowledge, such communities are not unchanging, not unaffected by processes of communication and interconnection. This is precisely where they are seen to have an emerging source of strength. The injustice of states cannot be counteracted through the state's judiciaries; and capitalism cannot be resisted through its markets. Hope for the future is not to be found in the substitution of peoples' authentic nature with futile, difference-eroding struggles in conditions determined by their oppressors. That is to say, the master's tools are *not* the best way to bring down the master's house; better to avoid their corrupting power by using one's own. Hope is to be found in new forms of collaboration, beyond the reach of the powerful, outside the corrosive formalities of law, in the combined forces of the many who share those basic forms of knowledge and attachments to heritage that, over the long term, can produce a spiritual-political awakening that will change the world.

I have tried to show that, through the public dynamics of rights claims, the same kind of hope can be expressed *within* legal institutions, not necessarily through disengagement from them. The UN meeting room, as a permissive space that connects with a global network of sympathetic actors, is thus a site for the expression of the most cherished opinions, not limited to the expression of rights claims and grievances, but extending to cosmologies of world-renewal. The "divine spark" foundations of human rights have created a space for the expression of spiritual identity. Such expression can also be found in truth and reconciliation commissions, in the encounter (direct or indirect) between survivors – the once-powerless given voice – and those who stand in for the moral wrong of states – the perpetrators or agents of harm by a past, illegitimate regime. Those individuals and peoples who are the subjects and claimants of rights do not maintain an exclusive focus on the practical contests of law, politics and development, but often express ideas and sentiments that are more elemental, that have to do with the spiritual cultivation of humanity and, through reform of the cosmological foundations of human relations, usher in a long awaited era of global peace.

One pathway to the recovery of traditional knowledge and values, which complicates the often taken-for-granted connection between juridification and disenchantment, is centered in institutions normally associated with instrumental reason, the state-centrism of international law, and the promulgation of a legally inscribed global society. The institutions of global governance are not just orderly mechanisms acting on the powers of reason and science. The global management of culture reveals that bureaucracies can also be places of re-enchantment and extravagant hope, of nostalgic longing and memories seeking security.

Publics are not just moved into action by ideas about justice. As interpreted by publics, rights claims must carry with them demonstrable implications for collective suffering, possibilities for human improvement, and identifiable forms of testimonial expression. There is a process of juridification at work here, in which legal agencies themselves become the producers and promoters of significant categories of belonging, and in which rights claimants subsequently create community, formulate history and invest pride – all through the mirror and moral persuasion of public visibility.

References

Aboriginal Healing Foundation. 1999. *1999 Annual Report*. Ottawa, www.ahf.ca/about-us/annual-reports. Accessed August 30, 2009.

Abu-Nimer, Mohammed. 1999. *Dialogue, Conflict Resolution and Change: Arab-Jewish Encounters in Israel*. Albany: SUNY Press.

Allen, Lori. 2009. "Martyr Bodies in the Media: Human Rights, Aesthetics, and the Politics of Immediation in the Palestinian Intifada," *American Ethnologist*, 36 (1): 161–80.

Amselle, Jean-Loup. 1998. *Mestizo Logics: Anthropology of Identity in Africa and Elsewhere*. Stanford University Press.

   1999 "Ethnie et espaces: pour une anthropologie topologique," in *Au coeur de l'ethnie: Ethnie, tribalisme et État en Afrique*, ed. J.-L. Amselle and Elikia M'Bokolo. Paris: La Découverte, 11–48.

Anaya, James. 2004. *Indigenous Peoples in International Law*, second edn. Oxford University Press.

Antze, Paul and Michael Lambek (eds.) 1996. *Tense Past: Cultural Essays in Trauma and Memory*. New York: Routledge.

Baker, Keith Michael. 1990. *Inventing the French Revolution*. Cambridge University Press.

Barsh, Russel. 1999. "Putting the Tribe in Tribal Courts: Possible? Desirable?" *Kansas Journal of Law and Public Policy*, 8: 74–97.

Barth, Fredrik. 1969. *Ethnic Groups and Boundaries: The Social Organization of Culture Difference*. Bergen/Oslo: Universitetsforlaget; London: George Allen & Uwin.

Blelloch, David H. 1941. "The International Labour Organisation and the Indigenous Workers of the Americas," *Revista América Indígen*, 1 (1): 35–7.

Bloch, Marc. 1993 [1949]. *Apologie pour l'histoire ou métier d'historien*. Paris: Armand Colin.

References

Boltanski, Luc. 1999. *Distant Suffering: Morality, Media and Politics*. Cambridge University Press.

Bosum, Abel. 1994. "The Human Rights of Indigenous Peoples at the United Nations," Workshop on Indigenous Peoples' Rights, The John F. Kennedy Library, Dorchester, MA, December 10.

Bourdieu, Pierre. 1998. *Acts of Resistance: Against the Tyranny of the Market*. New York: The New Press.

Brasfield, C. 2001. "Residential School Syndrome," *B.C. Medical Journal*, 43 (2): 57–112.

Braudel, Fernand. 1993. *A History of Civilizations*, trans. Richard Mayne. New York: Penguin.

Bruckner, Pascal. 2006. *La tyrannie de la pénitence: essai sur le masochisme occidental*. Paris: Bernard Grasset.

Brundtland, Gro Harlem. 1999. "International Consultation on the Health of Indigenous Peoples." Geneva: World Health Organization. Unpublished document, www.who.int/director-general/speeches/1999/english/19991123_indigenous_people.html. Accessed July 2, 2010.

Canada, Royal Commission on Aboriginal Peoples. 1996. *People to People, Nation to Nation: Highlights from the Report of the Royal Commission on Aboriginal Peoples*. Ottawa: Minister of Supply and Services Canada, www.ainc-inac.gc.ca/ap/pubs/rpt/rpt-eng.asp. Accessed November 13, 2009.

Clifford, James. 1988. "Identity in Mashpee," in *The Predicament of Culture: Twentieth-Century Ethnography, Literature, and Art*, ed. James Clifford. Cambridge, MA: Harvard University Press, 277–346.

Cohen, Alex. 1999. "The Mental Health of Indigenous Peoples: An International Overview." Geneva: Department of Mental Health, World Health Organization.

Curry, B. 2009. "Residential Schools Inquiry to Move West," *The Globe and Mail*, August 27, A4.

Daes, Erica-Irene. 1996. "Working Paper by the Chairperson-Rapporteur, Mrs. Erica-Irene A. Daes, on the Concept of 'Indigenous People.' United Nations Economic and Social Council, Commission on Human Rights. UN doc no. E/CN.5/Sub.2/AC.4/1996/2.

2001. "Striving for Self-determination for Indigenous Peoples," in *In Pursuit of the Right to Self-Determination: Collected Papers and Proceedings of the First International Conference on the Right to Self-Determination and the United Nations, Geneva 2000*, ed. Y.N. Kly and D. Kly. Atlanta: Clarity, 50–1.

Danilevsky, Nicolai. 1969 [1869]. "The Slav Role in World Civilization," in *Readings in Russian Civilization. Volume II: Imperial Russia, 1700–1917*, second edn, ed. Thomas Riha. University of Chicago Press, 383–9.

Dennis, Anthony J. (ed.) 2001. *Letters to Khatami: A Reply to the Iranian President's Call for a Dialogue among Civilizations*. Bristol, IN: Wyndham Hall.

References

Douglas, Mary. 2002. *Purity and Danger: An Analysis of the Concepts of Pollution and Taboo*. London: Routledge.

Eagleburger, Lawrence. 1998. "Foreword," in *The Psychology of Peacekeeping*, ed. H.J. Langholtz. Westport: Praeger, vii–ix.

Ehl, Sibylle. 1995. "Ein Afrikaner erobert die Mainmetropole. Leo Frobenius in Frankfurt (1924–1938)," in *Lebenslust und Fremdenfurcht: Ethnologie im Dritten Reich*, ed. Thomas Hauschild. Frankfurt am main: Suhrkamp, 121–40.

Ellinor, Linda and Glenna Gerard. 1998. *Dialogue: Rediscovering the Transforming Power of Conversation*. New York: John Wiley & Sons.

Espiell, H. Gros. 1980. *The Right to Self-Determination*, UN doc. E/CN.4Sub.2/405/Rev.1.U.N. Sales No. E.79.XIV.5.

Foucault, Michel. 1995. *Discipline and Punish: The Birth of the Prison*, trans. Alan Sheridan. New York: Vintage.

Foucault, Michel. 2000. *Power*, ed. James Faubion. New York: The New Press.

Frobenius, Leo. 1925. *Erlebte Erdteile: Ergebnisse eines Deutschen Forscherlebens*. Vol. I. Frankfurt am main: Frankfurter Societäts-Druckerei.

1993 [1933]. *Kulturgeschichte Afrikas: Prolegomena zu einer historischen Gestaltlehre*. Wuppertal: Peter Hammer Verlag and Frankfurt: Frobenius–Institut.

García Linera, Álvaro, Marxa Chávez Léon and Patricia Costas Monje. 2008. *Sociología de los movimientos sociales en Bolivia: Estructuras de movilización, repertorios culturales y acción política*. La Paz: Plural.

Gellner, Ernest. 1992. *Postmodernism, Reason and Religion*. London and New York: Routledge.

Gibney, Matthew. 2004. *The Ethics and Politics of Asylum: Liberal Democracy and the Response to Refugees*. Cambridge University Press.

Giddens, Anthony. 1990. *The Consequences of Modernity*. Stanford University Press.

Goffman, Erving. 2007. *Asylums: Essays on the Social Situation of Mental Patients and Other Inmates*. Piscataway: Aldine Transaction.

Habermas, Jürgen. 1984. *The Theory of Communicative Action*, Vol. I, trans. Thomas McCarthy. Boston: Beacon.

1987. *The Theory of Communicative Action*, Vol. II, trans. Thomas McCarthy. Boston: Beacon.

1991 [1962]. *The Structural Transformation of the Public Sphere: An Inquiry into a Category of Bourgeois Society*. Trans. Thomas Burger with the assistance of Frederick Lawrence. Cambridge, MA: The MIT Press.

Harten, Hans-Christian. 2004. "Utopie," in *Historisches Wörterbuch der Pädagogik*, ed. Dietrich Brenner and Jürgen Oelkers. Weinheim and Basel: Beltz.

Harvey, David. 2000. *Spaces of Hope*. Berkeley: University of California Press.

Hathaway, Oona. 2002. "Do Human Rights Treaties Make a Difference?" *Yale Law Journal*, 111 (8): 1935–2042.

References

Hayner, Priscilla. 2001. *Unspeakable Truths: Confronting State Terror and Atrocity.* New York: Routledge.

Heinrichs, Hans-Jürgen. 1998. *Die fremde Welt, das bin ich: Leo Frobenius: Ethnologe, Forschungsreisender, Abenteurer.* Wuppertal: Peter Hammer Verlag.

Helton, Arthur. 2002. *The Price of Indifference: Refugees and Humanitarian Action in the New Century.* Oxford University Press.

Herman, Edward and Noam Chomsky. 2002. *Manufacturing Consent: The Political Economy of Mass Media.* New York: Pantheon.

Hewstone, Miles and Rupert Brown (eds.). 1986. *Contact and Conflict in Intergroup Encounters.* Oxford and New York: Blackwell.

Hodgson, Dorothy. 2002. "Precarious Alliances: the Cultural Politics and Structural Predicaments of the Indigenous Rights Movements in Tanzania," *American Anthropologist,* 104 (4): 1086–97.

Huntington, Samuel P. 1993. "The Clash of Civilizations?" *Foreign Affairs,* Summer, 22–49.

   1996. *The Clash of Civilizations and the Remaking of World Order.* New York: Simon & Schuster.

International Fund for Agricultural Development. 2004. "International Day of the World's Indigenous People." www.ifad.org/media/events/2004/ip.htm. Accessed September 13, 2007.

Karlström, Mikael. 1999 "Civil Society and its Presuppositions: Lessons from Uganda," in *Civil Society and the Political Imagination in Africa: Critical Perspectives,* ed. J.L. Comaroff and J. Comaroff. University of Chicago Press.

Kelly, Fred. 2008. "Confessions of a Born Again Pagan," in *From Truth to Reconciliation: Transforming the Legacy of Residential Schools,* ed. Marlene Brant Castellano, Linda Archibald and Mike DeGagné. Ottawa: Aboriginal Healing Foundation, 11–41.

Khatami, Mohammad. 1998. *Islam, Liberty and Development.* Binghamton: Global Academic Publishing.

   2006. "Dialogue Among Civilizations: A Necessity for Living in Peace and Non-Violence, Bridging the Development Gap among Nations, and Building a Global Citizenship." U. Thant Distinguished Lecture, United Nations University, Tokyo, August 25. www.unu.edu/uthant_lectures/index.htm. Accessed November 19, 2007.

Kunhardt, Philip B. Jr, Philip B. Kunhardt III and Peter W. Kunhardt. 1995. *P. T. Barnum: America's Greatest Showman.* New York: Alfred A. Knopf.

Kymlicka, Will. 2007. *Multicultural Odysseys: Navigating the New International Politics of Diversity.* Oxford University Press.

Latour, Bruno. 1993. *We Have Never Been Modern*, trans. Catherine Porter. Cambridge, MA: Harvard University Press.

Legrand, Pierre. 1996. "European Legal Systems are Not Converging," *International and Comparative Law Quarterly*, 45 (1): 52–81.

Lemkin, Raphaël. 1933. "Les actes constituant un danger général (interétatique) considérés comme délits du droit des gens." www.preventgenocide.org/fr/ lemkin/madrid1933.htm. Accessed October 16, 2009.

    2008 [1944]. *Axis Rule in Occupied Europe: Laws of Occupation, Analysis of Government, Proposals for Redress*, second edn. Clark: The Lawbook Exchange.

Lévi-Strauss, Claude. 1966. *The Savage Mind*. London: Weidenfeld and Nicolson; and University of Chicago Press.

Maine, Henry. 1917 [1861]. *Ancient Law*. London: Dent; New York: Dutton.

Malinowski, Bronislaw. 1984 [1922]. *Argonauts of the Western Pacific*. Prospect Heights: Waveland.

Maresch, Rudolf and Florian Rötzer (eds.). 2004. *Renaissance der Utopie: Zukunftsfiguren des 21. Jahrhunderts*. Frankfurt am main: Suhrkamp.

Maritain, Jacques. 1943. *The Rights of Man and Natural Law*. New York: Charles Scribner's Sons.

Marrus, Michael. 2002. *The Unwanted: European Refugees from the First World War Through the Cold War*. Philadelphia: Temple University Press.

Martínez Cobo, José. 1986. *Study of the Problem of Discrimination against Indigenous Populations*, Vol. V. UN doc. E/CN.4/Sub.2/1986/7/Add.4.

McKinley, James C. 1996. "At a Ceremony in Kenya, A Harsh Rite of Passage for a Brother and Sister." *New York Times*, October 5. http://query.nytimes.com/ gst/fullpage.html?res=9E00EEDB103FF936A35753C1A960958260&sec=healt h&spon=&pagewanted=all. Accessed August 22, 2008.

Merry, Sally Engle. 2006. *Human Rights and Gender Violence: Translating International Law into Local Justice*. University of Chicago Press.

Minnow, Martha. 2000. "The Hope for Healing: What can Truth Commissions Do?" in *Truth v. Justice: The Morality of Truth Commisions*, ed. R. Rotberg and D. Thompson. Princeton University Press, 235–60.

Morgan, Lewis Henry. 1962 [1851]. *League of the Iroquois*. Secaucus: Citadel.

Muteshi, Jacinta. 2009. "Women's Advocacy: Engendering and Reconstituting the Kenyan State," in *Human Rights NGOs in East Africa: Political and Normative Tensions*, ed. Makau Mutua. Philadelphia: University of Pennsylvania Press.

Niezen, Ronald. 1993. "Power and Dignity: The Social Consequences of Hydro-Electric Development for the James Bay Cree," *Canadian Review of Sociology and Anthropology*, 30 (4): 510–29.

References

2000. *Spirit Wars: Native North American Religions in the Age of Nation Building.* Berkeley and Los Angeles: University of California Press.

2003. *The Origins of Indigenism: Human Rights and the Politics of Identity.* Berkeley and Los Angeles: University of California Press.

2004. *A World Beyond Difference: Cultural Identity in the Age of Globalization.* Oxford and Malden: Blackwell.

2008. "Postcolonialism and the Utopian Imagination," in *Postcolonial Theory and the Arab-Israeli Conflict,* ed. Philip Salzman and Donna Robinson. New York: Routledge.

2009a. *Defending the Land: Sovereignty and Forest Life in James Bay Cree Society,* second edn. Upper Saddle River: Prentice Hall.

2009b. *The Rediscovered Self: Indigenous Identity and Cultural Justice.* Montreal and Kingston: McGill-Queen's University Press.

2009c. "The Aufklärung's Human Discipline: Comparative Anthropology according to Kant, Herder and Wilhelm von Humboldt," *Intellectual History Review,* 19 (2): 177–95.

2009d. "Self-Destruction as a Way of Belonging: Understanding Cluster Suicides among Aboriginal Youth in Canada," in *Healing Traditions: The Mental Health of Aboriginal Peoples,* ed. Lawrence Kirmayer and Gail Valaskakis. Vancouver: University of British Columbia Press.

Nye, Joseph. 2007. *Understanding International Conflicts: An Introduction to Theory and History,* sixth edn. New York: Pearson/Longman.

Oblate Fathers in Canada. 1958. "Residential Education for Indian Acculturation, Workshop I: General Principles." Ottawa: Deschâtelets Residence library, doc. no. 8D1/21.

Oelschlaeger, Max. 1991. *The Idea of Wilderness: From Prehistory to the Age of Ecology.* New Haven and London: Yale University Press.

Parker, Karen. 2001. "Understanding Self-determination: The Basics," in *In Pursuit of the Right to Self-Determination: Collected Papers and Proceedings of the First International Conference on the Right to Self-Determination and the United Nations, Geneva 2000,* ed. Y.N. Kly and D. Kly. Atlanta: Clarity Press, Inc., 63–73.

Perkins, Edward J. 1998. "The Psychology of Diplomacy: Conflict Resolution in a Time of Minimal or Unusual Small-Scale Conflicts," in *The Psychology of Peacekeeping,* ed. H.J. Langholtz. Westport: Praeger, 41–56.

Raath, Jan. 2009. "Mugabe Torturers Confess as Church Starts Quest for Reconciliation," *The Times,* April 17, 2009, www.timesonline.co.uk/tol/news/world/africa/article6108799.ece. Accessed April 19, 2009.

Ramos, Alcida Rita. 1998. *Indigenism: Ethnic Politics in Brazil.* Madison: University of Wisconsin Press.

Ranger, Terrence. 1983. "The Invention of Tradition in Colonial Africa," in *The Invention of Tradition*, ed. Eric Hobsbawm and Terrence Ranger. Cambridge University Press, 211–62.

Renaud, P.A. 1958. "Education for Acculturation," in Oblate Fathers in Canada, "Residential Education for Indian Acculturation, Workshop I: General Principles." Ottawa: Deschâtelets Residence library, doc. no. 8D1/21.

Richards, Audrey. 1982 [1956]. *Chisungu: A Girl's Initiation Ceremony among the Bemba of Zambia*. New York: Routledge.

Richland, Justin. 2005. "'What Are You Going to Do with the Village's Knowledge?' Talking Tradition, Talking Law in Hopi Tribal Court," *Law and Society Review*, 39 (2): 235–71.

Robert, G. and S. Sholto-Douglas. 2000. *The Bushman Myth: The Making of a Namibian Underclass*, second edn. Boulder: Westview.

Ross, Fiona. 2003. *Bearing Witness: Women and the Truth and Reconciliation Commission in South Africa*. London: Pluto

Rostkowski, Joelle. 1995. "Deskaheh's Shadow: Indians on the International Scene," *Native American Studies*, 9 (2): 1–4.

Saage, Richard. 2000. *Politische Utopien der Neuzeit*, second edn. Bochum: Winkler.

Sarfaty, Galit. 2007a. "Doing Good Business or Just Doing Good: Competing Human Rights Frameworks at the World Bank," in *The Intersection of Rights and Regulation: New Directions in Sociolegal Scholarship*, ed. Bronwen Morgan. Surrey: Ashgate.

2007b. "International Norm Diffusion in the Pimicikamak Cree Nation: A Model of Legal Mediation," *Harvard International Law Journal*, 48 (2): 441–82.

Saugestad, Sidsel. 2001. *The Inconvenient Indigenous: Remote Area Development in Botswana, Donor Assistance and the First People of the Kalahari*. Uppsala: Nordic Africa Institute.

Saunders, Harold. 1999. *A Public Peace Process: Sustained Dialogue to Transform Racial and Ethnic Conflicts*. New York: St. Martin's Press.

Senghaas, Dieter. 2004. *Zum irdischen Frieden*. Frankfurt am main: Suhrkamp.

Solway, Jaqueline. 2009. "Human Rights and NGO 'Wrongs': Conflict Diamonds, Culture Wars and the 'Bushman Question,'" *Africa*, 79 (3): 321–46.

Spencer, Herbert. 1995 [1850]. *Social Statics*. New York: Robert Schalkenbach Foundation.

Steady, Filomina. 2006. *Women and Collective Action in Africa*. New York: Palgrave Macmillan.

Stiglitz, Joseph. 2003. *Globalization and its Discontents*. New York: W.W. Norton.

Sylvain, Renée. 2005. "Disorderly Development: Globalization and the Idea of 'Culture' in the Kalahari," *American Ethnologist*, 32 (3): 354–70.

References

Tarde, Gabriel. 1969 [1901]. *On Communication and Social Influence*, ed. Terry Clark. University of Chicago Press.

   1999. *Monadologie et Sociologie*. Le Plessis-Robinson: Institut Synthélabo pour le progrès de la connaissance.

   2001. *Les Lois de l'Imitation*. Paris: Les empêcheurs de penser en ronde/Éditions du Seuil.

Teitel, Ruti. 2000. *Transitional Justice*. Oxford University Press.

Tirum, Nicolas Lucas. 2009. "Mensaje de los Mayas de Ayer y de Hoy para el Futuro de la Humanidad: Un Compromiso Imperativo de los Estados y Gobiernos en el Marco del Trece B'aqtun." Unpublished presentation to the 8th meeting of the Permanent UN Forum on Indigenous Issues, New York, May 27.

Toynbee, Arnold J. 1946. *A Study of History*, Vols. I–VI, abridged by D.C. Somervell. Oxford University Press

Tutu, Desmond. 1999. *No Future Without Forgiveness*. New York: Doubleday.

UNESCO, "Definitions for 'Intangible Cultural Heritage' (Replies to Questionnaires sent to National Commissions in February and August 2000)," www.unesco.org/culture/ich/doc/src/00078-EN.pdf. Accessed October 30, 2009.

   2006. "UNESCO and Indigenous Peoples: Partnership to Promote Cultural Diversity," http://unesdoc.unesco.org/images/0013/001356/135656M.pdf. Accessed September 10, 2007.

UNESCO, "Diversity of Cultural Expressions; Intergovernmental Committee for the Protection and Promotion of the Diversity of Cultural Expressions"; Paris, April 3, 2008, UNESCO doc. CE/08/1.EXT.IGC/3. http://unesdoc.unesco.org/images/0015/001598/159868E.pdf.

UNHCR. 2006. *The State of the World's Refugees: Human Displacement in the New Millennium*. Oxford University Press.

United Nations. 1998. "General Assembly Resolution 53/22, United Nations Year of Dialogue among Civilizations." UN doc. A/RES/53/22, November 16, 1998.

   2001a. "United Nations Year of Dialogue among Civilizations: Report of the Secretary General." United Nations General Assembly, fifty-sixth session. UN doc. A/56/523.

   2001b. "Letter Dated 27 September 2001 from the Permanent Representative of Austria to the United Nations addressed to the Secretary-General." UN doc. A/59/419.

   2004a. "The Concept of Indigenous Peoples, Background Paper Prepared by the Secretariat of the Permanent Forum on Indigenous Issues." UN doc. PFII/2004/WS.1/3, 2004.

   2004b. "'The Concept of Local Communities,' Background Paper Prepared by the Secretariat of the Permanent Forum on Indigenous Issues for the Expert Workshop on the Dissaggregation [*sic*] of Data." UN doc. PFII/2004/WS.1/3/Add.1.

2006. *Alliance of Civilizations: Report of the High-Level Group, 13 November 2006*. New York: United Nations.

2007. "Message of Louise Arbour, United Nations High Commissioner for Human Rights and Rodolfo Stavenhagen, Special Rapporteur on the situation of human rights and fundamental freedoms of indigenous people, on the occasion of the International Day of the World's Indigenous Peoples." Office of the High Commissioner for Human Rights, August 2007. www.unep.org/indigenous/pdfs/Statement-Louise-Arbour-Aug2007.pdf. Accessed May 3, 2008.

United Nations Development Programme. 2001. *Human Development Report 2001: Making New Technologies Work for Human Development*. Oxford University Press.

Wax, Emily. 2005. "A Place Where Women Rule; All-Female Village in Kenya Is a Sign Of Burgeoning Feminism Across Africa," *Washington Post*, July 9, A.01.

Weber, Max. 1948. *From Max Weber: Essays in Sociology*, ed. Hans Gerth and C. Wright Mills. London: Routledge & Kegan Paul.

2002 [1904–5]. *The Protestant Ethic and the Spirit of Capitalism*, trans. Stephen Kalberg. Los Angeles: Roxbury Publishers.

Wilke, Helmut. 2003. *Heterotopia: Studien zur Krisis der Ordnung moderner Gesellschaften*. Frankfurt am main: Suhrkamp.

Wilson, Richard A. 2000. "Reconciliation and Revenge in Post-Apartheid South Africa: Rethinking Legal Pluralism and Human Rights," *Current Anthropology*, 41 (1): 75–87.

York, G. 1990. *The Dispossessed: Life and Death in Native Canada*. London: Vintage.

Legal references

International instruments

Constitution of the United Nations Educational, Scientific, and Cultural Organization, November 16, 1945.

Convention Concerning Indigenous and Tribal Peoples in Independent Countries (C169), International Labour Organization, June 27, 1989, 72 ILO Official Bull. 59; 28 ILM 1382.

Convention Concerning the Protection and Integration of Indigenous and other Tribal and Semi-Tribal Populations in Independent Countries (C107), International Labour Organization, June 26, 1957, 328 U.N.T.S. 247.

Convention on the Elimination of all Forms of Discrimination against Women (CEDAW), GA Res. 34/180, 34 UN GAOR, 1981, Supp. (No. 46) at 193, UN doc. A/34/46; 1249 UNTS 13; 19 ILM 33 (1980).

References

Convention on the Protection and Promotion of the Diversity of Cultural Expressions, General Conference of UNESCO, October 20, 2005.

Convention Relating to the Status of Refugees, July 28, 1951, 189 U.N.T.S. 150.

Convention for the Safeguarding of the Intangible Cultural Heritage, General Conference of UNESCO, October 17, 2003.

Covenant of the League of Nations, January 10, 1920.

Declaration on the Granting of Independence to Colonial Countries and Peoples, GA Res. 1514 (XV), UN GAOR, 1960, UN doc. A/4684/1961.

United Nations Declaration on the Rights of Indigenous Peoples, UN GAOR, A/61/L.67/Annex (2007).

Universal Declaration on Cultural Diversity, General Conference of UNESCO, November 2, 2001.

National statutes and agreements

Canada

The Indian Residential Schools Settlement Agreement. An Agreement among Canada, as represented by the Honourable Frank Iacobucci, Plaintiffs, as represented by the National Consortium and the Merchant Law Group, Independent Counsel, the Assembly of First Nations and Inuit Representatives, The General Synod of the Anglican Church of Canada, the Presbyterian Church of Canada, the United Church of Canada and Roman Catholic Entities. May 8, 2006. www.residentialschoolsettlement.ca/Settlement.pdf. Accessed January 22, 2010.

James Bay and Northern Quebec Settlement Act. 1976–1977, c. 32, July 14, 1977 (Published in *James Bay and Northern Québec Agreement and Complementary Agreements*. Québec: Les Publications du Québec, 1991).

Spain

Declaración de Fiestas de Interés Turístico Nacional e International. RI §1017322, Orden ITC/1763/2006, May 3, 2006. www.iustel.com/v2/diario_del_derecho/noticia.asp?ref_iustel=1017322. Accessed January 22, 2010.

Index

Index

Index

Eagleburger, Lawrence, 19
Eastmain River, 84
Ecuador
  refugees, 64
Edmonton, 199, 212
education, 192, 198
  aboriginal, *see* residential schools
Egypt
  UN and, 156
enchantment, 167
  legal, 175
Enlightenment, 7, 9, 50, 56,
  106, 107
environmentalism, 78, 80, 81, 82, 83
Eritrea, 170
ethnic cleansing, 17
ethnic groups, 143
ethnic minorities, 5
ethnicity, 25, 97, 111
ethnography, 68, 99, 164, 168, 171,
  172
ethnology, 143, 144, 171
Europe, 161
European Union, 219
evolutionism, 140, 163
extractive industries
  opposition to, 125

female circumcision
  FGM, 88
Fontaine, Phil, 202
Fort George, 81
Fort George Island, 76
Foucault, Michel, 16, 17, 37, 191
Frankfurt, 169
French Revolution, 8
Frobenius, Leo, 144, 165, 169, 171, 172
FUNAI, 44
functionalism, 166

Gathering Strength, 188, 201
Gellner, Ernest, 106
gender, 210
  justice campaigns, 87
genocide, 11, 17, 24, 100, 109, 146, 147,
  180
Germany, 146, 161

UN and, 156
global diplomacy, 159
global governance, 41, 96, 108, 116, 119,
  124, 125, 137, 146, 148, 160, 163, 174,
  177, 222, 223, 227, 231, *see* United
  Nations
Global Youth Exchange Programme
  Japan, 157
globalization, 149, 163
Globe and Mail, 198, 205
Goffman, Erving, 191
Golden Gate Bridge, 27
Gramsci, Antonio, 37
Grand Council of the Crees, 75, 78, 80
Great Britain
  UN and, 156
Great Whale River, 78, 80, 81, 82,
  83, 84
Greenland, 55
Griaule, Marcel, 144
Guatemala, 86

Habermas, Jürgen, 7, 219
Haddon expedition, 15
Haiti, 41
Harper, Stephen, 202
Hebron, 53
hegemony
  concepts of, 37
Helton, Arthur, 61
Herder, Johann Gottfried, 107, 232
heritage, 68, 82, 128, 130, 134, 146,
  148, 149, 150, 151, 153, 173, 227,
  see also culture; tradition
Herman, Edward, 38
Herzegovina, 11
Hinduism, 158
Hollywood, 64, 109
Holocaust, 59, 146
human genome research
  resistance to, 125
human rights, 2, 5, 6, 7, 10, 11, 12, 13,
  19, 22, 25, 29, 36, 42, 48, 49, 51, 58,
  70, 85, 93, 98, 106, 118, 123, 125,
  127, 180, 182, 198, 203, 210, 214,
  225, 230, 231, 233, *see* truth and
  reconciliation commission (TRC)

Index

Index

Index